WITHDRAWN

# SUNSET OF THE SIKH EMPIRE

MAHARAJA RANJIT SINGH (1780-1839) RECEIVING
RAJA DHIAN SINGH (1796-1833)

# SUNSET
## OF
# THE SIKH EMPIRE

SITA RAM KOHLI

EDITED BY
KHUSHWANT SINGH

ORIENT LONGMANS
BOMBAY • CALCUTTA • MADRAS • NEW DELHI

ORIENT LONGMANS LTD.
Regd. Office : 3/5 Asaf Ali Road, New Delhi 1
Nicol Road, Ballard Estate, Bombay 1
17 Chittaranjan Avenue, Calcutta 13
36A Mount Road, Madras 2
1/24 Asaf Ali Road, New Delhi 1

LONGMANS, GREEN & CO. LTD.
48 Grosvenor Street, London W. 1
Associated companies, branches and representatives
throughout the world

DS
485
P3
K63

FIRST PUBLISHED 1967

© ORIENT LONGMANS LTD., 1967

Price Rs. 15.00

PRINTED IN INDIA
by R. K. Jain at Today & Tomorrow's Printers & Publishers, Faridabad
and Published by K. L. Kohli, Manager, Orient Longmans Ltd.,
Asaf Ali Road, New Delhi 1.

*Dedicated to the Memory of
Sita Ram Kohli
A Great son of the Punjab
and
Chief Chronicler of the Sikhs*

# About this Book

IN THE summer of 1962 when I was engaged in writing my volumes on the History of the Sikhs I came across a mass of conflicting data regarding the sequence of events which led to the first war between the Sikhs and the English. Not being a trained historian, I was unable to sift fact from fiction and I decided to seek the guidance of Principal Sita Ram Kohli. I had read his works and had borrowed liberally from his *Khalsa Durbar Records* and his life of Ranjit Singh (by far the most reliable account of the Maharajah) to write my own biography of the Sikh ruler. Although I had never met Principal Kohli I took the liberty of writing to him and questioning his authority for the exact date when the Sikh army crossed the Sutlej and so precipitated hostilities with the forces of the East India Company. (In the preface to Shah Mohammad's ballad of the first Anglo-Sikh war, Principal Kohli had mentioned a date which did not tally with the English records). Principal Kohli was at the time living in retirement in Rohtak, and unknown to me, seriously ill. It was a long time before he replied to my questionnaire. I treasure his letter, wherein he also said, "I only hope God will give me the strength to complete this work on which I have been engaged for the last ten years." In July 1962, death overtook Principal Sita Ram Kohli.

Students familiar with Principal Kohli's books know how thorough and painstaking he was in his work. No historian of the Punjab, dead or living, set the same high standard for his research or achieved it in the same measure. This book was his last child but destined to be born after its sire had ceased to be.

The book deals with the most vital period in the history of the Punjab—the ten years between the death of Maharajah Ranjit Singh and the annexation of the state by the British Government. It has all the elements of a great tragedy; its pages drip with blood; they arouse emotions which often lie too deep for tears.

Principal Sita Ram Kohli's manuscript was given to me after it had been through many hands. By then some pages had been lost and the last three chapters which were still in his handwriting were terribly mutilated. I have done the best I could to delete repetitions and fill in some omissions without taking too much liberty with the original.

Authors Club  
London, S.W.1.

Khushwant Singh

# CONTENTS

| Chapter | Page |
|---|---|
| 1. The Builders | 1 |
| 2. A Bolt from the Blue | 10 |
| 3. The Heel of Achilles | 30 |
| 4. Nemesis | 39 |
| 5. Hira Singh as Prime Minister of the Punjab | 67 |
| 6. The Last Year of Freedom | 90 |
| 7. The Beginning of the End | 101 |
| 8. The Kingdom of Lahore Becomes the State of Lahore | 121 |
| 9. Rising at Multan and the first Siege | 141 |
| 10. The Hazara Episode and the Defection of Sher Singh | 158 |
| 11. The Curtain Falls | 172 |
| Index | 193 |

# ILLUSTRATIONS

*Plate No.*

1. Maharaja Ranjit Singh receiving Raja Dhian Singh  ........  *Frontispiece*
2. Maharaja Kharak Singh
3. Maharaja Sher Singh
4. Raja Dhian Singh
5. Map of the Punjab.  1st Anglo-Sikh War
6. The Second Lahore Durbar
7. Jawahar Singh
8. Diwan Mul Raj
9. Sher Singh Attariwala
10. Maharaja Gulab Singh
11. Map of the Punjab.  2nd Anglo-Sikh War
12. Lord Dalhousie

## Chapter 1
### THE BUILDERS

THE theme of the volume now presented to the reading public unfolds the story, "how the kingdom of the Panjab lost its sovereignty." In the normal course of events this should have followed an account of "how the Panjab became a sovereign power." This was my original intention and I had planned the whole range of the subject (1748-1849) accordingly. However, because of other preoccupations and my own indifferent state of health during the last ten years, the volume dealing with the earlier part of the story could not be written. It may, therefore, be necessary to explain in bare outline the theme with which the earlier volume was to have dealt. Hence this unusual way of adding a small introductory chapter to the text.

The Khalsa as a political power assumed its proper form during the period of anarchy that followed the invasions of Nadir Shah and Ahmad Shah Abdali. Nadir occupied Delhi in March 1739; and for the time that he stayed at the imperial capital, the *Khutba* was read in his name, as if the Mughal Emperor did not exist. The Shah thus completely exposed the utter helplessness of the Mughal ruler. Ten years later, Ahmad Shah Abdali commenced his series of invasions and further bled the already bleeding empire. In 1753, he cut off a big slice of the Panjab from Delhi, and appointed a governor to rule on his behalf. This completed the process of Mughal expulsion from the stage of Panjab politics. During the next thirty to forty years the main contestants in the Panjab were the Afghans and the Sikhs; the former determined to retain their conquered dominion while the latter were resolved to rule their own homeland. The Mahrattas who did not take long to recover from the disaster to their arms on the battlefield of Panipat (1761) also made a couple of half-hearted attempts to grab the fertile plains of the Panjab in the name of the Mughal Emperor; but these proved abortive.

## Rise of the Khalsa power

After the execution of Banda Bahadur (1716) the Sikhs were left without a spiritual or secular leader. The government of the day made full use of this opportunity to suppress the Sikh movement. A series of repressive measures were adopted against the Sikhs with the result that many were forced to remove the exterior symbols of their faith (unshorn hair and beards) and once again became Hindus. However, the more determined among them preferred to face tyranny than to submit to unwarranted interference in their practices. They left their homes and took refuge in the foothills of the Himalayas and in the jungles. The number of these staunch votaries of Guru Gobind did not exceed two thousand men. Nevertheless, so firm was their faith in their cause and so strong the conviction that victory would ultimately crown their efforts that they were able to vanquish mercenaries, more numerous and better trained than themselves that the Mughals or the Afghans sent against them. These two thousand have, indeed, played a significant role in the making of the Panjab during the two decades of struggle between Afghans and Sikhs. One institution which deserves particular notice was a semi-military organisation, the *misldari*, which they evolved. Men from a clan or *gotra*, a village or group of adjoining villages, or from one occupational group would band together under the leadership of the most venturesome of their comrades and form a small independent politico-military group known as a *misl*.

The only means of subsistence left open to these small groups of religious enthusiasts was to prey upon their adversaries. The booty thus acquired was divided equally among them except that one got an additional share for the *Sardari* or leadership. The *misls* functioned independently of one another. Their number went on increasing as the hold of the Mughals weakened on the Panjab. According to one estimate, at one time there were sixty-five *misls* operating in the Panjab.

## Rise of the Dal Khalsa

Ahmad Shah Abdali first invaded northern India in April 1748. Within a couple of years he annexed the Panjab to his kingdom. This was a novel situation for the Khalsa. Their

## The Builders

homeland was gradually going out of the feeble hands of the Mughals of Delhi into the vicious grip of the Afghans of Central Asia. Hitherto they had been largely engaged in pillaging and marauding. Now for the first time they realised that theirs was a crusade to expel a foreign usurper and their destiny to become masters of their motherland. The litany, *Raj Kareyga Khalsa* (the Khalsa shall rule) became a part of their daily prayer.

At a meeting of the *Sarbat Khalsa*, the entire body of the Khalsa Panth on the 1st of Baisakhi, 1748 at Amritsar the one question that exercised the minds of the old and the young was how they were to rid themselves of this new yoke of Central Asian Afghan devising. The *Gurumatta*, or resolution, given by the synod was, "we shall fight them." With the hour comes the man, they say; and so it happened with the Khalsa in their hour of trial. There came into prominence the celebrated Kapur Singh of Faizullapur and his equally resourceful, younger colleague Jassa Singh Ahluwalia. Kapur Singh convinced his Khalsa brethren that the only chance of defying the Afghans, and, the only way to preserve themselves, lay in uniting their forces under a central command; on his advice all *Jathedars*, leaders big or small, agreed to pool their individual resources for the service of the *Panth*, and consented to fight under the banner of the Khalsa. The new body was given the significant name, *Dal Khalsa*, National Army of the *Panth*. Command of the *Dal* was invested in Jassa Singh, leader hitherto only of the Ahluwalias.

For two decades the Khalsa waged relentless war against Abdali's Afghans, a grim battle for survival against Central Asian hordes who set out to destroy everything: trade, commerce, agriculture and industry in their course. Peasants, artisans, entrepreneurs all cried out for protection, looking to the Khalsa as their only hope. The *Dal Khalsa* responded with a special scheme for the protection of the populace, which came to be designated *Rakhi*, (literally, to take care of). The *zamindars* (land-owners) readily agreed to give one-fifth of the produce of their estates in return for this service. The *Rakhi* system created a new sense of values. For the people it provided the assurance of a powerful army to defend them; for the Khalsa the *Rakhi* tax meant both revenue and responsibility, a realisation of sovereignty. Leaders of various sections of the *Dal* were assigned one or more districts for *Rakhi* duty. Each was expected to establish his *dehra* (camp) at a strategic point, to repair old Mughal forts or build *garhis* (mud fortresses) for the security of his neighbourhood. The scheme worked well. Intervals between Afghan invasions afforded the Khalsa time to consolidate its gains, and opportunity for most of the Central Panjab districts to accede to the protective system. Thus was delineated for the Khalsa their path to power.

The Sikhs were not unaware of the superiority of the Afghans in numbers as well as arms and training, and that Ahmad Shah Abdali was one of the greatest generals of the time. As against these odds, however, the Khalsa had two clear advantages, the *dhai-phut* (hit-and-run) tactics of guerilla warfare, highly developed; and a religious zeal which impelled its soldiers to engage the enemy disregarding peril. The hit-and-run, strategy gave the Afghans little opportunity of making their superior equipment tell, deprived them of initiative, and wore them out to the point of exhaustion.[1]

In May 1765, Ahmad Shah, having accomplished his eighth invasion of India, re-crossed the Attock to return to Kabul. The leaders of the *Dal* re-occupied their territories, and resumed the collection of *Rakhi*. Jathedars Gujjar Singh and Hari Singh of the Bhangi *misl*, ejected Diwan Kabuli Mal, Abdali's viceroy from Lahore, and proclaimed the sovereignty of the Khalsa Panth.

Ahmad Shah Abdali made two more attempts to recover his former conquests but age and health prevented him from doing so. He died in 1773, and the Sikhs were left free to consolidate and extend their territories. Within a decade, most of the Panjab was in their grasp. Power changed the complexion of the Khalsa Panth. Its conquests were the result of the efforts of individual *Jathedars* made in the name of the Khalsa commonwealth. Revenue had been collected on behalf of the Khalsa. The *Jathedar* or Sardar, who commanded a military unit and had charge of one or more districts for purposes of *Rakhi*

---

[1] The one occasion and probably the only one, on which the *Dal* was forced to fight a pitched battle with Abdali's trained army was at *Kup Rahira* near Malerkotla, in February 1762. In this action they lost about twenty thousand men, the event being still remembered in Sikh history by the name *wadda ghalughara* (the great holocaust).

## The Builders

was a custodian appointed by the Commonwealth for these purposes. But as the Afghan menace dwindled, the concern of the *Jathedar* over territory in his care became personal. There ensued an urge to partition the territory acquired in a common cause. This came to be accepted as a basis for arrangements least likely to cause bickering and jealousy. The leader of a unit of the *Dal*, to whom was assigned the *Rakhi* of a particular territory was now, formally acknowledged as *misldar* of that area, and he subdivided this among his own following, according to the general custom of sub-infeudation. As a result twelve *misls* acquired prominence, six within the Panjab proper, viz. between the Indus and the Sutlej rivers, and six east of the Sutlej extending up to the Jumna. These two groups gave rise to a distinction between Manjha and Malwa Sikhs.

Each *misl* then, had a territorial habitat, a standing army, a regular source of revenue from the cultivated land and a ruler in the person of its *misldar*, in short it became a small state, an independent political entity owing no allegiance to a superior political authority. Yet, the Sikh chieftain and every individual Sikh paid deference to the *Sarbat* Khalsa or the *Panth*, consecrated by Guru Gobind Singh. Theocracy had changed into a theocratic commonwealth and then into a federation of feudal chiefs. The next step in the process of evolution, whereby the *misls* were consolidated under a monarchy, was effected by Ranjit Singh of the Sukerchakiya *misl*, before the turn of the century.

**Kingdom of the Panjab**

The creation of a monarchy had become a necessity for the Khalsa. A glance at a map of the Panjab reveals how divided it was at the close of the eighteenth century into a number of small states. The following four groups were of special importance: (1) the twelve Sikh *misls* occupying the plains of Central Panjab and Sirhind and the foothills from Kangra to Jammu; (2) hill states ruled by Rajput princes with their strongholds on the inner ranges of the Himalayas between Jammu and Spiti-Lahaul; (3) territories of the martial clans of Panjabi Mussalmans, organised under tribal leaders, viz. the Pathans of Kasur, Chhathas of Rasulnagar, Sials of Jhang, Tiwanas of Shahpur, Biloches and Awans of Khushab and Sahiwal, and (4) principalities of Multan-

## Sunset of the Sikh Empire

Bahawalpur, Dera Ghazi Khan, Mankera, Bannu, Tonk and Peshawar and the uplands of Hazara. These were ruled by Pathan chiefs on behalf of the kings of Kabul, but for all practical purposes, were independent.

There was little prospect of drawing these groups together or inducing them to work in harmony as members of a federation. On the contrary, their relations were too often animated by mutual distrust and hatred. The Panjab was a house divided, and its disunity a standing temptation to neighbouring powers to absorb it piece by piece. The Mahrattas, who held Delhi from 1773-1803, made many forays into Sirhind; Zaman Shah of Kabul made three attempts (1793-98) to recover the territory which his grandfather, Ahmad Shah Abdali had conquered; and when the British had replaced the Mahrattas in Delhi, they too began to cast designing glances in the direction of the petty Panjab states. The only way to save the Panjab from disintegration and foreign conquest was to bring its disparate groups under one effective government. Only a bold, resolute and resourceful spirit could accomplish such an arduous feat. This was to be discovered in Ranjit Singh.

It may seem astonishing that an unlettered peasant lad should have the foresight and sagacity to perceive that the political condition of his country was fraught with dangerous consequences. Such, however, was his vision. He was, in addition, that rare phenomenon, a true leader of men, whose by no means moderate ambition was tempered by political wisdom.

Ranjit Singh, a *misldar* himself, was aware of the qualities and weaknesses of his fellow *misldars*, but stood apart, in his sense of the danger to which the Khalsa community stood exposed, by internecine disputation. The history of the last twenty years had been nothing but a list of wars waged by the *misldars* against one another, and that, in spite of the fact that their territories were encircled by those of non-Sikh chieftains, either distinctly hostile, or indifferent to Sikh aspirations. Thus hemmed in, and enfeebled by internal disharmonies the power, so staunchly wrested from the Mughals and Afghans was liable to be squandered. It was against this tide, that Ranjit Singh set himself. It does appear as though the Guru was his guide, informing him of what was to be done, and when. For the first ten years of his career, Ranjit

## The Builders

Singh was chiefly occupied in establishing his equation with the other *misldars*. With the Kanhya and Nakai chiefs he made marriage alliances; with Fateh Singh of the powerful Ahluwalia *misl*, he exchanged turbans, an act symbolising brotherhood and abiding friendship. He brought low the Bhangis and seized their possessions, including Lahore, Amritsar and Gujarat. In 1807 he succeeded in annihilating the Pathan colony of Kasur, which was uncomfortably close to the capital, Lahore. The Nawab of Kasur was pensioned off with a *jagir* in Mamdot beyond the Sutlej. Two years later Ranjit Singh clashed with the Gurkhas over possession of the fort of Kangra. He led his troops against the hillmen and achieved a notable victory. This was a double blessing. It drove the valiant Gurkhas to a respectable distance from Sikh terrain, and provided Ranjit Singh with the command of the entire Kangra valley.

Ranjit Singh's policy of subjugating other principalities succeeded because he took care to provide liberal compensation. Some of the princes were glad to accept *jagirs* and live a secure, retired life; others more active, to serve under the Maharajah, and merge their forces with the state army. As a result, the major portion of Ranjit Singh's cavalry consisted of the *ghorcharah* supplied by dispossessed Sardars. It was with the aid of soldiers such as these that Ranjit Singh, eventually, subdued the Mohammedan chieftains of Central and West Panjab.

During the ensuing span of twelve years, Ranjit Singh's energies were directed to breaking the cordon of Muslim principalities which checked his westward expansion. This had become a matter of the utmost urgency to him, since the grievous blow his prestige had suffered when in 1809, the British forced him to accept the Sutlej as the eastern limit of his dominion, and renounce the dream he had cherished of bringing the cis-Sutlej Sikh states into the Khalsa kingdom. He would not abide another setback, by allowing the Mohammedans on his side of the Sutlej to defy him, either singly, or by making common cause against his authority.

Of the Sikh Sardars who were compelled to barter their independence for service in the Lahore Darbar, the most notable were, Nidhan Singh Kanhya of Gurdaspur, Nidhan Singh Hathu of Daska, Jiwan Singh of Sialkot, Amir Singh of Sheikhupura, and

## Sunset of the Sikh Empire

the chiefs of the Ramgarhia clan. Muslim tribal leaders whose territories were made part of the expanding kingdom of Lahore were the Tiwana Maliks of Shahpur, the Biloches of Khushab, the Awans of Pind Dadan Khan and Sahiwal, the Sials of Jhang and the Pirzadas of Pakpattan. In 1813, the strategic fort of Attock fell into Ranjit Singh's hands and a little later, the hill principalities of Bhimbar and Rajauri became a part of his kingdom.

After bringing to heel, the zamindars and chieftains of the Doabs, which lie between the rivers Sutlej, Beas, Ravi, Chenab and Jhelum, he felt strong enough to take on the Pathan kingdoms of Multan, Dera Ismail Khan, Mankera, Dera Ghazi Khan, Kashmir and Peshawar. Rulers of these, had the support of the Pathan tribes of the North West Frontier and the kings of Kabul. Undeterred, Ranjit Singh subjugated each of them in turn. When the kingdoms of Multan, Mankera and Kashmir had capitulated, (1818-1821) the last vestiges of Afghan authority, *de facto* and *de jure*, were gone.

The problem that next faced Ranjit Singh was that of the trans-Indus region including Peshawar. The fort of Attock on the eastern bank of the Indus, which guarded the highway to Kabul, was already his, but beyond it lay the strongholds of the Amir of Afghanistan. A conflict was inevitable, because for both Afghans and Pathans on the one side and Sikhs on the other, the possession of the region round Peshawar, had become an issue touching upon *izzat* (honour). So great was the fear of Ranjit Singh's name that the brothers, Sultan Mohammed and Pir Mohammed, Governors of Peshawar, both agreed to send tribute to Lahore. The Amir of Afghanistan, however, was not prepared to accept this humiliation. At his behest, Sardar Mohammed Azim Khan, Wazir of Kabul came to Peshawar and exhorted the Pathan tribesmen to join him in a crusade against the infidel Sikhs. Ranjit Singh accepted the challenge and marched from Lahore at the head of his troops, encamping at Attock to supervise the transport of heavy artillery and baggage trains, across the Indus. His artillery, and Misr Diwan Chand's skilful manoeuvring, won the day. A decisive battle was fought at Naushera in which Azim Khan was trounced. He fled, leaving ammunition and camp equipment to the triumphant Sikhs. This victory extended

## The Builders

Ranjit Singh's dominion to the Khyber Pass. From the Khyber Pass his domain ran southward along the Suleiman range to Shikarpur, while on the east the Sutlej divided his kingdom from that occupied by the British. Ranjit Singh's kingdom then comprised an area of 1,40,000 square miles, and his revenues, including tribute from the hill-states, Bilaspur, Chamba, Suket, Ladakh and Iskardu, amounted to Rs. 3,02,67,000 per annum. The army, including troops sent by the feudal chiefs, was 79,000 strong; maintained at a cost of Rs. 12,527,000, it claimed more of the Maharaja's attention than any other department of state. This was chiefly because of his suspicions of British designs; the British were not only his immediate neighbours, but had begun to interest themselves in the commerce and politics of countries west of the Indus.

The Lahore Darbar of the later years of the Khalsa Raj, came to wear a distinctly different aspect from that of the early years of Ranjit Singh's rule. Most of the Sardars who surrounded him in the earlier phase, were comrades-in-arms, and of mature age. With a few exceptions, they were of Jat-Sikh peasant origin, proud however of their contribution to the glory of the Khalsa. As time passed these veterans were removed from the scene by death. But their places were not filled by Jat Sikhs or even Panjabis. Adventurers from European countries, Dogra Rajputs from the Jammu hills, Gaur Brahmins from Uttar Pradesh, and Pandits of Kashmiri Brahmin stock, were employed by the Maharaja, and in course of time some of them came to occupy very high positions in the Darbar. The Jat Sikhs were represented by a few, derived from such families as the Attariwallas, the Sindhanwalias, and the Majithias. This development altered the character of the court and created fresh problems. The Sikhs, though they had produced no such great administrators as Raja Dhian Singh Dogra or Fakir Aziz-ud-din, nor skilful generals of the calibre of Raja Gulab Singh Dogra, Court, Ventura and Avitable, were resentful of the foreigners who had gained predominance in their land. The Darbar, therefore, split into many factions fiercely opposed one to the other; held only in a semblance of harmony by the towering personality of the Maharaja. When Ranjit Singh died on Thursday 27 June 1839, these factions came to a head-on clash.

## Chapter 2
### A BOLT FROM THE BLUE

PRINCE KHARAK SINGH was the eldest son of Ranjit Singh and Dhian Singh Dogra, in the opinion of all who were competent to judge, the most influential and the most capable man in the Panjab, to perform the duties of a chief minister. It was widely believed that peace and order in the State, could only be ensured if Dhian Singh remained at the helm of affairs.[1]

Succession according to the wishes of the dying monarch, was confirmed by the ladies of the harem. On the night of 27 June, Rani Mehtab Devi, the Katoch princess of Kangra, made the Dogra and the new Maharaja exchange mutual pledges of confidence and good-will, place their hands on the body of Maharaja Ranjit Singh and then on the holy scriptures, swearing to abide by their bond.[2] The funeral obsequies were performed next day, 28 June. The court observed full mourning thereafter, for three days and partial mourning for another nine.[3]

Two days after the cremation, the ashes of the Maharaja and his four wives who had offered themselves for *Sati*, were collected and despatched in five palanquins to Hardwar for immersion in the waters of the Ganges. The bag containing the ashes[4] was placed before the Holy Granth, and then on the palanquin in which Ranjit Singh used to ride. The mounted bodyguard of the Maharaja, a corps of 2000 cavalry, together with two infantry battalions, marched in front of the palanquin, while the Princes and chiefs followed after, then came elephants and lines of horses. "As the procession emerged from the Taxali Gate of the city," writes Munshi Sohan Lal, "the guns from the ramparts of the fort and city walls fired the first salute." This was

---

1 Hugel, p. 287; Fane, v. 1, p. 127; Wade & Mr. Clerk's letters to the Governor-General. P.G.R.
2 S. L. d. iii. (v) p. 156; also Punjab Akhbarat, 1839-41, N. Arch. Delhi.
3 S. L. d. IV(I) pp. 1 & 10.
4 This bag was specially stitched for the occasion from the skin of deer (*Mirgan-i-Ahu*) which is considered holy or sacred by the Hindus S. L. d. iv (I) pp. 1-10,

## A Bolt from the Blue

followed by a second salvo when it passed through the Delhi Gate, on to the Trunk Road. The five-mile route from the Delhi Gate to the Shalimar Gardens was lined by seven thousand of the élite corps of infantry, cavalry and artillery. As the palanquin passed, each unit presented arms. The last salute was given near the Shalimar Gardens. Then the Chiefs returned to the city leaving the remains of their departed master in the charge of Bhai Gurmukh Singh, Sardars Dhana Singh Malwai and Rattan Singh Gadwai, who were appointed to accompany them to their destination.[1] Sohan Lal relates that as the remains of the Maharaja passed through the estates of his own chiefs, and then through territories of other Indian Princes and the British, ceremonial offering of presents and *nazranas*, salutes by guards of honour was observed as it had been during his lifetime.[2]

With the ceremony of *Kirya* on the thirteenth day, the period of mourning came to an end.

### Prince Sher Singh's Bid for the Throne

Even those thirteen days, however, were not free from anxiety for Kharak Singh. His stepbrother, Kanwar Sher Singh, also aspired to the throne. He was reported to have increased the force on his estate in Mukerian, to 1500 men during the last week of June. On receiving the news of his father's death, he hastened to Kangra and tried to induce the Commandant of the fort to hand over possession to him. About 2 July, he sent a confidential message to the British Agent at Ludhiana, "urging his superior merits on the attention of the Governor-General," and was said also, to have assured the British authorities that whatever aid might be afforded him, would be rewarded by a cession of territory on the left bank of the Sutlej.[3]

Sher Singh's bid for the throne may seem odd in view of the fact that Kharak Singh was the eldest son and Ranjit Singh had explicitly nominated him for the succession. Moreover, Sher Singh's paternity had been a matter for speculation. It was said

---

1 Sohan Lal states that the Bhai was advanced Rs. 10,000 to meet incidental expenses at Hardwar.
2 A.L. d. IV(I) pp. 2-4 & 9-10 some of the important towns en route to Hardwar where such ceremonies were observed are mentioned; Kapurthala, Phillaur, Ludhiana, Ambala, Jagadhari and Saharanpur.
3 MacGregor, vol. II, p. 8; Cunningham, p. 224.

that Rani Mehtab Kaur, being barren adopted the baby of a dyer's wife and presented this infant, Sher Singh, to Ranjit as their child. As against this, Sher Singh was fortified by the fact that the Maharaja had censured any who entertained the rumour casting doubt on his antecedents and entrusted him with distinguished civil and military commands. Moreover, Sher Singh was mentally better equipped than Kharak, who was, virtually, an imbecile. He was popular with the army, conversant with European ways and a favourite with the Europeans.

Court chronicles of Lahore record many encounters between Prince Sher Singh and British dignitaries in India. In March 1837 he met Sir Henry Fane, Commander-in-Chief of the British forces, and eight months later received Lord Auckland, when the Governor-General visited Lahore and Amritsar. Prince Sher Singh, assisted by Sardar Lehna Singh Majithia, was entrusted with the important duty of looking after this distinguished guest. The Prince, indeed, had several opportunities of meeting senior British officers in the Governor-General's entourage. Miss Emily Eden, Lord Auckland's sister, who accompanied him, spoke of Sher Singh as "our dear friend," and feelingly remarked that "during the regime of the foolish Kharak Singh, it is just possible, his dear head will be chopped off unless he crosses to our side of the river" (Sutlej).[1] William Osborne, military secretary to the Governor-General, mentioned Sher Singh in terms which distinctly indicate that he had succeeded in enlisting the interest and sympathy of the British.

When reports of Sher Singh's activities in Kangra were received in Lahore, Raja Dhian Singh lost no time in taking steps to avert the danger. Any contest for succession, he believed, was certain to be exploited by the British, who were as anxious to extend their influence over the court of Lahore, as they had recently done in the domain of the Amirs of Sindh. In fact, Lord Auckland, during his meeting with Ranjit Singh (December 1838) had openly expressed his wish to install a British Resident at Lahore. The Maharaja had firmly turned down the proposal. Nevertheless, the British made their proximity felt through their cantonment in Ferozepur and recently established military posts in Sindh.

---

1 Up the country, p. 221, 1839, London.

## A Bolt from the Blue
### Dhian Singh in the Saddle

Dhian Singh allayed the fears, real or imaginary, of high functionaries of the Darbar by assuring them that their estates, privileges, *jagirs* etc. would be maintained under the new regime. He also considered it expedient to make an early announcement of the date for the formal ceremony of accession (*Raj Tilak*). Tentatively, a date in September was arrived at. Precautions were taken to prevent Sher Singh from creating disturbances. Immediately on receipt of news from the commandant of the Kangra fort, express orders were sent to the governor of the province with copies to commandants of other garrisons in the valley, Nadaun, Haripur, Kotla and Nurpur to be vigilant, to trust no one, "friend or foe, subject or stranger," nor permit any such, *khwesh-o-begānā*, to come within the precincts.[1] Dhian Singh addressed personal letters to Princes Sher Singh and Nau Nihal Singh. He guaranteed to the former, security for his person, position and property, and advised him to come to Lahore to take part in what remained of his father's obsequies. This was followed by an official communication[2] signed by Kharak Singh, confirming Dhian Singh's words. Nau Nihal Singh, at the same time, was fully apprised of the situation.[3] Sher Singh was by then in a chastened mood. The British response to his appeal had not been encouraging. The Governor-General, on the advice of his Political Agent, Captain Wade, made it clear that as far as the British were concerned, Kharak Singh was Maharaja of the Panjab.[4] Wade had stated "for the interests of the British Government and the tranquillity of the country no arrangements could, in my opinion, be more favourable than those which the Maharaja is desirous of establishing."

1 S.L. d. IV (I) p. 5.
2 S.L. d. IV (I) p. 5. It is stated that Bhai Ram Singh and a couple of other senior members of the Darbar had also signed this communication as witnesses to its authenticity.
3 In acknowledgement, Nau Nihal Singh expressed appreciation at the promptness with which Sher Singh's efforts in Kangra had been challenged.
4 Wade to Government, 27 June 1839, Book no. 147, PGR. Wade, being then engaged in helping to install Shah Shujah-ul-Mulk on the throne of Kabul, the Shah, in possession merely, of Kandahar, with the main body of British troops, and he himself held up in Peshawar, any contest for succession in the Panjab would have been acutely embarrassing.

## Investiture of Kharak Singh, 1839

The actual ceremony of investiture took place on the eighteenth of *Bhadon* (1 September 1839) that is, about two months after the death of Ranjit Singh. In accordance with rites prescribed in the Shastras, Kharak Singh was bathed in water brought from the Ganges, and seven other sacred rivers of India (*ab Shri Gangā Jal-o-digar haft āb*), and later, dressed in pure white (*poshāk sufed*) with the Koh-i-Nur diamond displayed on his arm, took a seat in the Darbar. The Darbar on this special occasion was arranged under a beautiful canopy set up in the forty-pillared hall, (*Zer takhtgāh chhahil satūn*) erected by the Mughal sovereigns within the fort. The *Purohit* (priest) was then called in to lead the *puja* (worship) of *nau grah*, and apply a saffron mark (*qashqā zāfrān*) to the forehead of the Prince. He was followed by Bhai Rupa and the three well-known Sikh priests of the Lahore Darbar, Bhai Ram Singh, Bhai Gobind Ram and Bhai Gurmukh Singh, who each in turn, applied the *tilak* of saffron water. The Darbaris then made their obeisances, and in deference to his rank, Prince Sher Singh was given precedence over all chiefs and Sardars in the assembly.[1]

The absence of Prince Nau Nihal Singh, Kharak Singh's only son, on this occasion did not escape attention; in fact it soon became hot gossip in the bazaars. The Prince had left Peshawar and was on his way to Delhi. This information had been received by the Maharaja, through the agency of the Peshawar news-writer. Yet he did not wait for his son's arrival. The ceremony was rushed through a day or two before he could be expected to appear. It seemed as though the Maharaja and his young companion, Chet Singh Bajwa, apprehended some mischief from the Prince.[2]

Prince Nau Nihal Singh and the Minister, Dhian Singh Dogra, may have been perturbed about Kharak Singh's friendship with Chet Singh, but there is no evidence for the supposition that the Prince intended to usurp his father's rights, nor anything to support

---

[1] S.L. d. IV (I) p. 25.
[2] The news-letter from Peshawar was received on 12th Bhadon, which stated that the Prince had already left for Lahore. S.L. d. IV (I) pp. 23-25. Punjab Akhbarat, 1839-41 (N. Arch, Delhi). It is stated that Kharak Singh was advised to hasten the ceremony, to forestall the possibility of his ambitious son being won over by Dhian Singh.

PLATE 2

MAHARAJA KHARAK SINGH

## A Bolt from the Blue

Captain Wade's opinion that "it was fortunate for the Sikh Government that Prince Nau Nihal Singh and several other influential Sardars were at a distant place like Peshawar, because this prevented for the moment all chances of a contest."[1] What the Prince wished, was to see the establishment of an efficient government, so that the prestige of the Khalsa should be maintained. He knew that his father had neither talent nor energy, and that Chet Singh was an evil influence. He was also aware of other dangers that beset the monarchy: Sher Singh's popularity with the army and in the councils of the British Government; the Dogras, immensely influential and firmly entrenched in office, with the backing, of the Bhais, family priests of the Maharaja. In this situation the Prince might well have felt it incumbent to put his energies to the task of preserving the State.[2]

### Assassination of Chet Singh and Kharak Singh's fall

Maharaja Kharak Singh had no intention of sharing confidences with his son or his Chief Minister, preferring instead to consult Chet Singh[3]. Chet Singh was an impudent youth, with little to recommend him beyond good looks and a smooth manner. His wife was the niece of Sirdar Mangal Singh, whose sister, Ishar Kaur was one of Kharak Singh's favourite Ranis. It was this tenuous relationship that enabled him to gain the Maharaja's confidence, and then to oust his benefactor Mangal Singh from the lucrative position of manager of Kharak Singh's estate.

---

1 Wade to Government of India, Foreign Department, 2 July 1839, N. Arch. D.

2 Nau Nihal Singh, had, in April been posted by Ranjit Singh, to arrange (1) the despatch of 5000 troops of the Lahore kingdom to Kabul as agreed upon in the Tripartite treaty and, (2) to see that British forces accompanying Shahzada Taimur and Captain Wade, *en route* to Kabul, via the Khyber Pass should be unmolested. But, as soon as he received news of the Maharaja's illness, in May, he requested permission for a personal visit to Lahore. He was directed to stay at his post and, according to the court annalist, one letter to this effect dated 7th Har (19 June) bore the *Sahi* (signature) scribbled personally by the sick Ranjit Singh to emphasize authenticity (*Sahi as dast-i-Mubarik andakht*) S.L. d. IV (I) p. 146.

3 This was anticipated by Captain Wade (27 June 1839); from Peshawar he wrote to his government, "I do not know how it would affect the Sirdars, but the influence of Chet Singh is so much on the Prince, that I am doubting if Dhian Singh will be able to pursue the salutary system which the Maharaja has, in his present state of health, had the wisdom to make for the conduct of his government." Book 147, P.G.R.

Kharak Singh was known to publicly extol Chet Singh's capabilities, and treat him on the same level as other ministers of government. This gave rise to apprehensions in the minds of Dhian Singh and other dignitaries of the court who had been affronted by the young man's pretensions and arrogance.

Dhian Singh and Chet Singh each plotted for the other's downfall. It is a matter for surmise, which of the two started first, but in the execution Dhian Singh achieved priority. It had for some time been rumoured that Chet Singh was in league with the British to bring about the subjugation of the Panjab. There is no evidence to substantiate this, but the suggestion, enabled the astute Dogra minister to persuade Rani Chand Kaur, Kharak Singh's senior Maharani, to agree to a change of government in favour of her son, Nau Nihal Singh. Mother and son were sworn to secrecy, and the Dogra Raja then enacted a preparatory charade. A deputation of important courtiers was organized to wait upon Prince Nau Nihal Singh and remonstrate against the high-handed Chet Singh and his interference in the administration. Sohan Lal Suri, the Chronicler of the Lahore Darbar, records: "A deputation consisting of Raja Dhian Singh, the Sindhanwalia Sardars, Jamadar Khushal Singh and Sardar Lehna Singh Majithia, waited upon the Kanwar (prince), and gave him to understand that although their loyalty and devotion towards him and his family remained unshaken, they were not prepared to carry out the orders of Chet Singh. If the Prince could set things right, well and good; otherwise their resignations called for acceptance, and they should be relieved of their respective duties at the court." (7 October 1839). The Prince promised to mend matters.[1]

After this opening manoeuvre, Dhian Singh could not afford to lose time particularly as certain influential men such as Misr Beli Ram, head of the treasury, his brother Ram Kishan, controller of the Maharaja's household, and the Bhais, Ram Singh and Gurmukh Singh, were known not to be inimical towards Chet Singh. Dhian Singh posted his own guards at the gates, and in the early hours of the morning of 8 October his party forced an

---

1 S.L. d. IV (I) p. 38.

entry into the Maharaja's sleeping apartments. Kharak Singh took his friend into a protective embrace, But Dhian Singh was inexorable. Regardless of decorum, he snatched Chet Singh from his master's arms and hacked him to pieces.[1] Beli Ram and his brothers were seized and thrown into a dungeon. Kharak Singh was compelled to retire from active administration and Prince Nau Nihal invested with authority to carry on the affairs of government in the name of his father.

Chet Singh's assassination and the enforced retirement of Kharak Singh proved to be the first of a series of violent acts which led ultimately to the dissolution of the Sikh kingdom. It is unfortunate that of all the state dignitaries, the Prime Minister should have been the first to stain his hands with blood. "If Kharak Singh had followed the advice of his father in reposing trust in Dhian Singh and not yielded to the insinuations of Chet Singh," observed Dr. Honigberger, "everything would have proceeded in a prosperous manner."[2]

## Nau Nihal Singh

Nau Nihal Singh was nineteen when he became ruler of the Lahore kingdom.[3] He assumed supreme power but allowed Kharak Singh the courtesy title of Maharaja. In judging Nau Nihal's conduct towards his father it should be stated that he was not actuated by any sordid motive but the good of the state. To leave things to the whims of Kharak Singh who added to his inherent inability to govern a constant recourse to alcohol and opium would have amounted to criminal connivance at

---

1 Chet Singh's brother, Gurdit Singh, was murdered, and a number of his relatives rounded up.

2 Although none of the European officers of the state had joined in the deputation to Prince Nau Nihal, yet among them, too, the feeling was expressed, that a speedy removal of Chet Singh from the councils of the state, would be in its interests. On one occasion General Ventura had gone as far as to suggest to the Maharaja, that if Prince Nau Nihal and Raja Dhian Singh were given a free hand, the administration would run more smoothly.

3 Sohan Lal relates that Ranjit Singh often said in open Darbar that Prince Nau Nihal was worthy of holding the reins. (*Laik deheem-i-khilifa ast*). Holding him thus in esteem he appointed a proven soldier, Hari Singh Nalwa, to be his tutor. The Nalwa Sardar was with the young prince on the expeditionary force sent to annex Peshawar (1834) and when he was commissioned to proceed to Dehra Ismail Khan and take possession of Bannu and Tonk two years later.

## Sunset of the Sikh Empire

maladministration.[1] Furthermore, to maintain the Sikh character of the state—and Sikhism was its basis and its strength—the prince felt that it would be wrong to leave a Dogra Hindu, however capable, in sole charge of the kingdom. As executive head of the State, Nau Nihal Singh was scrupulous in following the advice of Dhian Singh and Aziz-ud-din in matters touching upon relations with neighbouring powers, particularly the British. But in domestic affairs he made decisions himself. He proved a stern administrator. He put down vigorously the spirit of insubordination that had begun to manifest itself in certain parts of the kingdom. Report was received that Baba Bikram Singh Bedi of Una had murdered his nephew (3 December 1839) and seized his estate. Relying on his priestly rank, the Baba paid no heed to remonstrances from the Darbar and refused to make amends. The Prince despatched a small force under General Ventura to bring him to book. In Palam and Jathera, another small principality, the sons of Dhan Chand, Mian Rattan Chand and Mian Prithi Chand, were compelled by a body of 500 Dogra cavalry sent from Lahore, to hold their peace.[2]

In the outlying districts of the North-West, unrest was more widespread. The Pathans of the areas beyond Attock refused both revenue and obedience to the Darbar. They regarded the Sikhs as usurpers and, with the death of Ranjit Singh, hoped to throw off their yoke. The Zamindars of the uplands of Muzaffarabad were quick to make trouble. But more menacing was defiance by Painda Khan of Darband of the authority of the Sikh governor of Hazara.[3] The jagir of Darband which was granted to Painda Khan by Ranjit had, for some reason, been resumed by the Darbar. Painda Khan collected a force of tribesmen and ravaged the entire countryside between Pagh Dhamtaur and Muzaffarabad and seized the fortress of Kishengarh from its Sikh commandant. For two months, January and February 1840, pillaging continued until the Lahore government restored Painda Khan's jagir.

1 Sir Alexander Burns after a meeting with Kharak Singh at Peshawar, August 1837, observed, "his imbecility is such that he can scarcely return an answer to the most simple question." (*Cabool*, p. 123)... Sir William Osborne, after an interview in Lahore (1837) pronounced him "little better than an imbecile." (*Court and Camp of Ranjit Singh*, p. 193.)
2 Ibid. p. 12.
3 1. S.L. d. IV(I).

## A Bolt from the Blue

Another scene of disturbance was the country round Hassan Abdal where the banditti of Gandgarh looted neighbouring towns and villages. They made the highway between Rawalpindi and Attock unsafe and brought the caravan trade between Northern India and countries of Central Asia to a standstill. As the activities of these bandits remained unchecked for a time, the Chief of Gandgarh became audacious enough to defy the government (January 1840). This stirred the Darbar to action. Chattar Singh of Attari, who held a jagir in Hazara, was ordered to proceed in person to Gandgarh to bring Khan Zaman to book and restore order in the region.[1]

The tardiness of governors of outlying districts in remitting revenue seriously affected the state treasury. Sohan Lal Suri states that during the five weeks preceding the death of Ranjit Singh, a sum of rupees thirty-one lakhs was drawn in cash and cheques from the central treasury for purposes of charity. This was only a supplement to the gold and silver, richly caparisoned horses and elephants, milch cows and utensils, regularly given to religious institutions.[2] Failure of the monsoons during two successive years (1837-39) impoverished the peasantry so that they could not pay their dues. Nau Nihal Singh summoned Diwan Sawan Mal from Multan and General Mian Singh from Kashmir and ordered them to clear their arrears. He exhorted Darbar officials to discharge their duties with more than customary despatch.

### Expedition to Iskardu, 1840

In conquering Ladakh in 1834, Ranjit Singh had provided a base from which the dominion of the Lahore Darbar could be extended beyond the Himalayas. When the Dogra General, Zorawar Singh, returned triumphant from Ladakh and came to pay homage to the Maharaja, he sought permission to extend the frontier further into Tibet. Ranjit Singh was wise in not wishing to grasp more than was tenable. He did not want to provoke the Chinese and the British and forbade Zorawar Singh from undertaking another expedition.

1 2. Ibid. pp. 55-56.
2 S.L. d. iii (V) p. 153 & p. 149.

## Sunset of the Sikh Empire

Nau Nihal was persuaded to lay aside caution by Dhian Singh who had personal interests in the region concerned. Zorawar Singh was in the service of the Dogra, Raja Gulab Singh, Dhian Singh's elder brother, and a powerful chief in his own right. The Dogra brothers had extensive estates in Jammu and Kashmir, and, therefore, had good reason to believe that a successful forward policy in that region would greatly increase their power. Moreover, the sepoys considered best fitted to fight in Tibetan territory were the Dogras.

Zorawar Singh, gifted as much in intrigue as in military command, took advantage of dissensions within the Iskardu ruling house, and by playing off one member against the other, was able to make Iskardu tributary to Lahore in May 1840. But complications with the British, narrated later, induced the Darbar to suspend operations in the area for the next twelve months.

### Expedition to Mandi and Kulu, 1840

When sanction was accorded to Zorawar Singh for the expedition against Iskardu, General Ventura and Sardar Ajit Singh Sindhanwalia were ordered to march with their troops to the hill states of Mandi and Kulu to enforce from their rulers payment of their stipulated dues to Lahore. The Sikh army encountered considerable resistance from local soldiery stationed at strategic points, so that reinforcements had to be sent from Lahore.[1] However, Nau Nihal's attentions being divided between a variety of claims, the expedition against Mandi and Kulu, like the one against Tibet, was suspended.[2]

### Relations with the British

Political relations between the Sikhs and the British had deteriorated. It called for tact and firmness on the part of the Sikh ruler

---

[1] The total number of trained troops despatched to Kulu and Mandi, inferred from the pay rolls of the army: 9 infantry battalions; 6 *derahs* (artillery units) with an approximate strength of 9000 men and 50 guns; the Sindhanwalia regiment, irregular cavalry about 500 strong; a number of camel swivels. For further details see KH.D.R. vol. I, pp. 55, 56 & 116.

[2] Cunningham suggests that the real reason for such a show of force in Mandi and Kulu, was to intimidate the Dogra chiefs into keeping their proper place and moderate their capactity for mischief; hence the selection as leaders of General Ventura and Ajit Singh Sindhanwalia, neither being well disposed towards Dhian Singh's family.

## A Bolt from the Blue

to restore them to normality, as to his credit, Nau Nihal Singh was able to do. The British army which accompanied Shah Shujah to Kabul (November 1838), entered Kandahar in May 1839, stormed Ghazni in July, seized Kabul in August, and proclaimed Shujah, King of Afghanistan.[1] Upon this British prospects in Afghanitan appeared fair. British authorities in India and at home approved of the proceedings and Macnaghten, the ambitious political officer in Kabul, at once began to devise schemes for extending the British-cum-Durrani kingdom. He advanced westward to acquire Herat and advised his government to seize the district of Peshawar from the Sikhs. This was a flagrant betrayal of friendship and a violation of the Tripartite Treaty, which had made possible the restoration of Shah Shujah to the throne of Kabul and had at the same time guaranteed to the Sikhs, in its very first article, their possessions between the Indus and the entrance to the Khyber Pass.[2] British policy under Auckland had indeed, as admitted by one English historian, "fallen to a lower level of unscrupulousness than ever before." Macnaghten and his colleagues established contact with chiefs of the Yusafzai and other important clans living within the jurisdiction of the Sikh province of Peshawar and inflamed religious sentiment against the Sikhs, not only by words, but also with gold and *khilaats*. Captain Wade invited the chiefs of Jalalabad to a meeting (August 1839) and tempted them with gifts and cash to break their relations with the Sikhs.[3] In like manner Lt. Connolly conferred *khilaats* on Yuzafzai subjects of the Sikhs.[4] In April 1840, Macnaghten proposed to his government the desirability of declaring the Yusafzai clans of

---

1 Dost Muhammad and his sons escaped and continued desultory warfare for another year. The father surrendered on 4 November 1840, and was sent to India as a state prisoner, but Muhammad Akbar Khan, the elder of the brothers remained at large, to organize the general insurrection, which compelled the British to retire from the country in January 1842.

2 This article reads as follows: The Shah disclaims all title on the part of himself, his heirs and successors and all the Suddozies, to all the territories lying on either bank of the river Indus, that may be possessed by the Maharaja, viz. Kashmir, including its limits east, west, north and south, together with the fort of Attock, Chhuch, Hazara, Khubul, along with its dependencies on the left bank of the aforesaid river and, on the right bank; Peshawar with the Yuzafzai territory, the Khattaks, Hastanagar, Michna, Kohat Hangu, and all places dependent on Peshawar as far as the Khyber Pass.

3 S.L. d. IV (I) p. 55 states that Macnaghten himself had gone there.

4 *Lahore News*, March 1840, N. Arch.

Swat and Buner independent of the Sikh government.[1] He expected that this proposal would be accepted and asked Darbar officials in Peshawar to stop collecting revenues from the area pending an enquiry into their claims. At the same time he persuaded the Zamindars and Jagirdars of the Yusafzai to consider themselves subjects of the Kabul government.

To camouflage his anti-Sikh activities, Macnaghten concocted a charge against the Lahore Darbar of having encouraged and given shelter to the Ghilzai refugees who had fought against Shah Shujah and promised monetary aid to the fugitive, Dost Muhammad Khan, who was reported to be preparing an attack on Khorasan. Prince Nau Nihal was mentioned specifically as being implicated in this.

The Lahore Darbar strongly resented this double-dealing by British functionaries and deputed Fakir Aziz-ud-din to meet Mr. George Russell Clerk at Ludhiana and discuss the matter with him. The British Agent was convinced that the Lahore Dabar's claims upon the Yuzafzai territory were valid and dissuaded his government from entertaining Macnaghten's proposals. "The Sikhs," he wrote, "may not be debarred of the possession of the territory, which, for the convenience of other parties, and the wishes of the Afridi Zamindars, may be expedient to do; and it can only be done by abandoning the English version of the tripartite treaty." Lord Auckland's government, however, adhered to a contrary view so that the issue was prolonged, without any final decision.[2]

It was, therefore, with a background of mutual distrust and suspicion that the representatives of the two governments met to discuss some necessary business: questions such as the passage of British troops returning from Kabul, adjustment of boundaries between Sikh and Afghan dominions in the vicinity of Peshawar, maintenance of the Derajats, status of the 5000 Muhammedan troops at Peshawar, and the regulation of tolls on the Indus and Sutlej. The most urgent of these was in regard to safe conduct through the Panjab of British troops returning after storming Ghazni.

1 Macnaghten to Government, 28 April 1840, N. Arch. D.
2 The Lahore government, too, adhered to its view so rigidly that some among the British advocated the use of "the mailed fist". Macnaghten, in fact, proposed it. Kay's *The War in Afghanistan*, vol. I, pp. 515-16.

## A Bolt from the Blue

Ranjit Singh had refused permission to the British troops to pass through his territory on their way to Kabul forcing them to take a circuitous route through the Bolan Pass. But during Lord Auckland's visit to Lahore he agreed that they might return by way of the Khyber and Peshawar.[1] When, however, in September 1839, Russell Clerk went to Lahore to felicitate the new Maharaja and ask for confirmation of Ranjit Singh's concession, this was refused, as was at the same time a request of the British government regarding supplies for the returning soldiers. The British Agent did not give up hope of achieving his point. While continuing to try and assuage the feelings of the Darbar, he went out of his way to pay a courtesy call on Prince Sher Singh,[2] hoping perhaps, that a touch of insecurity might make Nau Nihal and Dhian Singh more amenable to his cause. This manoeuvre appears to have succeeded. When the subject was re-opened a few days later, the Darbar agreed to the British proposal on condition that the passage of troops through their territory be only for this one emergency; that its route should be via Dehra Ismail Khan not Lahore, and any act of sacrilege rigorously forbidden. The British Agent accepted these conditions.[3]

After three months the question of passage for British troops was again raised. This time for a small military escort and for supplies and stores being conveyed to Kabul for the benefit of a portion of the army that remained in Kabul (since it had been discovered that Shah Shujah would be unlikely to maintain his position without such support). Meanwhile, unfortunately for the British plea, Captain Wade had resumed his position of Agent in Ludhiana. Relations between him and Nau Nihal Singh were strained[4] and the tone of his letters was not such as to mollify. The Darbar could with justice emphasise that they did not wish their territories to be used as a highway for foreign troops and

---

[1] Sohan Lal states, "the Maharaja accepted the request of the Governor-General, to permit the returning British troops to pass through the Panjab only once. But he would not give this in writing."
[2] S.L. d. IV (I) p. 28.
[3] The Governor-General was not satisfied with this pledge. Cunningham, p. 226; S.L. d. IV (I) pp. 17-19.
[4] When the Prince was Governor of Peshawar, Captain Wade, escorting a small body of troops, stayed there, and expressed, in letters to government, suspicions regarding the conduct of his host.

that the terms made with Russell Clerk were framed so as to preclude this happening. Yet the isolated section of the British army in Kabul was in dire need and Lord Ellenborough decided to restore Russell Clerk to his post in Ludhiana (March 1840) in the hope that he might, once again, appease the Darbar.[1] Mr. Clerk was successful in restoring confidence and received permission for supplies and a military convoy to proceed to Kabul by the Khyber route. It was agreed, moreover, that the allegation made by Macnaghten of complicity between Nau Nihal Singh and the fugitive Dost Muhammad be officially withdrawn and their intercepted correspondence (so called) admitted to be false and forged.[2] The Darbar, in its turn, made over the Ghilzai refugees to the British. Credit for these smooth and reasonable dispositions must go to both Russell Clerk and the Prince.

Another matter that concerned the two governments was in regard to a contingent of 5000 Muhammedan soldiers which the Darbar had undertaken to keep in readiness at Peshawar in case Shah Shujah should require their services. Captain Wade and Macnaghten discounted the value of this arrangement and found fault with the discipline of the men: they recommended to their government that Article 15 of the Tripartite Treaty whereby Shah Shujah had promised to pay a sum of two lakhs of rupees[3] towards the maintenance of this force should be abrogated. The Darbar objected to this, not only as a breach of contract, but because it would lose them a point of entrée into Afghan affairs. To meet British criticism regarding discipline, Prince Nau Nihal Singh offered to take over command of the contingent himself, whereupon Russell Clerk recommended that the unwelcome abrogation should not take place. This was agreed to by the Governor-General.

---

[1] S.L. d. LV (I) p. 46; Cunningham, p. 227.

[2] The kind of situation, which prompted L. I. Trotter to write: "there remains the undoubted fact that Macnaghten paid, by a violent death, the penalty of his rash attempt to fight the Afghans with their own weapons of deceit and double dealing." Lord Auckland, p. 157; Clerk to Govt. and Govt. to Clerk, 1 & 9 Oct. 1840; *Mohan Lal Kashmiri*, by Dr. H. R. Gupta, p. 35.

[3] S.L. d. IV (I) p. 63. The contingent, the actual strength of which exceeded 6000 men, including 3 Mussalman battalions and 3 irregular ones formed by detaching Muslim officers and men from other regiments. Vide Kh., vol. 1, pp. 42-50: Shahamat Ali, pp. 332-35. This cost the Sikhs Rs. 500,000 per annum. The Afghan contribution, they chose to regard as tribute, and confirmation of prestige.

## A Bolt from the Blue

The British government next took up the revision of a commercial treaty dealing with the navigation on the Indus river. Such a treaty had first been concluded with the Lahore government in 1832, revised in 1834, and again in 1839. The Sikhs had raised no objection to the changing policies of their allies even though it was evident that their purpose was not only commercial but also political. Merchant steamers could easily, if the need arose, be converted into gunboats, and the Indus made a channel for transporting troops and artillery (as in fact it was by the British when they seized the kingdom of the Amirs of Sindh two years later). At this point, however, the new provisions related to toll rates and the declaration of certain articles, such as grain, wood and limestone, duty free. Decisions were amicably arrived at. In all these negotiations Nau Nihal Singh proved himself as informed and tactful as his grandfather. He showed willingness to parley with the British without relaxing vigilance in regard to the interests and dignity of the Sikh kingdom.

**Internal Administration**

One of Nau Nihal Singh's problems on the domestic front was to keep his wayward father, Maharaja Kharak Singh, in good humour. He had not accepted his deposition with equanimity and, till the close of 1839, continued to reside in the fort-palace and preside over the Darbar. He was particularly bitter about the imprisonment of Misr Beli Ram and his brothers, and in his frustration about obtaining their release, often raved like a madman threatening very often to invoke the aid of the British. In December 1839, when he was apprised of Sir John Keen's intended visit to Lahore, he looked forward to it as an opportunity for speaking his mind to the Commander of the British forces. Thoroughly chagrined at the treatment he met with on 19th Poh (31 December 1839), he stole away from the palace, causing much embarrassment to the court.[1]

Nau Nihal Singh was aware that expediency required maintaining a facade of propriety in the relations between the Maharaja

---

[1] S.L. d. IV (I) p. 55. The Maharaja had recently shifted his residence from the palace to his house, *haveli*, inside the town, which explains his being able to escape un-noticed from the city. The Prince, thereupon, rode out with a few trusted courtiers, found him at Sheikhupura and brought him back.

and the *de facto* government, and that open rupture between himself and his father might serve as an excuse for British intervention, as his close association with Dhian Singh Dogra had already threatened to do. He therefore ordered that the Misr family should be released. Beli Ram having submitted an apology for his past conduct and having undertaken to comply with Dhian Singh's orders was produced before the Maharaja on the morning of 28th Poh, 10 January 1840.[1] Despite Nau Nihal Singh's tact, Dhian Singh continued to express dissatisfaction with the release of Beli Ram and his brothers.

Another source of anxiety were the aspirations of Sher Singh. Although he had failed in previous attempts to secure the throne, Nau Nihal Singh's difficulties with the British helped to keep his hopes alive. He applied for a month's leave of absence from the court on the pretext of visiting Hardwar and other holy places.[2] The leave was not sanctioned. He was informed that Maharaja Kharak Singh was contemplating a similar pilgrimage and it would be well if the brothers went together. There were few people whom Nau Nihal Singh could turn to for advice. Among those who had the necessary quality were Lehna Singh Majithia, Fakir Aziz-ud-din, Khushal Singh and Fateh Singh Kalianwala. But the ablest, without a doubt, was Dhian Singh. The Prince and the Chief Minister should have made an excellent team if both had earnestly striven to that end.

The difficulty with Dhian Singh was that he had become powerful independently. And instead of extending co-operation to the Prince as a matter of course for a loyal subject, he continually bargained for terms.[3] This attitude accentuated the friction that already existed between the Dogras and the Sikhs. The Prince had not only to keep the grandees of the Darbar (the youngest being twice his age) in their proper places, but guard

---

[1] S.L. d. IV (I) pp. 57-58 & 61.
[2] Wade's letters to Meddock, March 1840, National Archives, Delhi.
[3] Dhian Singh's family, jointly held estates with revenues of about Rs. 1800,000 per annum, and besides feudal levies maintained troops numbering not less than 25,000 men and a park of artillery. *Memoirs of Alexander Gardner*, pp. 190-91.

## A Bolt from the Blue

himself against their machinations. Yet for a time he got on well with the Chief Minister.[1]

The first time a serious difference occurred was over the release of Misr Beli Ram. Dhian Singh asked for leave to go home and was granted a fortnight (20 January 1840).[2] During his absence, the priest-barons Bhai Ram Singh and Bhai Gobind Ram, the Sindhanwalias, Ajit Singh and Attar Singh, and Jamadar Khushal Singh, all of whom were inimical to Dhian Singh, sought to widen the breach between the Raja and the Prince. The latter, however, was wise to their intention, and made use of the Minister's absence to try to soften his father's sentiments towards him and to make clear to the other ministers his own regard for Dhian Singh's abilities. Bhai Ram Singh was deputed to bring the Dogra back. Meanwhile Beli Ram and his brothers remained out of office.[3] Then came a bolt from the blue.

Kharak Singh had been ailing for some time. By September 1840, there was little hope of his recovery. Soon after the Dussehra and Divali celebrations were over, the camp at Amritsar was broken up and the ruling family left for Lahore. Maharani Chand Kaur and Prince Nau Nihal Singh accompanied the sick Maharaja for some distance; then branched off to Fatehgarh to spend a few days with the Maharani's parents, while the Maharaja was conveyed to Lahore by easy stages. The strain of the public celebrations at Amritsar seems to have aggravated his condition and he died in the early hours of 5 November. Nau Nihal Singh was summoned immediately to perform the last rites of his father. But the very day when he was expected to succeed to the throne proved to be his last.

Nau Nihal Singh's death was so sudden and unexpected that it gave rise to much speculation. Sohan Lal, the official diarist, has, however, made an effort to put the relevant incidents into

---

[1] Shahamat Ali, *The Sikhs & the Afghans*, pp. 26-27 states "the Raja is the channel for conveying the petitions and representations of the people . . . . when he returns from court he is in the habit of holding a darbar in his own house attended by officers of the army as well as the Sirdars."
[2] S.L. d. IV (I) p. 61.
[3] The despatches of Mr. Russell Clerk can give a misleading picture of relations between the Prince and Dhian Singh. This may be due to the author's bias against Dhian Singh, so that the Prince's toughness as an opponent in negotiation was attributed to the Minister, whereas, particularly in relations with the British, the two were almost invariably in accord.

orderly sequence. While Kharak Singh's funeral pyre was still burning, the Prince suddenly felt very ill. He vomited and complained of stomach-ache and was removed to the shade near the shrine of Maharaja Ranjit Singh; the Bhais, Ram Singh and Gobind Ram administered medicine for sunstroke. Later, when the mourners proceeded to leave the cremation ground, making for the river to perform the traditional ablutions, the Prince felt strong enough to join them; he took the hand of his friend Mian Udham Singh, son of Raja Gulab Singh, and as he was passing beneath the archway of the city gate, stones and tiles crashed down on his head. When the debris was cleared, it was discovered that Udham Singh was dead; Prince Nau Nihal's skull was fractured and an arm broken. Bhai Gobind Ram felt his pulse and pronounced him dying: "*waqt-i-akhri-ast*."[1] Among others who suffered injuries were Raja Dhian Singh and Dewan Dina Nath.

The Prince was removed to the *baradari* of the Hazuri garden and the premises cleared of people; Dhian Singh, personally, using 'hand and stick' to persuade any who lingered. Only such as the two Bhais, the Fakir brothers, Aziz and Nur-ud-din, the Sindhanwalia Sardars and Jamadar Khushal Singh remained. The gates of the garden were closed.[2]

An emergency meeting of the Sardars was called to make interim arrangements for government. Raja Dhian Singh was invested with the highest executive authority and this fact communicated to officials in Lahore and the muffasil. They were instructed to treat as valid only those orders that bore the *sahi* and seal of Raja Dhian Singh (*bar bar parwana ki sahi Raja buda bashand, bar an amil shawand*). Towards the evening the body of the Prince was conveyed to the fort but the fact of his death was kept secret. By way of camouflage, *Hazūri lāngris*, his personal cooks, were ordered to prepare his favourite dishes. Late at night Bhai Mohan Singh, Prince Sher Singh's confidential agent, was summoned to the palace and sent with a personal letter from

---

[1] Nau Nihal Singh met with the fatal accident on the afternoon of 5 November, and expired probably the same day, just three days short of thirteen months since Chet Singh's assassination had made him *de facto* ruler.

[2] S.L. d. IV (I) pp. 64-66.

## A Bolt from the Blue

Dhian Singh to the village of Kahnwan, 80 miles from Lahore, where Sher Shah had gone on a shooting expedition and relays of horses posted on the way to speed his journey to the capital. Upon his arrival on the 7th, the news of Prince Nau Nihal Singh's death was officially released. The obsequies were performed next morning.[1]

Since Dhian Singh was then the chief functionary of the state and had played a conspicuous part in the proceedings of the two previous days; his enemies and rivals found it easy to cast aspersions on his integrity. Some went as far as to allege that the sudden fall of masonry was contrived by him and Gulab Singh through the agency of men who had cause to fear Nihal Singh's censure. But no evidence was forthcoming and the circumstances were such as to make it extremely unlikely that the execution of such a plot could pass without detection. A Russian traveller, Soltykoff, who visited the neighbourhood a year afer the accident wrote: "I can quite understand the likelihood of sutch an occurrence, for I tremble every time I pass a gateway of Amritsar on an elephant and there are many such gates, half ruined and threatening to fall at any time." Sayyed Mohammad Latif, likewise writes: "the prolonged roaring of the cannons in the morning which had announced the death of Kharak Singh had shaken the old fort to its foundations; that a part of it should have fallen at this particular juncture is not very extraordinary."[2]

That Nau Nihal Singh's death at that particular moment was accidental is fairly well established. But the impact of the tragedy was tremendous. Even the careful reporter, Sohan Lal, was impelled to see in it the workings of providence. It was veritably a bolt from the blue.

---

1 The records of the Sikh government Kh. D.R., vol. II, p. 312 give 7 November as the official date on which Nau Nihal's rule ended; also S.L.d. IV (I) pp. 74-75; also Clerk's letter to Torrens 7 Nov. 1840.

2 Among contemporary writers who subscribe to the view of accident are Dr. Honigberger and Munshi Sohan Lal; Sir Lepel Griffin in the early sixties of the same century examined courtiers, who witnessed the scene and were convinced of the impossibility of foul play. Dr. G. L. Chopra stigmatised statements to the contrary by Smyth and Alexander describing them as "notorious for inventing facts and passing them on as true history by investing them with fabricated evidence." Paper on the death of Kanwar Nau Nihal Singh, Indian Historical Records Commission, 1942.

## Chapter 3
### THE HEEL OF ACHILLES

NAU NIHAL SINGH's death left six princes with claims to the throne: Sher Singh and his twin brother Tara Singh born in 1807; Peshaura Singh (b. 1818) and his brother Kashmira Singh (b. 1819); Multana Singh (b. 1819) and Dalip Singh (b. 1838). Of these Sher Singh was the eldest and the only one who had been privileged to a seat in the Darbar with the heir-apparent, Kharak Singh. He had failed in his attempt to get precedence over Kharak Singh, but now that the senior line of succession had been cut off, his claim was admitted and the notables of the Darbar agreed, on the afternoon of 5 November to place him on the throne. He was presented with the traditional embossed seal bearing the title of Maharaja before his name. Sher Singh's succession was formally proclaimed, and the Sardars paid him homage on 9 November 1840.[1] But at this juncture, Rani Chand Kaur, wife of Kharak Singh, backed by the Sindhanwalia chiefs, put forward a claim to rule on behalf of her prospective grandchild. She declared that Sahib Kaur, the widow of Nau Nihal Singh, was in the third month with child and demanded that she be accepted as regent during the pregnancy. It was immediately admitted that the claim of Nau Nihal Singh's child was superior to Sher Singh's, but the question remained as to whether until the child came of age, the Rani or Sher Singh should be placed at the head of the government. Over this issue most important courtiers came to be divided into two sharply opposed groups. Among Chand Kaur's supporters were the chiefs of the Sindhanwalia family, Attar Singh, Lehna Singh and Ajit Singh, the two Bhais, Ram Singh and Gobind Ram, Jamadar Khushal Singh and his nephew Tej Singh, Sardar Fateh Singh Man, Sardar Gulab Singh Povindia and Sheikh Ghulam Mohi-ud-din. The Dogra brothers, Gulab

---

[1] Sher Singh mentioned these facts in his *Kharita* addressed to Russell Clerk, Agent to the Governor-General at Ludhiana, who communicated them to his govt. (11 Nov. 1840). National Archives, Delhi.

## The Heel of Achilles

Singh and Dhian Singh, Bhai Gurmukh Singh Granthi, Sardar Sham Singh Attariwala, Sardar Dhanna Singh Malwai, Fakir Aziz-ud-din and his two brothers, and the senior European officers, including Ventura and Court, were in favour of Sher Singh.

Dhian Singh Dogra urged that it would be highly inadvisable to have a woman at the helm of affairs while conditions were unsettled specially emphasising the fact that the British were continually sending troops, stores and ammunition across the Panjab to Kabul. The Rani's supporters insisted, however, that the interests of the unborn child would hardly be considered safe in the hands of the ambitious Sher Singh. Dhian Singh considered it expedient to suggest a compromise whereby both the Rani and Sher Singh be represented in power. This was the more readily acceptable to the former as it contained a tacit admission of the facts of Sahib Kaur's pregnancy. Dhian Singh's proposal was that administration should be carried on in the name of Maharaja Kharak Singh, that his seal (not Sher Singh's) be used on official documents; that Rani Chand Kaur's approval be obtained on all important matters but that Sher Singh be appointed executive head *afsar-i-kalan* of the state. Dhian Singh endeavoured to convey to the Rani that Sher Singh's position would be merely titular, *dar-alam-i-zahiri*, that he would not be in a position to override her wishes and undertook to serve her as Chief Minister with Fakir Aziz-ud-din as council *mashir-i-Khasa*. This scheme was also communicated to the British Agent at Ludhiana.[1]

Having gained her point in earlier negotiations, Rani Chand Kaur flatly refused to accept these proposals when they were spelled out in detail. Proud of her birth and station (she was the grand-daughter of Sardar Jaimal Singh, chief of the Kanhyas, and senior daughter-in-law of Ranjit Singh) this middle-aged but attractive woman disdained association with Sher Singh whom she looked upon as the illegitimate offspring of a dyer of clothes. Dhian Singh, devised a new scheme; that Chand Kaur be the chief authority and Sher Singh president of a council of chiefs composed of Attar Singh Sindhanwalia, Lehna Singh

---

[1] Clerk's letter dated 11 November, also S.L.d. IV (II) pp. 5-8.

## Sunset of the Sikh Empire

Majithia, Khushal Singh, Fakir Aziz-ud-din and Dhian Singh, and that Sher Singh be specially charged with seeing to drill and discipline in the army, a task which a woman could not be expected to enjoy. It was arranged that Sher Singh should preside over the morning session of the council held in Hazuri Bagh, and later in the day, state documents be submitted to the Rani for approval. This clumsy form of co-regency did not last long as Chand Kaur made no secret of her desire to exclude Sher Singh from the government and even threatened to demand help from the British.

Dhian Singh tried yet another method of appeasing the vain and cantankerous lady.[1] On the 16th day of Maghar, 27 November 1840, an agreement was drawn up by unanimous consent of the grandees to the effect that till such time as Nau Nihal's widow should be delivered of her child, Sher Singh retire to his estate leaving his minor son, Partap Singh, to represent him on the council. Chand Kaur became regent with four ministers—Dhian Singh, Attar Singh Sindhanwalia, Khushal Singh and Lehna Singh to advise her.

The document which was drawn up to regulate the succession ran as follows: "At this time, we all, with one heart and one tongue, swear to abide by the stipulations agreed upon among us, that Singh Sahib Sher Singh ji shall remain on his own Jagir, and that Partap Singh ji, son of the Singh Sahib take his place; if Sher Singh ji shall agree to this, it is well; if not, we taking joint action will compel him to agree.[2] Likewise we will make the exalted Bibi Sahiba (Rani Chand Kaur) consent. What has been above arranged will hold good until the birth of a son or otherwise, when we will make other arrangements."[3]

Thus Chand Kaur's party seemed to have won. But when it came to actual working, the administration was found to be still impeded by a factional spirit. Little better could be expected with Chand Kaur and Sher Singh both impelled by ideas of self-

---

[1] S.L. d. IV (II) pp. 6-7. Also Clerk to govt. 5 December, which suggests that the Rani had won over Gulab Singh by promising to restore the estate of Munawar which her late husband had appropriated from him.

[2] Sher Singh wrote in a letter that he was actually forced to accept and sign by Diwan Dina Nath who came with a Gurkha battalion and another from the *campu-i-muala*.

[3] Of the sixteen persons, who witnessed this document, only 5 could write; others just used the *sahi* mark of approval.

## The Heel of Achilles

aggrandisement, without the ability to achieve a clear victory, or the wisdom to leave things in the hands of competent ministers. In addition, Dhian Singh's colleagues were jealous of him; his sharp intelligence and quick grasp of knotty administrative problems, instead of stimulating co-operation incited them to put as many obstacles as possible in his way. In sheer disgust Dhian Singh refused to come to his office for five weeks, and when he realised that even Chand Kaur was a party to the misconduct of the ministers, he decided to espouse the cause of Sher Singh.

He applied for leave, which was readily granted. He proceeded to Jammu[1] to devise a plan to secure for the Prince and himself, supremacy at Lahore. "The Raja," Sohan Lal writes, "while leaving Lahore, had sent a secret message to Prince Sher Singh to hold himself in readiness, and had also advised the officers of the army in whom he had confidence, to join the Prince when the call came. They were given hopes of increased pay and emoluments and also some additional money gifts.[2] Dhian Singh's influence with the army, particularly those regiments that had European officers, was considerable. Sher Singh, on his part, tried to sound the British as to the probability of their recognising him as Maharaja. He was told that having been allies for thirty-two years they wished to see a strong and stable government in the Punjab. He took this to mean that they favoured his claim.

During Dhian Singh's absence the administrative machinery was completely thrown out of gear and, in the words of Sohan Lal, *khalīl-i-azam dar arākīn-i-saltanat rahyāb gasht*, feelings of confusion and dismay came to possess the minds of its members.[3] At long last Chand Kaur was forced to admit that Dhian Singh was indispensable. She sent frantic messages asking him to return to Lahore, assuring him that his advice would be followed and his authority upheld. He paid no attention to these belated entreaties. Then he struck at the opportune moment. He sent word to Sher Singh to proceed to Lahore. The Prince obeyed leaving Batala with an escort of 300 men, and reached the vicinity of Lahore on the morning of 13 January, to encamp on

---

1 S.L. d. IV (II) p. 8 gives Poh as the month in which the Raja left.
2 Ibid.
3 S.L. d. IV (II) p. 9, his remark is significant

the site of an old brick kiln known as *Budhu dā Āwā*[1] about six miles south-east of the city. This mound commanded roads leading to three major cantonments of Lahore, Naulakha, Begampur and Mianmir. The Prince took up residence in a large building on top of the kiln, and his *mukhtiar*, Jawala Singh, himself a brave and popular soldier as well as an astute politician, opened negotiations on behalf of his master with the troops in the cantonments. Men and officers already sounded by Dhian Singh and General Ventura,[2] came forward to side with the Prince. Desertions to his camp began as soon as the news of his arrival gained currency. Soldiers were followed by civilians. *Budhu dā Āwā* became a rival court... Rani Chand Kaur was not idle. While Dhian Singh was wooing the troops in the cantonments, she won Gulab Singh Dogra to her cause. He, Teja Singh and Attar Singh Sindhanwalia, became busy buying the support of soldiers quartered about the fort. Gulab Singh took upon himself the defence of the city and the citadel, moving from bastion to bastion to distribute coins by the handful to the guards on duty. It is estimated that Gulab Singh gave away three lakhs and Sher Singh five during the twenty-four hours before hostilities commenced on the morning of 16 January. Love of gold had so corrupted the Khalsa soldiers that they abandoned any attempt at discrimination between right and wrong and sold their blood to the highest bidder, sometimes avowing allegiance to each side in turn. By the evening of 15 January, Sher Singh had a force of about 26,000 infantry, 8000 cavalry and a park of artillery comprising 45 guns, also Generals Ventura, Court and Mahtab Singh Majithia, in his train. He marched from his camp two hours after sunset and appeared before the wicket gate of the city adjoining the Badshahi mosque. Dhaunkal Singh's battalion, which was on guard, promptly betrayed the cause of the Rani and opened the gate. The same occurred at three other gates, the Delhi, the Yakki and the Taxali. Thus, before sunrise on 16 January, Sher Singh

---

1 S.L d. IV (II) p. 9.
2 Sher Singh had met General Ventura when the latter was returning and requested him for help. The writer of an article in the *Calcutta Review*, 1844, p. 483 states "the General (Ventura) finding the army disgusted with the Mai, (Chand Kaur) encouraged them to make a new *baṇdobast* with Sher Singh."

## The Heel of Achilles

was master of most of the city.¹ He called upon the defending troops to surrender. Rani Chand Kaur spurned his offer of safe conduct and prepared for battle. She pinned her hopes upon the fidelity of Gulab Singh, Teja Singh and Attar Singh Sindhanwalia. That Gulab Singh Dogra should find himself thus in opposition to his brother remains something of a mystery. It is probable that desiring to hold the administration together till Dhian Singh's return from Jammu, he had found it necessary to support the Rani, and the rapid march of events found him unprepared² for any considered re-alignment.

As soon as Rani Chand Kaur's decision was made plain, Sher Singh ordered his artillery to open fire on the fort. The Hazuri Bagh gate was blown off by a battery of twelve guns and a band of two to three hundred Nihangs made a frontal charge in an attempt to take the citadel. The defending Dogra gunners stood firm and met the onslaught by firing two cannons simultaneously. Nearly a hundred Nihangs bit the dust. Before a second attack could be launched, the Dogras had their guns reloaded and the second Nihang charge met the same fate. Meanwhile Dogra infantry poured deadly fire from their muskets upon a dense mass of besiegers who had approached the walls of the fort. "In ten minutes," observed Major Smyth, "the Hazuri Bagh was cleared of besiegers who left behind them about fifty prisoners, taken during a sally of the Dogras, sword in hand."³ During the ensuing confusion Sher Singh fled back to his quarters. An attack on the eastern gate was repulsed by the skilful tactics of Gulab Singh and his men; the whole operation having proved a triumph for the small force of Dogras against a vastly superior (if reckoned numerically) Sikh army.

For two days there was a stalemate. Meanwhile Ajit Singh Sindhanwalia,⁴ who had been sent by the Rani to ask for aid from

---

1 S.L. d. IV (II) p. 10-12; also Mohd. Latif, p. 503.
2 Kahan Singh of Banga, a contemporary Punjabi poet expressed this view in a ballad, *Jangnama*, verses 90-94; also Clerk in a letter dated 12 January.
3 *Reigning Family of Lahore*, pp. 55-59.
4 Ajit Singh left Lahore about the 10th, happening to meet Sher Singh on the way at Pul Kanjari. S.L. d. LV (II) pp. 9-10. Clerk refused Ajit an interview as the Governor-General was not in favour of being party to the domestic quarrels of the Sikhs. Ajit Singh wrote: "as I was not encouraged in my ideas by the Governor-General, therefore this time I have not taken a definite course." P.G.R.

the British Agent at Ludhiana, had drawn a blank. She then directed Bhai Ram Singh to see Clerk's munshi, Harsarn Das, who was stationed in Lahore, and communicate to him, verbatim, what she had proposed in her letter to Clerk. As a result, Harsarn Das wrote to Clerk in detail: The Rani, apparently had declared herself willing to accept a British Resident in Lahore and to be guided by him in forming a ministry. She offered, if the British would come to her help, to transfer to them either the province of Kashmir, or one-fourth of the annual revenues of the entire Punjab, and one year's revenue from Kashmir as a personal gift for Russell Clerk. She added that State troops in Lahore numbered no more than 20,000, and it would take only eight British battalions to bring them under control. (Bhai Ram while pressing the Rani's suit, found fit to interpolate an idea on his own that Chand Kaur herself being without an heir, and Sahib Kaur's expected child a doubtful proposition, the British would have a chance of obtaining the Punjab by escheat; he only asked, in view of this contingency that the Sardar's jagirs be guaranteed in perpetuity).[1]

Sher Singh, desperate because of Gulab Singh's continued support of the Rani, sent an urgent summons to Dhian Singh in Jammu.[2] With his arrival on 18 January, the Prince and the Minister rode into the city, mounted on the same elephant amid the acclamation of the troops and the relief of the populace.

The few days of fighting had wrought untold misery on Lahore. When Sher Singh entered the city during the severest phase of winter, the soldiers engaged in an orgy of pillaging and violence. Merchants and traders closed their places of business and removed what goods they could get away with to hiding places in narrow unlit streets, where people huddled together without food or drink. In their absence, soldiers broke open the shops and looted what they could find. They killed anyone who offered resistance—then they killed for sport. The *Gulab Khana* that in Ranjit Singh's time had been stocked with delicacies, wines, dried fruits, nuts and preserves of all kinds, was made free for all, and according to Sohan Lal, the Khalsa sepoys feasted on its

[1] The text of his letter re. this is worth perusal showing so patently, a willingness to barter away political freedom, while holding on to personal gains.
[2] S.L. d. IV (II) p. 13.

## The Heel of Achilles

contents for two days. They smashed all the rare glass and pottery.[1] (This particular act of vandalism might well serve to point for the historian the end of a long spell of peace and prosperity, which had continued unbroken for Lahore, ever since Ranjit Singh occupied it in 1799. The present generation of men and women had known no other condition, and discovered at this juncture, their own countrymen behaving as they had been led to believe only the barbarous Afghan hordes of Abdali's time, could be expected to do).

Dhian Singh's terms for peace required that Chand Kaur renounce all claim to the throne; that she be given a jagir valued at Rs. 900,000 per annum, and be treated with the respect and honour that befitted her rank. Raja Gulab Singh and his Dogra troops were to be granted a safe conduct out of the fort; Sher Singh was to be Maharaja and Dhian Singh Chief Minister.

These terms being accepted by the Rani, the fort was vacated by Gulab Singh's army and occupied by Sher Singh on 20 January 1840.[2] Gulab Singh and the treasurer, Misr Beli Ram, then paid homage to the new sovereign and Gulab Singh presented to him on Chand Kaur's behalf the *Koh-i-Noor* and was given permission to return to his home in Jammu. So ended the seventy days of Chand Kaur's misrule. They turned out to be significant[3] in that they exposed the Achilles heel of the Sikh kingdom, the vulnerable point in the body politic, which the British were to discover and turn to their own advantage.

Sher Singh and Chand Kaur had each offered slices of Ranjit Singh's kingdom to the British. It was only too evident that this was not to preserve what remained of the state but to forward their own personal interests. Moreover, their tortuous negotiations exposed to the British Agent a great deal of valuable information regarding personnel in the Sikh state. The Agent was in a strong position in advising his government on how best to use a particular Sardar, a family or an official, to further British ambitions. It is not surprising then, that soon after the accession of Sher Singh Lord Ellenborough began making plans for the conquest of the Punjab.

---

1 S.L. d. IV (II) p. 12.
2 Ibid.
3 Ibid. pp. 15-16.

## Sunset of the Sikh Empire

Seeds of yet another weakness had been sown during the ten weeks' interregnum. In wooing the army, members of the ruling family had failed to realize that they were creating in many a rude untutored soldier an exaggerated notion of his own importance. The army had in fact been invested with the role of king-maker to the detriment of the prestige and dignity of the state and the sovereign. To check the forces that had thus been released would have been a difficult task for any man, more so for Sher Singh who was in large measure responsible for the situation.

MAHARAJA SHER SINGH

## Chapter 4
## NEMESIS

The formal ceremony whereby Sher Singh was invested as Maharaja took place on 20 January 1841. Baba Bikram Singh Bedi of Una put the *qashqā*, (saffron mark) on the forehead of the Prince, and blessed him and his son, Kanwar Partab Singh. The chiefs present paid homage and presented the customary *nazars*. Among these were Attar Singh Sindhanwalia and others who had sworn earlier that they would compel Prince Sher Singh to retire to his jagir and support Rani Chand Kaur as regent at least for eight months.[1] At this moment things promised well. The supporters of Chand Kaur were in a chastened frame of mind, or else departed from the court. Ajit Singh Sindhanwalia had already left; his uncle, Attar Singh, was soon to follow. The British attitude seemed to indicate tacit acceptance of the investiture. But hopes of tranquillity were short-lived.

The army, already out of hand and a menace to peaceful conducting of business, now demanded the emoluments and rewards they had so rashly been promised, not only by Sher Singh but his Chief Minister, Dhian Singh, and his friend, Jwala Singh. There was little money in the treasury to honour these commitments. The period of unrest had inevitably resulted in governors in the provinces becoming remiss in submitting revenues to the capital. In addition, Chand Kaur and Gulab Singh had taken advantage of their unmolested exit by including in their baggage cartloads of cash, gold and jewellery from the *Toshā-khānā*. The government, therefore was obliged to ignore the demands of the soldiers, who in their turn, felt fully justified in helping themselves. For days, the soldiers made it a practice to desert their posts, claiming that the government owed them arrears, that the pay-clerks were fraudulent (this particular grievance was well founded),[2] and

---

[1] S.L. d. IV (II) p. 17.
[2] The *Punjab Akhbarat* (Feb. 1841) states that even some of the *Maulvis* (distinguished scholars) were roughly handled, because suspected of teaching the *munshis* the art of devious account-keeping.

that their commanders were unnecessarily harsh. They assembled in bazaars and squares and marched in a body to plunder homes and shops, but also to hunt, maltreat or kill the fraudulent *munshis*, (clerks) and those officers, who had come to be regarded as rigid or even over-particular about discipline,[1] among them being General Court, Jamadar Khushal Singh and Lehna Singh Majithia. For eight to ten weeks, according to Sohan Lal, the city was turned into a veritable hell. The common sepoy became so overbearing that the peaceful citizens were allowed no quarter, and people of rank were not immune. Ministers and secretaries of government were mocked and jeered at, and Sher Singh, himself greeted with the refrain that unless he paid up, Rani Chand Kaur would be restored.[2]

Insubordination soon spread to other parts of the kingdom. Reports of excesses committed by troops in the provinces poured in. From Srinagar, came news that the governor, Man Singh, had been hacked to pieces (19 April) *Jism-i-nāzim rezā rezā kardand*;[3] from Mandi came the report of the murder of Commandant Foulkes[4] (March 1841); from Hazara the murder of Major Ford (8 April) and from Amritsar, of the garrison commander, Sobha Singh. General Avitable was constrained to abandon Peshawar and seek shelter at Jalalabad, and Diwan Sanwan Mal, governor of Multan, only escaped the wrath of his troops by a ruse. He paid them at the enhanced rate they demanded and gave them leave, *raza*, to go home, but arranged for Pathan dacoits to relieve them of the cash on the way.

This state of lawlessness continued with brief intervals of quiet for at least six months. It is the less understandable considering that in the past both Sher Singh and Dhian Singh had been popular with the soldiery. Dhian Singh had charge of the whole of the westernised section of the military force. Recruitment, postings, transfers, promotions, leave and incidental

---

1 Court fled to Ferozepore to seek refuge with the British. Ventura was rescued by the Maharaja's personal guard.
Ibid. *Akhbarat* dated 8 Feb. 1841.
2 S.L. d. IV (II) pp. 18-19 & 34.
3 S.L. d. IV (II) p. 29.
4 Foulkes, Moulton and Holmes were left in charge of the brigade in Mandi when Ventura returned to Lahore in early March; the two latter escaped.

favours, were all in his provenance,[1] and when he had chosen to espouse Sher Singh's cause, the response had been most gratifying. Moreover, the financial demands of the army were, at least partially met. The pay-rolls of March 1841-February 1842, show that the scale of pay was raised, in the case of the sepoy by one rupee per month, for company commanders, from one to three; regimental commanders were given both promotion and additional salary. And each man was rewarded with a gratuity amounting to one month's salary.[2]

It seems probable that the grievance of the army had its origin in the conduct of the battle against Chand Kaur. The fact that Gulab Singh persisted in his allegiance to the Rani was a reverse for his brother in more than one way. The Dogra schism in itself was a source of uneasiness to the army; to this was added the lamentable failure of Sikh soldiers to gain the citadel by assault and the heavy punishment inflicted upon them by the Dogras, kinsmen of Dhian Singh, who they were trying to restore to office. This was enough to make him unpopular, as subsequently, did the measures he was forced to take to check the turbulence of the soldiers. He was responsible for a policy whereby the more violent elements in the army, very often Sikhs, were transferred from important military stations to others where scope for making trouble was slighter, and of recruiting new men, mostly non-Sikhs, from Jammu and the other Punjab hills. Between the months of June 1841 and February 1842, some six thousand of these hillmen were formed into 8 battalions of infantry and 3 units of light artillery.[3] This, very naturally, aroused suspicion of him, both as a disciplinarian and a Dogra.

Perhaps the root cause of the trouble was that the form of devotion the Sikhs had learned to cultivate was that prescribed by Guru Gobind Singh: it was devotion to the *Panth*. Believing in their theocratic political system they were distressed to see its disintegration through dissension between members of the ruling family, their shameless exhibition of selfish motives, and their willingness to dismember the state in order to ingratiate them-

---

1 This had been so since 1834, when Ranjit Singh had his first stroke of paralysis, and was forced to delegate heavy work.
2 For details see Kh. S.R. vol. 1, pp. 51 & 56-57.
3 For details see Kh. D.R. vol. 1, pp. 56-57.

## Sunset of the Sikh Empire

selves with the British. It was feelings such as these which led the Khalsa soldiers to decide that the duty of preserving the state now devolved on them, and to the formation of *Panchayats*, and from this, to the concept of the *Sarbat Khalsa* a body of men, who regarded themselves as truly representing the Sikh people, and fitted by virtue of their own prestige and power to discuss matters with the government.[1]

Although Sher Singh had the throne and the grandees of the Darbar acknowledged him, his mind was not at ease. The possibility of Nau Nihal Singh's widow giving birth to a male child, could not be ignored; nor could the fact that two of Rani Chand Kaur's staunchest supporters, Attar Singh and his nephew, Ajit Singh Sindhanwalia, had escaped to British India and were active in promoting her claims. Sher Singh became so obsessed with the feeling of insecurity that he could only think of murder to alleviate his condition. His first victim was the pregnant Kanwarani Sahib Kaur. Having noised it abroad that her pregnancy was a fiction invented by Chand Kaur who was planning to smuggle a male child into the zenana at the appropriate moment; a slave girl was bribed to administer drugs to Sahib Kaur which brought about a miscarriage, and a young Kashmiri girl *zanka*[2], inveigled into the Darbar to spread the lie. When the dignitaries were assembled, she entered and made a statement: "since the time I was conceived, Rani Chand Kaur began to take an interest in me. One day she whispered to me that if I bore a baby boy, he would be placed on the throne of Lahore."[3] The Darbaris, accustomed to the dignity of Ranjit Singh's court, were amazed by this charade being enacted before them. Sohan Lal concludes his account of the episode by quoting a famous couplet of Saadi: "If your king calls the day, night, you must at once, say in response, 'yes Sire, we see the moon and the stars;'

---

1 The much-maligned military *panchayats* had come into being at the suggestion of the Govt. When Sher Singh and Dhian Singh were convinced they could not control the fierce spirit of the Khalsa soldiers, they asked them to present their demands in a more orderly way through some representative body. The institution of a *panchayat* was familiar in every village, so an obvious one for the purpose; two men from each unit of infantry, cavalry and artillery (officers being excluded) were chosen to serve as emissaries from the soldiers to the government.

2 Diminutive of Persian, *zan* or woman; age usually ranging from 8-10.

3 *Har gāh az bātan-i-tau pisrtalwallad shawadd o rā bar sarir-i-saltanat-o-jahāndari nishānidah khwāhad shud.* S.L. d. IV (II) pp. 19-20.

for remember that if you choose to act against the wishes of your sovereign, you must be prepared every moment to wash your stained hands with your own blood."[1] Sohan Lal's view was corroborated by Dr. Murray and also by Mr. Clerk. Dr. Murray stated: "the Lahore bazaars are whispering that Rani Sahib Kaur was delivered of a still-born child and it was not in the interests of Sher Singh that the child should be born alive."[2] The British Agent, who had his own private sources of information, did not believe in the Maharaja's version.[3]

Chand Kaur was the next victim. When she agreed to surrender the citadel to Sher Singh, she was by no means content, either with the *Jāgīr* bestowed upon her, or by Sher Singh's offers of marriage. However, the proposal gave her the excuse for leaving the palace to reside in her own *haveli* (mansion) within the city till Sher Singh took her back as a bride.[4] From this vantage point, she re-commenced her intrigues with the Sardars, the army and the British. Ajit Singh Sindhanwalia whom she had sent to the British Agent at Ludhiana, was now instructed to proceed to Calcutta to wait upon the Governor-General. Attar Singh was instructed to take up residence in Ferozepore, because of its proximity to Lahore, instead of Thanesar. She also employed secret agents to work among the troops, to inflame their grievances. When Sher Singh returned to the capital after attending Holi celebrations in Amritsar, the Khalsa soldiers surrounded the palace, also yelled at him saying that he owed his position to them, and threaten to replace him by Rani Chand Kaur.[5] The Maharaja considered it expedient to remain quiet, but resolved to rid himself of the nuisance.[6] It is probable that Dhian Singh was privy to his design, and possibly entrusted with the arrangements for carrying it out, while Sher Singh betook himself on a hunt in the direction of Wazirabad. Dhian Singh chose to work through the agency of Mahan Singh, Thanedar of Lahore, and Ichar Singh, Jamadar of

---

1 Ibid.
2 See also vol. II, p. 239. Allen & Co.
3 Clerk to Govt. also Vernacular Correspondence, letter no. 80, book no. 155, and letter no. 40, book no. 151. P.G.R.
4 Gulab Singh had suggested to the Rani that she and her daughter-in-law would be safer with him in Jammu, but she did not trust him any more than she trusted Sher Singh.
5 S.L. d. IV (II) p. 34.
6 L.G. p. 336.

the guard at Chand Kaur's *haveli*. Four of the Rani's women attendants were bribed with gifts, and promises of more to come, to kill their mistress! They first infused poison in a beverage she was in the habit of taking (*arq gulāb-o-bed mushq*). She refused to take it. Then while she was asleep, her skull was battered with a stone. After three days of agony, she died, on 12 June. She was cremated in the precincts of Mai Nakain's garden, near the mausoleum of Anarkali, where later, a modest monument was built to her memory.[1] Since the Maharaja was away at the time of the Rani's death it was left to Dhian Singh to dissimulate the nature of the crime, which he did by ordering that the perpetrators should have their hands cut off and be banished from the Punjab. (*kanīzkān mazkurā rā maqtā al oadd kardāh az shahar badar kardand*). It is difficult to fathom Dhian Singh's motives since Rani Chand Kaur could have been a valuable counterpoise to Sher Singh. What weighed with the Minister was a grudge against the Sindhanwalias and, perhaps more, the idea that the very act of complicity would put Sher Singh at his mercy. (*tā dam-i-hayāt-ākhir mummat sarkār-wālā marhun-i-minnat maufurāh-o-māmnun-i-nā māhsurā shuma khwāhad gardid*).[2]

Mention has already been made of a seal presented to Sher Singh which had, upon it both his name and the title Maharaja. On some of the state documents, his signature occurs, scribbled in Roman letters: Sher Singh. From a different source it is gathered that he ordered the minting of coins, to bear his name as sovereign, instead of the names of the gurus. These were not insignificant innovations. Maharajas Ranjit Singh, Kharak Singh and Nau Nihal Singh had never formally assumed the title, nor allowed their names or effigies to be engraved on the currency.[3] Their coins bore the names of the first and the last gurus, with a legend stating that it was through the grace of the gurus that the Khalsa had attained sovereignty.[4] It was thereby emphasised

1 S.L. d. IV (II) pp. 34-37. Mai Nakain was the popular name by which Ranjit Singh's senior wife, and the mother of Kharak Singh was known.
2 S.L. d. IV (II) p. 37.
3 A miniature of Ranjit appeared for the first and last time on a gold medal, *Kaukab-i-iqbal-i-Punjab*, which was struck on the occasion of Prince Nau Nihal's marriage.
4 The legend, which runs: *Deg o teg o Fateh o nusrat be darang yaft az Nanak Guru Gobind Singh*, was originally composed for the official seal of the Khalsa in the time of Gobind or Banda Bahadur. See *Mohd. Latif*, p. 270 & *Teja Singh & Ganda Singh*, vol. 1, p.87.

that the individual who occupied the *gaddi* at any particular time, did so by the authority of the Khalsa state *Sarkar Khālsā jeo*, as this concept was popularly rendered.¹

Ranjit Singh had respected this idea and deliberately avoided using any symbol that might have been construed as an arrogation of royalty to himself. He assumed no regal titles, nor sat upon a throne, or struck coins in his own name. It is possible that Sher Singh's departure from this tradition, was one more sign of his insecurity about the *gaddi*, but no serious notice appears to have been taken, of his attempts at innovation by the Sardars or by the body of the *Panth*.²

Sardar Jawala Singh had been appointed by Maharaja Ranjit Singh to administer Prince Sher Singh's jagirs. By conscientious work and honest dealings he was able to win the confidence of his young master, and in time, became not only his chief adviser, but a close friend. When Sher Singh marched on Lahore in January 1841, Jawala Singh was with him, and during Dhian Singh's absence from the scene (13-17 January), it was he who negotiated with the troops at Lahore and led the first attack on the fort. Later he was to perform the onerous duty of taking over the estates of the Sindhanwalias. Encouraged by his own success and the Prince's approbation, he began to aspire to the position of Chief Minister. But he proved no match for the Dogra's wiles. Dhian Singh insinuated to the Maharaja that Jawala Singh had conspired with the Sindhanwalia chiefs, and warned Jawala Singh that he had lost the Maharaja's good-will. The Sardar took alarm and decided to revolt. He won over the *Chahār Yārī* horse of irregular cavalry, one of the biggest divisions, comprising about 5000 men, and set up a camp near the Shalimar Gardens (May 1841). When summoned by the Maharaja, he refused to present himself. Then Dhian Singh intervened. He persuaded Sher Singh that, if strong measures were not promptly taken, treason was likely to spread and affect the

---

1 Guru Gobind invested the *Panth* with this authority; on initiating the first five disciples, he is said to have asked that they in turn should initiate him to the *Panth*. This was not unprecedented in the Punjab. The coins of the Yaudheyas, the Arjunayas and other republics bear legends invoking victory for the whole community e.g., *jaya yaudheya ganasya*. See Dr. B. Sahni's monograph, *Numismatic Society of India*, 1945.

2 An exception, was the refusal of the custodian of the Takht Keshgarh, to accept an offering made in the new coins.

nobility as it had the soldiers. The Maharaja marched in person against the rebels but the soldiers refused to surrender their leader. He was forced to parley with the army *panchs*. He only achieved his object when a cash donation of thirty thousand rupees was granted to them. Commenting on this concession Sir Lepel Griffin observes: "It is a remarkable proof of the lawlessness and power of the army at this time, that the very men of the *Chahār Yārī* horse and the Akalis who had on the first day of May supported Jawala Singh in mutiny and treason, on the second, demanded and obtained a donation of 30,000 rupees from Maharaja Sher Singh for having *not* compelled Jawala Singh to fight against him."[1] Jawala Singh was led into Lahore in chains. He was tortured. After forty days he died.

## The gallant Zorawar Singh

Though the Khalsa army was making trouble at home, some of the Maharaja's feudatories were engaged in extending the boundaries of his kingdom in far-off places and earning kudos for themselves and their country. Colonel Zorawar Singh, who had a year ago, rendered the small state of Iskardo tributary to the Lahore Darbar resumed hostilities against the Tibetans in April 1841. He demanded of the governor of Gartok (in the kingdom of Lhasa) the surrender of Rohtak district on the grounds that it was a dependency of Iskardo which was now a part of the kingdom of Lahore; he also desired, that all Lhasa's raw wool should be sent to Ladakh. Ladakh and Lhasa were the most important wool-producing centres in this region and the shawl manufacturers of Kashmir had been almost the entire market for it; recently however, a major portion of the Lhasa wool was being conveyed to cities in India by a route along the Sutlej passing through the British-protected state of Bushair. The conquest of Lhasa would ensure the diversion of its *pashm* back to Kashmir and make for the prosperity of its people. Zorawar Singh was, therefore, encouraged to pursue his expansive projects in the Tibetan regions, as far as he could do so on his own resources; he was warned that there was little chance of military aid from Lahore. The Dogra Colonel, having marched his forces through

1 L.G.P. 127.

this difficult terrain at least three times in the past did not lose any time. Early in May 1841 he proceeded against Gartok. He occupied the town with the help of Ladakhi troops in June. From there he moved towards Tuklakote. He was intercepted by a force sent from Lhasa, but he forced the Tibetans to withdraw (29 August) and succeeded in occupying Tuklakote. The town was of some size and importance near Lake Mansrowar, source of the Indus and Sutlej. He thus brought the dominion of Lahore close to the frontiers of Nepal.

Zorawar Singh decided to spend the winter in Tuklakote, to rest his troops and muster his resources, before undertaking the long march to Lhasa. The defences of the town were repaired and a couple of new forts built. The Dogra garrison thus found itself placed opposite the British outpost of Almora in the Kumaon hills.

The spectacular victories of Zorawar Singh alarmed the British who imagined that the object was to bring "the two Hindu kingdoms of Nepal and Lahore close to one another behind the screen of the Himalayas." The danger of losing the wool traffic from Lhasa was also of concern to them. Russell Clerk arrived at Lahore in October 1841 to remonstrate with the Darbar. He pointed out that the British had been at war with the Chinese and were now in process of making terms of peace; that if China were to think the Sikh offensive in Tibet were instigated by them, the chances of a satisfactory agreement would be jeopardized.[1] The Maharaja was therefore requested to recall his troops from Lhasa by the middle of December 1841. So very anxious was the British government to see this done, that Captain J. D. Cunningham (well known as a historian of the Sikhs) was appointed as special officer, to see the matter through, and also to arrange for the authority of the Lama to be re-established.[2] The Maharaja agreed to withdraw the Dogras. But before the order reached Zorawar Singh, the situation had taken a turn.

---

[1] This is a reference to the opium war (1839-42). The opium traffic between India and China was mostly in the hands of British merchants. When the Chinese government forbade the import of the drug, the British took to smuggling it on an immense scale; hence the war.

[2] Indian Historical Records Commission, vol. XX, part II, p. 4: Paper by M. S. Ahluwalia; also Cunningham, pp. 242-43.

The Chinese government had not been unaware of Zorawar Singh's movements and that he had penetrated as far into the interior as Lake Mansrowar. A well-planned counter attack was launched against him. One force, nearly 10,000 strong, marched from Lhasa; another of almost equal strength was sent via Gartok, and a division of 2,000 picked Chinese soldiers was held in readiness in Yarkand. Zorawar Singh realising the magnitude of the odds, and that retreat in mid-winter was out of the question, made overtures for peace. These being rejected, he moved out of Tuklakote, to give battle on the banks of Lake Mansrowar (10-13 December). The Dogras were not sufficiently acclimatised to fight at such an altitude and in such bitter cold. Some of them were actually frozen to death; others too benumbed to fire their matchlocks. The Chinese, on the other hand, were inured to frost and the mountains, and had superiority in numbers as well. The Dogras were overwhelmed. Zorawar Singh fighting in the van was struck and pierced by a lance.

The Lhasa army took the offensive and in the next five months recovered all it had lost, Tuklakote, Gartok, Rohtak and Iskardo and threatened Ladakh. There, Mian Munga Ram, with a garrison of 400 Dogras, defied the Lhasa troops till the close of May 1842, and when reinforcements arrived from Jammu led by Wazir Ratnu and Diwan Hari Chand, the Lhasa Commander hurriedly broke camp and retreated towards Gartok leaving Diwan Hari Singh in undisputed occupation of Ladakh. The Diwan resolved to punish the rulers of Ladakh and Iskardo for their treacherous conduct during the hostilities. Both of these tributary chieftains had refused to come to the help of Munga Ram and made common cause with the Chinese. After they had been chastised, Diwan Hari Singh and Wazir Ratnu went in pursuit of the retreating Chinese. By the beginning of August, their advance party had reached a spot whence it could easily retake the district of Garo, but when victory was in sight the British again intervened. They drew the Lahore Darbar's attention to the agreement concluded by Clerk in the previous year (October 1841) which recognised the authority of the Khalsa over Ladakh but not beyond it. Accordingly, Diwan Hari Singh was ordered to wind up the Lhasa expedition. He concluded an agreement with the Chinese officers and returned to

Jammu. However, he had been able to secure certain advantages for his government. He persuaded the ruler of Lhasa to send all raw wool and tea produced in his territory to Ladakh and to recognise the sovereignty of Lahore over Ladakh. Thus, was abandoned the prospect opened up by the gallant and intrepid Zorawar Singh. Raja Gulab Singh had not been in favour of renouncing the advantages which his officers had gained in the Lhasa territory and had urged his views on the Darbar, asserting that the British should refrain from interference, if not out of generosity, at least from gratitude, since they had grown used to the Sikhs fighting their battles in Afghanistan. On the other hand, Lord Ellenborough writing to the Duke of Wellington (7 June 1842) recorded "... I have already, as you are aware, said what I could to dissuade the Sikhs, or rather Dhian and Gholab Singh the Jammu Rajas, from their wild views of conquest beyond the Himalyas."

The assassination of Shuja-ul-Mulk on 5 April 1842, raised another issue between the two powers. The Tripartite Treaty had been signed by them and by the Shah at a time when the latter had no territory he could call his own. Upon his death the question of the validity of the treaty was considered and the British proposed a fresh treaty to the Khalsa government. The Darbar accordingly sent a draft to the British Agent in Ludhiana. This draft included clauses whereby (1) Sikh possession of Swat, Buner, and Panjtar would be formally recognised, (2) the practice of sending British troops through the Punjab be discontinued as it infringed on the sovereignty of the Sikhs.[1] The Agent, reporting the matter to his government stated he was prepared to accept (1) as an act of 'policy and clemency'; concerning (2) his comments were to the effect that the Sikhs were over-apprehensive in regard to their independence as a result of too much unguarded discussion about the future of the Punjab in the English press in India during the past few years. The Governor-General was not prepared to give up the concession of passage

[1] Clerk to Govt. 23 April and 19 July 1842. Panjab Govt. Records, Lahore. The Darbar has also proposed that Sultan Muhammad Khan Barakzai, a jagirdar of the Lahore govt. should be placed on the Afghan throne instead of his brother Dost Muhammad; that the revenues of Kabul be divided in three shares, one for Sultan Muhd., one for the Afghan chiefs who were helping the British and one to be divided between the Sikhs and the British.

for his troops, which his government had extorted from the Darbar on one pretext or the other. Further, he insisted that the Darbar permit Dost Mohammad to pass through the Punjab on his way to Kabul and provide him with an escort. He required also that the Sikh government should undertake "not to recognise any sovereign of Kabul whom we have not previously recognised." The Sikhs would not accept these terms.[1] Nothing came of the negotiations but the Darbar met the wishes of the British to the extent of permitting Dost Muhammad to pass through the Punjab. The Darbar contracted a treaty of amity and friendship[2] with Dost Mohammed independent of the British.

British garrisons were withdrawn from Afghanistan. Lord Ellenborough issued a declaration dated 1 October 1843, defining the future policy of his government in regard to the country of the Afghans.[3] With characteristic imperialist aplomb he stated "the Governor-General will leave it to the Afghans themselves to create a government amidst the anarchy which is the consequence of their crimes... the Governor-General will willingly recognise any government approved by the Afghans themselves, which shall appear desirous and capable of maintaining friendly relations with the neighbouring states..." Dost Muhammad was set at liberty and returned to Kabul as ruler.[4] On his way he stayed in Lahore (25 January-15 February 1843) as the guest of Maharaja Sher Singh and the opportunity was taken, of drawing up a friendly agreement. (Negotiations were carried through by Raja Dhian Singh and Sultan Mahmud Khan, a brother of Amir Dost Muhammad, who resided at Lahore as one of the feudal chiefs of the Sarkar Khalsa). The document which embodies the terms of alliance was in the form of a letter from the Amir, and is reproduced in Sohan Lal's book.[5] Its principal clauses were: (1) I will reciprocate fully the friendship of the Sarkar Khalsa;

---

1 Ellenborough to Wellington, 16 August 1842. Colchester.

2 The alliance was made with the knowledge, and perhaps, concurrence of the British govt. although they were not party to it.

3 This document was drawn up and signed on 10 Oct., but dated 1 Oct., as if to invite comparison with Lord Auckland's manifesto of 1 Oct. 1838. *Auckland* by Trotter, p. 206.

4 Dost Muhammed ruled till the ripe old age of 80, which demonstrates the mischievousness of British allegations of misrule, and the mistake that it was, to have placed Shah Shujah on the throne in his place, originally.

5 Div. III, p. 7. S. L. gives also the draft prepared by the Khalsa, to point out clauses the Amir had disapproved or altered.

and will be the friend of the friend and the enemy of the enemy of the Sarkar Khalsa, provided the Sarkar Khalsa maintains that attitude towards me.  (2) Of all my five sons, whoever is invited by the Sarkar Khalsa, will go to Lahore gladly and without harbouring any fear or feelings of mistrust.  (3) I will have no claim or concern with the trans-Indus territory, like Peshawar, Dehra Ismail Khan, Dehra Ghazi Khan, etc., now in the possession of the Sarkar Khalsa.  (4) The Fatehgarh *nullah* will continue to supply fresh water on the same terms as before and its channel will not be stopped or diverted.[1]  (5) The Punjab merchants who come to Kabul will not be harassed by my government for payment of customs duties, taxes etc. and their safety will be the concern of my government; and in the case of officers appointed by the government of Lahore for the purchase of horses for the use of the government, I undertake to help them personally in making a good selection.  (6) Should any one of the Princes or the Raja Sahib happen to come to Peshawar, I will be happy to meet them there with customary ceremonial presents.  (7) When the Sarkar Khalsa is at war, and a demand for help by my troops is made, I will give it, without demur or reluctance.  (8) In case of a joint expedition, my brother, Sultan Muhammad Khan, will be in command of the troops of the Sarkar Khalsa; and the booty will be divided in equal shares by our two governments.

## The Afghan Background

It is important to know something of the long history of violence and folly... which preceded the recoronation of Dost Mohammed.  The British tried to put Shah Shujah on the throne of Kabul.  But the Afghans were loath to accept as monarch someone brought in, as it were, in the baggage of a foreign power. Resentment against the Shah and the accursed *farangi*, exploded into violence in various parts of the country.  On the morning of 3 November 1841, an angry mob surrounded the houses of Sir Alexander Burns and Broadfoot and slaughtered every

---

[1] This streamlet was the only source of drinking water for the Sikh garrison in the fort of Fatehgarh, at the entrance to the Khyber pass.  Ranjit Singh used to pay Rs. 1200 annually for this water-supply to the tribes living in the pass.  See also *Sikhs and Afghans* by Shahamat Ali, p. 368.

inmate. General Elphinstone lost his nerve and decided to surrender. On 11 November he handed over to Muhammad Akbar Khan, son of the fugitive Dost Muhammad, 4,500 troops including 700 Europeans; and his guns and stores. Leaving at his mercy the old and the sick, women and children, he made an exit from Kabul on 6 January 1842. The Afghans fell upon the retreating foreigners in the defiles of Khurd Kabul. Two days later only 800 were left alive... Hunger, frost and Afghan bullets accounted for most of the others. Out of 16,500 men almost the sole survivor, Dr. Brydon "fainting from wounds, hunger and exhaustion," arrived in Jalalabad to tell the tale of disaster.

There remained some hundred and twenty British prisoners in Kabul;[1] a British garrison at Kandahar under General Nott; another at Ghazni under Colonel Palmer; one at Kelat-i-Ghilzai under Captain Craigie, and a fourth at Jalalabad, under Robert Sale, but all in desperate need of help. The Khyber route was the shortest, easiest and safest for a relieving force to take. Clerk (now Sir George) went to Lahore to request assistance. Maharaja Sher Singh readily agreed to render this in every possible way, provided the British assured him of support against Rani Chand Kaur, who was still actively plotting against him and whose agents were in British India. Clerk had no option but to give this assurance. British officers in Ludhiana and Ambala were instructed to see that the Sindhanwalias and others, who had fled from Lahore, were not allowed to "disturb Maharaja Sher Singh's reign."[2] The co-operation of the Darbar was thus made available and the British commander at Ferozepur assured that caravans and stores with military escort would be permitted to pass through the Punjab without let or hindrance.[3]

A small relieving force of four infantry regiments, without support of cavalry or artillery, was hastily collected and despatched from Ferozepore late in November to the garrison at Jalalabad. Maharaja Sher Singh sent instructions to his governor, Avitable in Peshawar, to supply Brigadier Wilde with a few pieces of

---

[1] Among the captives, some of the more prominent names are those of Lady Sale, Lady Macnaghten, Colonel Palmer, General Shelton, the political officer, E. Pottinger, and George Lawrence.
[2] Cunningham, p. 248.
[3] *Panjab Akhbarat*, January 1842. N. Arch. Delhi.

## Nemesis

artillery from the cantonment and render any other help that he might need. Raja Gulab Singh was asked to proceed from Hazara to Peshawar to supervise, personally, all arrangements and Clerk deputed Captain Henry Lawrence, liaison officer at Peshawar, to secure the good-will and co-operation of the Sikhs.

Brigadier Wilde took one month to traverse the 300 miles from Ferozepore to Peshawar, and having borrowed four guns from Avitable, forced his way through the Khyber pass on 3 January 1842, to reach Ali Masjid on the 15th. It was then discovered that much of his food supply had been left behind by an oversight. His force was ambushed by Afridis; among the injured was Brigadier Wilde himself. Shortage of provisions and the havoc wrought by snipers armed with long *jazails*, caused sepoys and officers, both Indian and British to lose heart. The first attempt to relieve Jalalabad failed and the troops returned to Jamrud (Peshawar territory) on 24 January.[1]

Meanwhile troops from all over northern India had been ordered to proceed to Peshawar, the rendezvous of the "army of retribution," commanded by General Pollock who arrived in Peshawar early in February. Pollock, to his dismay, found that Wilde's men were in no mood to accompany him. Moreover, some of the English officers shared the feelings of the sepoys.[2] He was forced to wait near Jamrud for his English dragoons and horse artillery till 29 March.

Another reason for delay was that Lieutenant Mackeson with the help of Avitable was trying to win over the Afridi chiefs who controlled the long narrow passage of the Khyber. When reports came in that a large body of Muhammad Akbar Khan's soldiers had arrived in the neighbourhood of Ali Masjid, Pollock was in a quandary. This meant that Jalalabad and other British positions were in graver danger than before. Yet his reinforcements (he was awaiting 4000 men) had not arrived. The 8000 he had, were not likely to be sufficient to risk the hazards of the pass,

---

[1] One reason for the failure, given by Edwardes and Merivale in their Life of Lawrence, was that the Muhammedan soldiers of the Najeeb Battalions sent by the Lahore government to accompany Wilde, refused to fight against their co-religionists, and marched back to Peshawar as the British army entered the Khyber pass. pp. 223-24.
[2] Auckland, R.I.S. p. 170,

and his rooted distrust of the Sikhs made it difficult for him to invoke their aid.[1] Pollock's reluctance was overcome by the political officers, Mackeson and Lawrence, who went to Attock to consult with Gulab Singh Dogra, appointed by the Darbar to assist the British expedition. Gulab Singh had a shrewd and penetrating mind. He understood the object of Major Lawrence's visit before the matter was broached. He perceived in it an opportunity of securing for himself the friendship of the British. He emphasised his difficulties. Sher Singh had shown himself disposed to co-operate with the British, but the feeling in the Darbar was, on the whole, against active help. Dhian Singh had shown reluctance; Ranjit Singh's acceptance of the Tripartite Treaty had not been enthusiastic; so it was easy for Gulab Singh to impress on Lawrence that if he helped out on this occasion' the obligation would be to him and not to the Lahore Darbar.'[2]

Lawrence was happy with the meeting with Gulab Singh. He secured both an assurance of immediate help and the prospect, when and if the need arose, of assistance in winning over other prominent members of the nobility in Lahore. He in turn assured Gulab Singh that his services would not be forgotten or go unrewarded (the reward being a guarantee of secure possession of the hill territory held by him and his family with some possible addition to it). He wrote accordingly to his government stating views and definite proposals.[3]

The British lost no time in sending Gulab Singh a *Kharita* through their Ludhiana Agent expressing appreciation of his help and assuring him of assistance and good will for the future.[4] Gulab Singh marched to Peshawar and used all the charm and skill at his command to persuade the Khalsa soldiers to put aside

1 Pollock to Govt. "the Chiefs are as far as I have observed, courteous and perhaps well-disposed to us, but the bearing of the soldiery one and all is insolent, and they scruple not to express their wish that we may meet with reverses: they are a disorganised rabble." *History of the Punjab*, vol. II, p. 243. Allen & Co.
2 See also Pannikar.
3 Edwardes and Merivale, p. 229; also Cunningham p. 249.
4 *Kharita* dated 8 April, 1842, quoted by Pannikar, p. 55. Although the half-promise of Jalalabad, or Peshawar, did not materialise, Gulab Singh had gained favour through the political officers, with the British, which may have been the basis of rather questionable activities before the battle of Sabraon 5 years later, see also Cunningham, p. 309, with footnotes.

*Nemesis*

hostile sentiments and make the British cause their own.[1] He even succeeded in persuading them to march through the Khyber by a longer route than the British were going to take.[2] Pollock left Peshawar on the afternoon of 5 April. He chose for himself what was known as the Shadi Bagiari route, seven miles longer. The Sikh contingent consisting of ten regiments under General Avitable, left an hour later and proceeded by the 14 mile route known as the Jubla Ka which converged with the other at Ali Masjid. The Sikhs had to fight all the way and thus drew away a large number of the enemy from the other route. This rendered Pollock's march through the Khyber a comparatively easy one. He arrived at Ali Masjid on April 6th, drove the Afghans from it and was joined two hours later by the Sikhs. The next objective was Jalalabad about twenty-five miles further which was held by Robert Sale and a small band of young officers. Out of the Lahore contingent about 3,300 men under Gulab Singh Pohoovindia accompanied the British army; the rest remained to guard the rear. Jalalabad was occupied on 16 April, by the joint efforts of the Sikhs and the British. Pollock did not immediately march on towards Kabul, partly because Lord Ellenborough was finding it difficult to make up his mind about the future of Afghanistan, and partly to allow Colonel Lawrence and Lt. Mackeson time to negotiate an honourable surrender of British prisoners with Muhammad Akbar Khan. When these negotiations failed, the march was resumed. Pollock was not in favour of taking the Sikh contingent beyond Jalalabad. He still doubted their faith and had a poor opinion of their discipline.[3] Under pressure from Colonel Lawrence, however, he agreed to take a part of Gulab Singh Pohoovindia's brigade.[4] After

[1] There were some 18,500 Sikh soldiers in Peshawar, far beyond the peacetime strength, which did not exceed 8000 infantry, 10 or 12 pieces of field artillery, and a division of irregular horse 500 strong. The large numbers had been moved up between May 1841 and Oct. 1842, and might have caused disaster to the British cause if not kept in good humour.

[2] Gulab Singh's biographer states that G. S. pointed out to the Sikh soldiers that it would be well if the British were safely conducted across the pass. Thereafter if they were defeated, their property in Peshawar would pass to the Sikhs; if not, the honours of victory would go to them.

[3] *History of the Sikhs*, vol. II, p. 243.

[4] Cunningham, p. 250 and Lepel Griffin, p. 371. Henry Lawrence's estimate of General Gulab Singh's sympathy with the British cause was justified by subsequent events. He and his son, Ala Singh most decidedly, helped the British during the Second Sikh war.

## Sunset of the Sikh Empire

engagements with Muhammad Akbar at Jagdalak and Tezin (14 and 15 September) the force reached Kabul and re-planted the British flag on the Bala Hisar. The services rendered by the Sikh contingent were mentioned favourably in official despatches by General Pollock and Lord Ellenborough. Considering the plight of the British in Afghanistan since the previous December, the help rendered by the Sikhs had indeed been opportune.[1] The dénouement of the Afghan War, has little bearing on the present subject. Under orders from Lord Ellenborough, Pollock and Nott evacuated Kabul on 12 October; but not before they had blown up the old and beautiful bazaar where the mangled body of Macnaghten had been exposed. This part of the city was the most important emporium of trade in central Asia. Vengeance thus fell on the trading community which had nothing whatever to do with the murder of Macnaghten and others of his company.[2]

For the British, the dismal nature of this Afghan war had meant a general loss of prestige in India. Lord Ellenborough desired therefore to make out of Pollock's recapture of Kabul a means of "regilding its tarnished fame."[3] As Nott and Pollock were leisurely returning across the Punjab with a force of 20,000, another force of the same strength, which the Governor-General was pleased to call "the army of reserve" assembled on the plains of Ferozepore to welcome the conquering heroes. The two armies met on the 17th of December. The town of Ferozepore presented a brilliant pageant the like of which it had never witnessed. Princes from all over India were invited. The Lahore Darbar was represented by Sher Singh's son, Prince Partap Singh and Dhian Singh Dogra. Pollock and Nott were knighted

---

1 Besides aid in the form of soldiers, the Lahore Darbar had helped General Pollock and Brigadier Wilde in procuring a large quantity of supplies, provisions and draught cattle, one item of many being somewhat more than 17,000 camels. Cunningham, p. 249, footnote.

2 Macnaghten, after signing the treaty with Muhammad Akbar Khan tried to seduce to his side some of Akbar's Ghilzai and Kazilbash chiefs. He failed in this but his design was betrayed, Muhd. Akbar, thereupon invited him to confer on 23 December; he and Mr. Trover were murdered but his other companions, George Lawrence and Mackenzie escaped with their lives. Alexander and his brother Charles Burnes and Lt. Broadfoot, who had incurred hatred in the Afghans by their personal "habitual and flagrant misconduct" were assassinated earlier on 3 November.

3 *History of India*, Innes, p. 241.

and a medal was struck, bearing the inscription, *Pax Asiae Restituata*.[1]

Despite the help they had received in the Afghan war, the British continued to cherish schemes for the conquest of the Punjab. Even in Ranjit Singh's time the Governor-General's military secretary, William Osborne, had proposed that immediately after the death of the Maharajah, the Sikh kingdom be invaded and occupied. Two years later Macnaghten wrote from Kabul, suggesting that the Sikh district of Peshawar be seized and a major portion of it made into an integral part of the new Durrani kingdom of Kabul. Six months later (February 1841), when Sher Singh's soldiers were running amok, the Governor-General's Agent at Ludhiana proposed "armed interference" in the affairs of the Punjab. He wrote "... the effects of the late revolution at Lahore, and principally among these, the outrages of the army, are producing consequences upon the Sutlej frontier which are quite incompatible with the general peace and security that ought to prevail on the border of a friendly state. The time seems to have arrived when it is incumbent on the British government to require restoration of order by the head of the state, to threaten if he fails, to interfere to restore it, and be prepared to undertake to do it."[2] To Maharaja Sher Singh he made an offer of help through the envoy of the Sikh government, Fakir Aziz-ud-din, of willingness to march to Lahore with an army of 12,000 British soldiers, which he believed to be adequate to subdue a force four times superior in number,[3] to restore peace and tranquillity in the Maharaja's kingdom, provided His Highness was prepared to cede his cis-Sutlej possessions for the maintenance of this force. Sir George Clerk and the British authorities at headquarters appear to have been quite in earnest about the scheme. Some ten to eleven thousand men were actually held in readiness under Sir James Lumley to move into the Punjab.[4] Clerk's proposal was, however, shelved partly because of Sher

---

[1] The "opium war," against China was also concluded about this time
[2] Clerk to govt., 14 February 1841. P.G.R.
[3] The reason for such an estimate was, that disunity among the Sikhs was expected to result in desertions. *Calcutta Review*, vol. VIII, pp. 478-80.
[4] *Calcutta Review*, vol. VIII, pp. 478-80.

Singh's vacillation,[1] and partly because of the advancing summer, and eventually abandoned because of the catastrophe in Kabul.

Further evidence of the fact that the British were contemplating the conquest of the Punjab while still avowing friendship, is to be found in the English press of India and in the correspondence of civil and military officers and their families. It was apparently talked of as a near possibility in Anglo-Indian circles. Mrs. Henry Lawrence, in a letter dated 26 May 1841, to her friend Mrs. Cameron, wrote "... Wars and rumours of wars are on every side, and there seems no doubt that next cold weather will decide the long suspended question of occupying the Panjab; Henry, both in his civil and military capacity, will probably be called upon to take part in whatever goes on."[2] To another friend, Mrs. Haye, she wrote on 5 June: "Nothing yet promulgated; but H. supposes the army for the Panjab will be divided into three columns; the main body accompanied by Mr. Clerk, our chief, and others by H. and Mr. Cunningham..."[3]

A couple of letters to Field Marshal the Duke of Wellington by Lord Ellenborough, the Governor-General designate, about the middle of October 1841, show also that the talk of impending invasion was not ill-founded or confined to Anglo-Indian society in India; that the project of a war against the Sikhs was actually engaging the attention of the British government, both at home and in India. Before he sailed for India, Lord Ellenborough solicited the expert military opinion of the Duke as to the manner in which a campaign against the Punjab could be successfully conducted. He wrote: "I have requested Lord Fitzroy to employ him (Henry Durand) at once in obtaining all information he can with respect to the Panjab and making a memorandum upon the country for your consideration. I am most anxious to have your opinion..."[4] (15 October 1841). However, on arrival

---

1 Sher Singh was afraid of losing his kingdom to the British; or his life to the Khalsa (if he ceded the cis-Sutlej states). On hearing of the proposition, he simply drew his finger across his throat. See also Cunningham, p. 237, footnote.
  Clerk's proposal, submitted to his govt. in Feb; the papers were not finalised till May. *Calcutta Review*, vol. VIII, pp. 478-80.
2 Quoted from Edwardes and Merivale, vol. I, p. 151.
3 Ibid.
4 Colchester, *Indian Administration of Lord Ellenborough*, p. 157.

## Nemesis

in India Lord Ellenborough found himself engaged in the Afghan trouble, and for the moment his chief concern was to obtain help from the Punjab.

Having provided help to the British, Sher Singh felt assured that the Governor-General would not forward the schemes of the "disturbers of his reign." He was unaware of the extent to which he had enemies within his own court, particularly among the Europeans in his employ. The Italian, General Avitable governor of Peshawar gave help and information to the British.[1] Jean Baptiste Ventura had been taken into the service of the Lahore government by Ranjit Singh in 1822, and he together with Jean Francois Allard, had been responsible for the reorganisation of the army. The latter having been on a year's furlough, returned to duty in October 1842. On a hint contained in a letter from the Duke of Wellington, Lord Ellenborough was encouraged to draw these French officers into his circle of informers. Lord Ellenborough's correspondence with the Duke and Queen Victoria shows that Ventura not only kept him posted about events in Lahore, but helped to shape them as the British desired.[2]

Another of the friends of the British was Gulab Singh Dogra. Henry Lawrence had suggested that the entire Jalalabad-cum-Peshawar territory be made over to him, and the only reason why this was not followed up was the change in the Governor-General. Ellenborough succeeded Lord Auckland. On the advice of Wellington, he favoured complete withdrawal from Afghanistan and strengthening the Sutlej border. The terms he offered to Gulab Singh were: that he will hold the Jalalabad-Peshawar territory; but relinquish Ladakh. To the Duke he wrote, "... If the Sikhs accept Jalalabad, they will be obliged to keep their principal force in that area, and the plains of Lahore and Amritsar will remain with insufficient garrison, within a few marches of

---

[1] Henry Lawrence wrote to his govt. from Peshawar "we need such men as the Rajah and General Avitable, and should bind them to us by the only tie they recognise, self-interest; The Rajas (Gulab & Dhian) secured in their territories, even with additions; General Avitable, guaranteed our aid in retiring with his property, and any other Sirdars aiding us cordially, be specially and separately treated for... "Edwardes and Merivale, Vol. I, p. 229; Cunningham, 249.

[2] Wellington to Ellenborough, 4 Feb. 1843; Ellenborough to the Duke, 11 May 1843; to the Queen, 2 Oct. 1843; Colchester, pp. 246-50 & 397-99.

the Sutlej, on which I shall in twelve days at any time, be able to assemble three European and eleven native battalions, one European regiment of cavalry, two regiments of native cavalry, two irregular cavalry, and twenty-four guns. The state of the Panjab will be under my foot."[1] This plan of occupying the Punjab was being made at the very time when the Sikhs were fighting Britain's battles at Ali Masjid, Jalalabad and Kabul, and while Ellenborough, himself was arranging to have a personal meeting with Maharaja Sher Singh and his ministers to thank them and to decide upon a policy in regard to Afghanistan.[2]

Under instructions from the Governor-General, Clerk arranged that a mission from the Lahore Darbar, should meet him at Ludhiana on 15 December. Accordingly, Sham Singh Attariwala, Fakir Aziz-ud-din and Lehna Singh Majithia went to Phillaur to be available on his arrival. Owing to a misunderstanding the meeting did not take place. Lord Ellenborough took this as an intentional slight and asked for an explanation, whereupon, the Maharaja, without investigating the facts,[3] but anxious to make amends, despatched three of his most prominent dignitaries, Raja Hira Singh, Raja Suchet Singh and Jamadar Khushal Singh to join Fakir Aziz-ud-din and proceed to Ferozepore where the Governor-General had gone. This was not good enough for the English autocrat who had desired that the Maharaja himself and the Chief Minister should present themselves to talk to him and to witness the military display that his government had organised at Ferozepore. Consequently, to appease the Governor-General's vanity, the heir-apparent and Raja Dhian Singh with a splendid military escort (which cost the treasury

---

[1] See Colchester's *Indian Administration;* Duke of Ellenborough, 2 April, Ellenborough's to Duke, 17 May, 17 June and 18 October 1842. Also Cunningham, p. 250.

[2] "The Sikhs have behaved beautifully hitherto. I mean to have an interview with the Maharajah in November, and I hope to be able to carry him and the Jammu Rajas with me, in the policy of leaving the Afghans to their own division." Ellenborough to the Duke of Wellington, 17 May 1842.

[3] Lehna Singh was to be received by the Governor-General in his camp at Ludhiana, conducted by Clerk. While Clerk awaited him half-way between Ludhiana and Phillaur, the Sardar remained at Phillaur, expecting to be found in his own camp. Cunningham, who with the G.-G., states that the Vakil of the Lahore Darbar, in league with Dhian Singh, deliberately misled Lehna Singh about the arrangment, in order to discredit him both with the Maharaja and the British. *History of the Sikhs,* p. 254.

## Nemesis

Rs. 1500,000.) were sent from Lahore to join the Ferozepore celebrations. Lord Ellenborough was sufficiently mollified to receive the young Partap Singh and pay a return visit to the Lahore camp.[1] Maharaja Sher Singh had excused himself on the grounds of an eye affliction, but it seems likely, as Cunningham suggests (p. 253) that he suffered from a want of confidence at the prospect of meeting face to face, a personage who, apart from his high office, was known as a man of intellect.

Sher Singh had little education; nor was he gifted otherwise in the handling of affairs. His weakness was inevitably exploited by others. The Sindhanwalia family were next of kin in Ranjit Singh's immediate family. During Ranjit's lifetime their influence was immense and their estates valued at upwards of Rs. six lakhs per annum. Attar Singh, Lehna Singh and their two nephews, Ajit and Shamsher Singh, represented the family at court. Besides his position as head of this distinguished family, Attar Singh was renowned as a soldier and had been acclaimed after Hari Singh Nalwa as a champion of the Khalsa.

The Sindhanwalias regarded Sher Singh as an upstart and usurper. They espoused the cause of Rani Chand Kaur against him, and tried to win sympathy for it both from the British and from Amir Dost Muhammad of Kabul. When Sher Singh came to power, Attar Singh sought refuge with Baba Bikram Singh Bedi at Una and was later joined by Ajit. But Lehna Singh and Kehr Singh who were still in charge of Darbar troops in Kangra, were brought to Lahore in chains, and dispossessed of their estates, weapons, stables, etc., valued at Rs. forty lakhs.[2]

Then events took a turn. On the one hand, Sher Singh began to tire of Dhian Singh's control of affairs. On the other, since Chand Kaur's death the Sindhanwalias having no candidate for the throne were inclined make peace with Sher Singh in order to regain their status at the court and challenge the supremacy of the Dogras. Though not so able and experienced as Dhian Singh, they were a match for the Dogras in cunning and intrigue. Attar Singh and Ajit Singh were advised by their friends and by

---

[1] Sohan Lal explains that the presence of Prince Partap Singh, was taken by the G.-G., as tantamount to the presence of the Maharaja. *bajāe sarkar tassawaridah-o-famidah*. S.L. d.LV(II) pp. 50-55.
[2] S.L.d IV(II) p. 27.

Clerk, the British Agent, who actually interceded with the Maharaja on their behalf, to return to the Punjab, and try to form an "all-party" government. At Clerk's suggestion, Ajit Singh made a formal request to the Maharaja to be allowed to return.[1]

The correspondence of Clerk and Richmond from Ludhiana shows very clearly that their interest in the 'reconstruction of the Lahore government" was directed towards the ousting from power of Dhian Singh, who alone retained in their view, the sort of prestige that made the Punjab a force to be reckoned with.[2] The desired reconciliation having been effected, Ajit Singh Sindhanwalia arrived in Lahore in the first week of November[3] while his uncle stayed at Thanesar to await news of his reception. Ajit Singh had his first encounter with the Maharaja in the course of a religious festival at the mausoleum of Ranjit Singh. He was welcomed and assured by the Maharaja that he harboured no ill feeling towards him. Sher Singh also made him a cash grant to tide over his immediate needs. A few days later the family property including their former residental house in Lahore was restored to the Sindhanwalia. Lehna Singh and Kehr Singh, who had been in jail at Mukerian, were released and received in Lahore with the honour due to their rank.[4]

Ajit Singh and Sher Singh had known each other since boyhood. They were both fond of the good things of life, and very soon resumed their drink-and-dancing soirées. Sher Singh began to neglect his duties. He failed to give audience to ministers and secretaries even when their business was urgent. When sober, the pleasures of the chase were more important to him than affairs of state. His ways became so scandalous that some of the elder Sardars, such as Lehna Singh Majithia, Lehna Singh Sindhanwalia, Fakir Aziz-ud-din, and Dhian Singh, felt it proper to draw

1 S.L.d. IV(II) p. 39, it appears that the Maharaja's views in this matter had already been ascertained by Clerk. S.L. writes "when Ajit Singh's petition was received in court, the Maharaja, who was *anxiously* awaiting it, was pleased to give orders for the return of the Sardar and invited him for an interview on Diwali Day."
2 Ludhiana Agency Correspondence, 1841-43. Clerk stayed in Lahore, March and April 1842, to supervise supplies and transport for Pollock's army, which provided opportunity also, for gauging the situation at court.
3 Ajit Singh's return coincided with that of the 20,000 British troops from Kabul, the winding up of the G.-G.'s summer office in Simla, and his projected meeting with Sher Singh at Ludhiana or Ferozepore.
4 S.L.d. IV(II) pp. 39-43.

## Nemesis

his attention to the dereliction of duty on his part.[1] Instead of heeding them Sher Singh began to think of means to rid himself of Dhian Singh. He despatched confidential messengers to Diwan Kirpa Ram, who had been driven from the court by Dhian Singh's hostility, to return to Lahore.[2] Bhai Gurmukh Singh, General Ventura, Bhai Gobind Ram and several others of the anti-Dogra faction, became his confidants. Distrust between the Maharaja and his Chief Minister grew. They had to swear good-will to each other every third day of the week. The crisis came in the month of July when Dhian Singh and Aziz-ud-din decided to leave Lahore in separate parties.[3]

The Sindhanwalia Sardars watched the situation. They hoped to exploit the misunderstanding between the Maharajah and the Chief Minister to get rid of both. The Maharajah they despised because of his supposedly humble origin; the Minister because they held him responsible for their years of exile.

Ambition in the Sindhanwalia Sardars to seize sovereignty from a cousin of the Sukerchakiya line that happened to be ruling was not a new thing. Within the past forty years, on at least two occasions a member of the family had attempted to do so.[4] Sohan Lal provides a detailed account of how matters developed this third time. Ajit Singh invited the Maharaja's attention to the fact that Clerk had deputed a special mission to escort his uncle, Attar Singh, to Lahore with instructions that 'the person of the Sardar was to be made over to the Maharaja on the behalf

---

1 Ibid. pp. 17-19.
2 Kirpa Ram was the son of Moti Ram and grandson of Diwan Mohkam Chand. His family at one time, held decidedly, the first place at the court of Ranjit Singh.
3 For a more detailed account of how matters developed at the court see S.L.d. IV(III) pp. 10-19.
4 Sir Lepel Griffin in *History of the Punjab, Chiefs and Families of Note* writes: "One morning (A.D. 1803) as Ranjit Singh came out of the Samman Burj, and was preparing to mount his horse, Amir Singh was seen to unsling his gun, prime it and blow the match. The bystanders accused him of seeking the life of his chief, and Ranjit Singh, who believed the charge, dismissed him from court. Amir Singh took refuge with Baba Sahib Singh Bedi of Una, at whose intercession, after some time, Ranjit Singh again took him into favour" . . . "in 1825 the Maharaja was in Rambagh at Amritsar, dangerously ill; his life was despaired of and he had become wholly unconscious. Sardar Budh Singh, who saw that on the death of Ranjit Singh the country would again be divided into separate chieftains, and supposing the Maharaja to be dying, determined to make provision for himself. He went at night with a force to the fort of Gobind Garh and demanded admittance in the name of the Maharaja. The Jamadar of the gate, Daya Ram, would

of the British government,[1] and that Attar Singh and his escort, were at the moment (23 March 1843) at Una. He suggested that as Attar Singh was the most senior living member of the family, it would be seemly if the Maharaja were personally to conduct him home. Sher Singh agreed but did nothing about it. Months later, the first of Bhadon (16 August) Lehna Singh and Ajit Singh sought private audience with him to press the matter. Sher Singh was once again cordial, but excused himself by saying that he had been advised by Dhian Singh that to comply with their wishes would not be in keeping with regal decorum, *munāsib dar ain badshāhān nest.*

This produced an explosion. Both Sardars are stated to have said 'one word from your Highness would be enough for us to finish this obnoxious Minister.' This is precisely what the Maharaja had wanted. It was decided to invite Dhian Singh to the palace and murder him. Ajit Singh went on to assure the Maharaja that Dhian Singh's own brother Suchet Singh was in accord with him and willing to undertake the responsibilities of government. The Maharaja agreed. But Dhian Singh got to know of the plot and excused himself. A month later, the day of reckoning came for him as well as the Maharaja.[2]

On the morning of the first day of Asuj (15 September) Ajit Singh went to the garden house at Shah Bilawal where the Maharaja was encamped. He took his newly raised levies with him, ostensibly for muster and inspection. After the parade he raised his doble-barrelled gun as if to make a present. The moment

not admit him without orders. Budh Singh accordingly went back, and induced by large bribes, the keepers of the seal to draw out an order for the fort to be given up to him and to this the seal was affixed. Budh Singh returned to the fort, but the Jamadar was not to be deceived. He would not look at the order, and declared that so late at night he would not open the gates to the Maharaja himself. The Sardar had to retire discomfited, and in the morning Fakir Imam-ud-din, the Kiladar, told the Maharaja, who had in some measure recovered. Budh Singh was given the Peshawar command in Yusafzai country... the Maharaja hoping that he would leave his bones in the Yusafzai hills and never return to disturb him."

[1] *Dastgiri Sardar aztarf Sahiban ba Sarkarwala kuna midah Dashad*, S.L.d. IV(III) p. 9.

[2] S.L. d. IV(III)pp. 26-27; also a letter from Lord Ellenborough to the Duke of Wellington, Calcutta, 13 August three days before the meeting of the Sardars with Sher Singh betrays a special knowledge of what was to come, "... the affairs of the Panjab will probably receive their denouement from the death of Sher Singh." Colchester, p. 367.

PLATE 4

RAJA DHIAN SINGH

## Nemesis

Sher Singh stretched his hand to take the gun, Ajit pressed both triggers aiming the charges at the Maharajah's chest. He then drew his sword and cut off Sher Singh's head.[1]

While Ajit Singh was thus engaged, his uncle, Lehna Singh, went in search of Prince Partap Singh, who was distributing alms in the garden of Jawala Singh. He seized the boy and with one blow severed his head from his body.[2]

The two regicides proceeded to the city attended by contingents of five hundred horse and foot. On the way they met Dhian Singh, who with a couple of personal servants, was going to the Shah Bilawal garden to pay his respects to the Maharaja. The Sindhanwalias pressed him to accompany them to settle the future of the government. Dhian Singh had no choice but to comply. The party had hardly reached the gun foundry inside the fort when a pistol shot from behind laid Dhian Singh in the dust and another ended the life of his devoted attendant, Fateh Khan Gheba.

The story given above is based on Sohan Lal's account in his diary (*Roznamcha*) of events in the court. But there are other versions: that Dhian Singh conspired with the Sindhanwalia's to bring about the destruction of his master; that the Sindhanwalia's wanted to kill only Sher Singh; that they wanted to kill only Dhian Singh, or as it actually transpired, to kill both. The fact remains that since these kinsmen of the Maharaja returned to Lahore, a contest for power was inevitable. One feature in the situation which is substantiated by the letters of Colonel Richmond, acting Agent to the Governor-General in Ludhiana, and letters from the Governor-General, was that the British were not only keenly interested but well-informed about developments in the Punjab. Lord Ellenborough, in a letter dated 20 September, writes: "The Maharaja of Lahore is pulling the house about his head; the catastrophe was nearly taking place three weeeks ago, but it is deferred".[3] Lord Ellenborough's letters were not made public at the time, but a note that appeared in a newspaper, 'the Friend of India,' edited by J. Karshman, dated December 1843,

---

1 S.L. d.LV(III) p. 29 states that Budh Singh, Nikka Singh and Ashraf, attendants of the Maharaja, who endeavoured to attack the assassins were killed on the spot; Sardar Hukm Singh Malwai was severely wounded.

2 The first day of the month of Asuj is considered as the harbinger of the cold weather, hence auspicious. Sohan Lal states that the two priests Hira and Jawahar who were conducting the ceremony were also killed.

3 Colchester. p. 393.

goes to show that politically-minded circles had reason for suspecting the complicity of British functionaries in the affairs of the Punjab: "we have no proof," says the writer, "that the East India Company instigated all the king-killing which has been perpetrated in the Panjab since the demise of Ranjit Singh, but keeping in mind their trade and the wonderful success which has attended their operations in that line in Bengal, the Carnatic and elsewhere both among the Mughals and Mahrattas, Rajas and Nababs, we must say that we smell a rat; we strongly suspect the Company's corrupt influence has been employed in fanning and fomenting these plots."[1]

Sher Singh's reign ended, as it had begun, in violence. The short period of two years and eight months during which he occupied the throne, was marked by events that accelerated the dissolution of the kingdom. The Prince was young when he came into power but had evinced his capabilities as a soldier. More than once he had held command in the most difficult region of the country, the district of Peshawar and the uplands of Hazara. In 1831 he had brought to a successful close a five-year-long conflict with Khalifa Sayyad Ahmad, which being in the nature of a *Jehad* had caused no small anxiety, and cost much to the state in terms of men and money. It was considerations such as these which caused many of the responsible personages at court to support him. But he belied their hopes. That he became a reckless sensualist and addicted to alcohol, can be gathered from many sources. The basic cause was no doubt, an uneasy mind. In his first attempt to seize the throne (June-July 1839), he failed because neither Dhian Singh, nor the British would suport him against Kharak Singh; later he allowed his position to be undermined by Rani Chand Kaur. When he did succeed, it must have been with no great confidence. The slur of doubtful heredity and his indebtedness to the Chief Minister may well have deprived him of ruling and suppressing the turbulent soldiers who had been instrumental in obtaining the throne for him. Finally, he proved incapable of holding his own against the villainous intrigues of the British. His own character, and that of many of those closest to him was maimed by insecurity and self-seeking.

[1] Quoted from: *Rise of the Christian Power in India* by Major Basu, p. 804.

## Chapter 5
### HIRA SINGH AS PRIME MINISTER OF THE PUNJAB

DHIAN SINGH'S younger brother, Suchet Singh, was a soldier of great repute: handsome, brave as a lion, the *beau ideal* of the Khalsa army. Since the days of Maharaja Ranjit Singh he had commanded the *Chahar Yari* troops, which formed one of the biggest divisions of the irregular cavalry, about 2,700 strong.[1] Hira Singh was a youth of twenty-five, who lived for the most part of those years in Lahore and became a great favourite of Ranjit Singh, whom he was used to address as *Bapu* (father), and was allowed a privileged seat in the Darbar, together with the Princes, Kharak Singh and Sher Singh.[2]

The news of the assasination of Dhian Singh was brought to Suchet Singh and Hira Singh by some men[3] who had managed to escape from the fort after witnessing the deed. Hira Singh did not lose his nerve. The issue to be settled was whether the Sindhanwalias or the Dogras were to wield power at the Sikh court. Dhian Singh had held it for nearly a decade and more than once, thwarted opponents who had tried to wrest it from his grasp. If feeling against Dogra dominance had been a reality, the opportunity now offered, for both Sikh and non-Sikh members of the nobility to close their ranks against the aliens. Nothing of the kind happened; on the contrary, the Khalsa army lent its full support to the Dogras, Hira Singh and Suchet Singh,[4] against the Sindhanwalias.

The moment the news of his father's murder reached Hira Singh, he proceeded to the barracks and obtained promises of help from the troops under the command of Generals, Court and Avitable. He then rode to the cantonment at Anarkali, where the *Fauj-i-Khas*, the brigade commanded by General Ventura

---
[1] Kh. D.R. v. I, pp. 113-14. The annual value of Suchet's personal jagirs amounted to Rs. 306,865. Shahamat Ali, p. 105.
[2] Ranjit conferred on him the title of Raja in 1828, and the more special *Farzard-i-khasi* 1835. His jagir amounted to Rs. 462,115.
[3] Sohan Lal mentions two names Chanda Singh Zargar and the son of Munshi Dilbagh Rai.
[4] In a sense, the Dogra dominance lasted till the close of Sikh sovereignty.

was encamped, and elicited a similar promise. He then addressed an assembly of the Sikh soldiers. It is said that he unbuckled his sword, laid it on the floor and bared his neck. The sword, he said had taken his father's life; he was now alone and defenceless but looked to the Khalsa for protection. If they did not wish to give this, they were free to use the sword to end his life as well. The youthful Dogra won the hearts of the soldiers. He then told them about the Sindhanwalias and their close relations with the British. He pointed out that the British Agent at Ludhiana had used his personal influence with Maharaja Sher Singh to restore the Sindhanwalias to position and privilege at court; he tried to impress upon his audience that in all the recent plots, intrigues and assassinations, the hand of the British was clearly discernible; that to leave power in the grasp of the Sindhanwalias amounted to handing over the Punjab to these foreigners. Hira Singh concluded his hangue by promising a substantial increase in pay for the army if it succeeded in destroying the traitorous Sindhanwalias. The effect of Hira Singh's appeal was dramatic. Mcgregor writes: "in their frenzied zeal, half-naked and half-armed soldiers, scorned the idea of waiting till morning, and in their impatient haste, they left their half-cooked meals, and got ready for the march within the hour."

On 16 September, before the night had advanced two or three hours, nearly 40,000 men with some 200 guns had taken up positions around the citadel of Lahore. Hundreds of the soldiers stole into the bazaars to loot shops and houses, and ravish any women they could find. But above this tumult continued the thunder of guns bombarding the walls of the fort. "For the citizens of Lahore" Sohan Lal was to write, "it was the veritable day of destruction, *Mamuna-roz-i-maha-shar numayan gasht*.[1]

The garrison under Lehna Singh put up a stout resistance. But with the dawn when they saw the numbers of besiegers, their spirits quailed.[2] A couple of breaches in the walls enabled the Khalsa to charge in sweeping everything before them. The defenders, not exceeding one thousand men, were annihilated almost to a man. Lehna Singh, who had earlier been wounded

1 S.L. d. LV(III) p. 32.
2 The author of the *Sher Singh Nama*, states that in the morning, General Ventura, Sardar Lehna Singh Majithia and Raja Suchet Singh, with his devoted friend, Raja Kesri Singh, had joined Hira Singh. p. 117.

in the thigh, was discovered hiding under a vault and promptly killed. Ajit Singh was shot dead while attempting to jump over the lofty wall of the fort. Hira Singh entered the citadel and ordered an immediate search for the body of his father. It was discovered in a foundry pit. It was conveyed with due honour to his mansion. Hira Singh carried the severed head of Ajit Singh to lay at the feet of his step-mother. "Now I am fully satisfied," she is reported to have said, and turning to Hira Singh added, "I will tell your dear father that you acted as a brave and dutiful son." Dhian Singh's body was cremated; with him his wife, Rani Pathani and seventeen concubines, were immolated as *satis*.

On the same day Sher Singh's obsequies were performed, (his body having remained at the spot where he was murdered). Hira Singh bore no ill-will towards the late Maharaja. Sher Singh's funeral rites were of the nature that befitted the ruler of the state.

Having reckoned with the Sindhanwalias, Hira Singh laid his punitive arm upon men of less prominence, who he believed, had some part in the murder of his father. Among victims of the purge were Misr Beli Ram, the Chief Treasurer and his brother Ram Kishen, Bhai Gurmukh Singh Granthi, religious adviser to the late Maharaja, Mehr Ghasita, manager of the Sindhanwalia estates and a host of their friends, relations and adherents. These men were secretly put to death, imprisoned or at the least, dismissed from service.

Thus three days, between the 15th and 17th of September, nearly a thousand men, including the Maharaja and his son, the Prime Minister and nine other leading dignitaries of the court, lost their lives.

Hira Singh had Prince Dalip Singh proclaimed Maharaja and himself assumed the position of Prime Minister. Dalip Singh, at this time five years old, was the youngest surviving son of Ranjit Singh.[1] Two other princes, Peshaura Singh and

---

[1] His mother, Rani Jind Kaur, came of a humble family of Jat peasants from Gujranwala; her father Manna Singh was one of the Jamadars appointed to look after Ranjit's kennels and was popularly known as Manna Singh, *kutianwala* (of the dogs). Neither mother or child had received much notice till this moment.

Kashmira Singh, had as good a claim[1] as the little boy, but neither suited Hira Singh's purpose. Both these Princes had received training in the army and the government—Kashmira Singh being perhaps the better equipped. According to Baron Hugel, he "possessed considerable talent and an intelligent and animated bearing."[2] But, they being about the same age as Hira Singh, with either as sovereign, he could not expect to enjoy the measure of authority he would have with Dalip Singh on the throne. Their claim was, therefore, deliberately ignored. This did not escape the attention of the people, or the diarist, Sohan Lal.[3] What remains inexplicable, is the acquiescence of the Khalsa in regard both to Hira Singh's own assumption of power and the role of king-maker.

Hira Singh arranged that Rani Jind Kaur should continue to look after her son, and that her brother, Jawahar Singh, should supervise his education. For the routine of administration, rules of procedure were laid down. Secretaries were instructed to submit their papers through Pandit Jalla, who was appointed *Mashir-i-Khas*, and whose recommendations regarding civil and revenue matters were to be regarded as final.

Hira Singh retained for himself charge of the army. In this capacity he immediately sanctioned the promised rise in pay; that of a common soldier was increased by Rs. 2 per month; of a junior officer Rs. 2 to 3; regimental staff were given liberal rewards in cash, *inams*, and *khilats*. Besides the general rise in salary,[4] all those who had actually taken part in the siege of 16-17 September, received a gratuity amounting to one month's salary. Having thus been given what was promised, the Khalsa troops were ordered to return to their cantonments and life was restored to normal within a few days.

1 They were the sons of Rani Mehtab Kaur, who Ranjit Singh had taken into his harem on the death of her former husband, Sahib Singh Bhangi of Gujrat. Peshaura Singh's birth was announced in 1818, a year after the conquest of Peshawar; Kashmira Singh's the next year, when the valley of Kashmir was occupied; the son of another of Sahib Singh's widows, also born in 1818, was named Multana Singh to celebrate the taking of Multan; Dalip Singh was born on 4 September 1838.
2 P. 221.
3 He writes "*sababh-i-jazh munafia-o-faida khuda ha az Kashmira Singh o-Peshaura Singh dida danista dasm posida tifal-i-saghir ra bar masnad-i-badshahi nisanidand.*" *Zamina mashiran-i-Saltanat-i-Singhan,* p. 4.
4 S.L. d. IV(III) p. 35; also Kh. D.R. v. I, p. 74.

## Hira Singh as Prime Minister of the Punjab

Hira Singh, being in the prime of life, might well have expected a long spell of peace and power. Yet, within ten weeks trouble began to brew. It began within his inner circle. In appointing Jawahar Singh guardian to the Maharaja, he had raised to the position of one of the most responsible dignitaries of the state a man who apart from his humble origin is described as 'ill-clad and loitering in the streets of Lahore with a hawk perched on his hand',[1] and also, 'drunken and debauched.' Jawahar Singh, very soon conceived the idea of ousting Hira Singh from power and began to intrigue to this end with Suchet Singh. In this design he had the approval of his sister Jind Kaur, who was said to have been intimate with Suchet Singh during the six years he had been manager of her household.[2] Suchet Singh readily accepted the offer of help from the Rani and her brother and prepared himself to make a bid for the Prime Ministership.[3] He was dissuaded by his elder brother, Gulab Singh, who came to Lahore to condole with Hira Singh, and attend the Dussehra Darbar. Foiled thus, Jawahar Singh tried another stratagem. He took the infant Maharaja on a state elephant to the cantonments outside the city, and told the soldiers who had assembled on parade, that as the Maharaja was not safe with Hira Singh, it was up to them either to remove the Dogra minister or to enable the Prince and himself to escape across the Sutlej and seek asylum with the British at Ferozepore. The troopers refused to be taken in, removed the Maharaja from Jawahar Singh's lap and informed Hira Singh. The latter displayed both firmness and tact. He rewarded the soldiers for their loyalty[4] and ordered Jawahar Singh to be taken in chains and incarcerated in the *haveli* of the late Maharaja Kharak Singh. His position in the young Maharaja's household was given to Lal Singh, a clerk of the *toshakhana*.

This did not prevent Suchet Singh from continuing to cause trouble. He hated Pandit Jalla. The hatred was reciprocated

---

1 *Tahquqat-i-Chisti*, p. 783.
2 Like other members of the Dogra family, Suchet Singh was handsome, and possessed of a noble and commanding bearing. It was Ranjit Singh who appointed him to look after the Rani's household.
3 It appears that Suchet Singh had also had some understanding with Lehna Singh and Ajit Singh when they were trying to dislodge Dhian Singh from his position.
4 The most deserving, turned out to be men and officers under the command of Misr Jodha Ram. Gupta, p. 32; S.L. d. LV(III).

in full measure. For a time Gulab Singh's restraining influence kept Suchet in peaceful, though restive retirement in Jammu. But not for long.

Gulab Singh's personal interest was to consolidate his own position in the hills where the family jagirs were situated. These estates value at more than Rs. 800,000 per annum formed a compact division of the country over which Gulab Singh exercised almost independent control. He had obtained as early as February 1842, an assurance from Colonel Lawrence that he would be allowed to retain his possessions in the event of the dismemberment of the Punjab if he remained loyal to the British.[1] He cared little therefore as to which of his brothers was Prime Minister. But he advised Hira Singh to hoard the treasure that Dhian Singh had amassed in the family fortresses in the hills. His own immediate problem was to get away from Lahore with his personal wealth without being challenged by the army. He decided to grease the palms of the soldiers and also feed their vanity. He published an *Ishtihar Nama*,[2] (public statement) to the effect that his own wealth and honour and that of other members of the family was entirely due to the support of the *Khalsa jeo*. At the same time he sent by way of *ardas* (offering) to be distributed to the troops, one thousand rupees for each infantry battalion, five hundred for each unit of artillery, and a lump sum of Rs. 70,000 for the cavalary.[3]

Gulab Singh's farsightedness was rewarded. He was able to get to Jammu unmolested. He then interested himself in Hira Singh's schemes for ejecting Kashmira Singh and Peshaura Singh from their *jagirs* in Sialkot very close to the borders of Jammu. Hira Singh charged the Princes on the basis of evidence provided by a single individual, Kapur Singh, one of the managers of Kashmira Singh's estates, with having conspired with the Sindhanwalias against Dhian Singh. Hira Singh requested Gulab Singh to seize the persons and property of the Princes and himself sent a contingent of Dogras to take the town of Sialkot. The Princes sought sanctuary in the monastery of Mahtab Singh at

---

[1] *Life of Lawrence*, by Major-General Sir Herbert Edwardes, p. 326.
[2] Drafted in most fulsome terms by Fakir Aziz-ud-din.
[3] S.L.D. LV (III) p. 39. Reference to the army payrolls, for an estimate of the number of soldiers present in Lahore, indicate that Gulab Singh must have spent Rs. 120,000 in this year.

## Hira Singh as Prime Minister of the Punjab

Kotli Loharan. Through the intercession of their saintly host, and the resentment of the Khalsa, Hira Singh was forced to stay his hand. The Princes were permitted to return after signing a pledge of loyalty to the government and undertaking to show clemency to Kapur Singh. Prince Kashmira Singh ignored his promise and a few weeks later had Kapur Singh flogged to death. This provided Hira Singh with an excuse for further proceedings against the Prince. Baba Mahtab Singh who had stood surety was summoned to Lahore and apprised of the situation; so too were the military *panchayats* of the Khalsa, which Hira Singh was inclined to keep in good humour.

The Princes, seeing no other way out for themselves, strengthened their garrisons at Sialkot and Kuryanwala, and despatched secret emissaries to the cantonments to secure support from the soldiers. Two regiments of irregular infantry (*Ramgols*) responded at once to the Princes' call; a little later, a number of men from irregular battalions on their way to Peshawar under orders of transfer, deserted their colours and took the road to Sialkot.[1] Kashmira Singh sent a confidential messenger to the British Agent, Colonel Richmond in Ludhiana; Suchet Singh, from Jammu was moved to offer help; and Mussulman *Najib* battalions of the Lahore army, who together with Dogras from Jammu were besieging Sialkot, declined to open fire upon the sons of their late Maharaja unless the Khalsa joined in.

The Princes were able to beat off small contingents which attempted to assault the fortifications of the town. Their strengthened position put Hira Singh in a predicament between the need of maintaining Dogra prestige and averting the wrath of the Khalsa. The old Dogra battalions of Dhian Singh then came forward and in one resolute attack forced the defenders to lay down arms. However, Hira Singh was forced to realise that in the circumstances, it would be prudent to let the Princes go without further molesting them.

The harassment of Kashmira and Peshaura Singh for three months roused the Khalsa against the Dogras. An air of unrest prevailed in the city of Lahore. Hira Singh thought it wise to stay

[1] News letter from the Punjab dated 13 March 1844. Gupta, p. 115. Sialkot was an important centre for the manufacture of fine paper; and of the manufacture of arms, which were made at Kotli Loharan. See *District Gazeteer* of Sialkot.

within his guarded mansion for a few days. The army *panchayats* held meetings on the 21st-23rd March, during which Hira Singh's administration was subjected to a searching examination. They decided that unless Hira Singh conceded certain demands, he must be forced to resign. Four representatives of the *Panchayats* appeared before him on the 24th when the Darbar was in session. They claimed that they had come on behalf of the *Sarbat Khalsa*, and after a brief preamble, conveyed to him the *hnkum*, (order) of the Khalsa: that he must release Jawahar Singh; remove the guard placed on the residence of Misr Beli Ram and set free his relatives and dependents; raise the siege of Kuryanwala and Sialkot, and give an undertaking that the Princes, Kashmira Singh and Peshaura Singh, would not be ill-treated in future. They also demanded the surrender of Misr Jalla, Sheikh Imam-ud-din and Raja Lal Singh.[1] "If he hesitated or refused," the delegates added, "the order was that he himself be seized." The language in which the message was couched, and the manner in which it was delivered in open Darbar, was in disregard of the rules of official decorum and in evident contempt of the authority of the government. Hira Singh did not allow the delegation's uncouthness to disturb his own demeanour, and readily promised compliance. One reason for this was the knowledge that Suchet Singh's return to Lahore had been solicited by the army, and he had set out from Jammu while their parleys were still in session. Later in the day he invited a thousand representatives of the Khalsa to his private mansion and sumptuously entertained them, hoping in this way to "let the thundering legions pass leaving him unhurt" (*az awazash-o-mufsaddah platan rustgari-o-rihaiyaft*").[2]

Suchet Singh having been advised that the moment was a good one for him to try out his chance of obtaining power, *hala Waqt bar amad, mudda-o-hasul matalab dil-i-shum nazdik rasidah*, had taken leave of his brother on the pretext of a big *shikar*, and

---

1 S.L. d. IV(III) pp. 45-46; Gupta, pp. 126-129; Broadfoot, pp. 227-229. Misr Jalla was regarded by the Khalsa as Hira Singh's evil genius; Lal Singh's sudden rise to the position of supervising the Maharaja's education, an,d his alleged illicit relations with Rani Jindan were common gossip; the newswriter Sheikh Imam-ud-din and his father were suspected of having defrauded the state, and to have caused a Hindu temple of be pulled down and replaced by a mosque, and also to have taken the lives of Misr Beli Ram and Bhai Gurmukh Singh, who had been placed in his custody by Hira Singh.

2 S.L. d. LV(III) p. 45.

arrived on the morning of 26 March. at Shahdara, on the outskirts of the capital, Accompanied by forty trusted men, including Rai Kesri Singh and Mian Bhim Sen, he crossed the river and made a dash for the encampment of soldiers who had invited him. By this time, however, the troopers had been won over by Hira Singh and saw little reason for taking side in a dispute between the Dogras, neither of whom was to their liking. Suchet Singh was advised by the Khalsa to go home. He was not in the mood to give up. He took up position in a ruined mosque and determined to fight it out with his forty devoted comrades.

When Hira Singh received the news he summoned Pandit Jalla for consultation. The Pandit, according to Sohan Lal, advised Hira Singh to avail himself of this "god-sent opportunity (*az parda-i-ghaib Shikar dar dam uftadah*)," to do away with his rival for ever.[1] Dewan Jawahar Mal, Ganda Singh Kunjahia and Mian Labh Singh, who desired to make a reconciliation between the nephew and uncle, were rebuked and dismissed from Hira Singh's presence.[2] A picked body of horse was posted on the bank of the Ravi to prevent reinforcements from crossing near Shahdara to Suchet Singh's assistance, and a force of about 20,000 men with fifty light guns despatched. Suchet Singh and his forty companions emerged to face this army. The Dogra addressed his last words to the Khalsa. "Relying on your good faith I came Lahore at your special invitation. You have forsaken me and have now come to kill me in such large numbers. I beseech you, at this moment to behave like true soldiers. Come on, one by one and let the world see the worth of a Rajput soldier."[3] The small band then fell upon their adversaries with such desperate violence they killed 150 and wounded another 200 before they were overcome and annihilated. (27 March).

Hira Singh hurried to the scene. He is said to have been moved to tears at the sight of his uncle's mangled corpse mingled with dust and blood. He attempted to make 'atonement' by giving Rs. 5000, to each of the brigades who had served him on the occasion; but this did not silence discontented elements in

---

1 Ibid. pp. 48-52.
2 Muhammad Latif, p. 526.
3 Report of the British news-writer, quoted by Dr. Gupta, p. 133.

the Khalsa, who continued to demand the surrender of Jalla, Lal Singh and Imam-ud-din.[1]

Disharmony that had existed between Hira Singh and Gulab Singh came into the open. Lamentations and demands for vengeance from Suchet Singh's widow added to the discord. Gulab Singh was not only the most senior member of the family, but also the doyen of the feudal nobility of the Punjab. His *jagirs* yielded seven lakhs of rupees annually. He was also the biggest revenue-farmer of the state, holding estates on contract, including salt mines worth about eleven lakhs. Most of his own estates and those of his dead brothers, Dhian and Suchet Singh, were in the hills alongside his personal domains. When his nephew became Prime Minister, Gulab Singh's territorial appetite became all the more voracious. He asked to be given on contract the vale of Kashmir, Hazara, Chhach and Rawalpindi and then Muzaffarabad, Ladakh and Gilgit. He offered five lakhs more than paid by Dewan Sawan Mal for his Multan contract.[2] Only Sawan Mal's integrity, and Gulab Singh's tardiness in paying his dues gave the Darbar excuse to turn down some of his bids.

Gulab Singh had taken a portion of Dhian Singh's estate. On Suchet Singh's death, he appointed his eldest son manager of Suchet's estate, on behalf of a younger son, Sohan Singh, who he claimed, Suchet Singh had adopted. Hira Singh was not willing to accept this arrangement nor were the army *panchayats* amenable to having Suchet Singh's property pass into the hands of Gulab Singh they demanded reversion to the State.[3] Argument interspersed with threats continued for a period of six months. Hira Singh threatened to confiscate Gulab Singh's property in the plains; Gulab Singh retaliated by threatening to seize the persons of Hira Singh's two brothers who lived in Kohistan.[4]

Both Hira Singh and Gulab Singh declared themselves ready

1 An intelligence report of the British news-writer, 28-29 March: "the talk among the soldiery is that Raja Heera Singh has done most wrong in killing his uncle and Rai Kesree Singh; but these Jammu Rajas, they say, are in reality an annoyance to everyone and they must be got rid of." Gupta, pp. 133-134.
2 Intelligence Reports, British news-writer, Gupta, pp. 139, 140, 147, 160.
3 British news-writer reports, Gupta, p. 272.
4 Ibid. p. 140.

## Hira Singh as Prime Minister of the Punjab

to make war on one another; but their well-wishers were able to point out that the split in the family might prove fatal to its interest especially in view of the Khalsa's indifference or hostility. With the help of intermediaries, a semblance of amity was restored. Gulab Singh sent his son Sohan Singh to reside at Lahore. The young man was welcomed with a salute of guns. Hira Singh sent his brother to visit Gulab Singh at Jammu.

Early in the spring of 1844, Hira Singh's ministry was threatened from another quarter. The monastary of Bhai Bir Singh in the village of Sarhali on the right bank of the Sutlej assumed the character of a princely court. It had an armed retinue of 1500 men; stables for horses and elephants. Bhai Bir Singh was greatly venerated, particularly by the Sikh peasantry and the people of Malwa. At the close of morning service and in the evenings the Bhai used to hold a regular court, (*do waqt darbar alishan arashtan pairastah me sakht*) in which affairs of the Lahore Darbar were freely discussed. Many disaffected chiefs had taken refuge in the monastery, which fast became a centre of agitation against Hira Singh: the general opinion being, that during the minority of the ruler, the Prime Minister should be a Khalsa Sikh. From this it was not a big step to the Bhai beginning to cherish the idea of himself becoming the supreme political authority, *mulkgiri-o-Sardari-i-Punjab*.

For a time the British became interested in Bhai Bir Singh as an alternative to Hira Singh. The feasibility of installing him in this position was discussed in the correspondence of the Ludhiana Agency. Colonel Richmond held the opinion that the 'austere views of a hermit would not satisfy the material cravings of the soldiery.'[1] But, like his predecessors, he believed that one of the Sikh chiefs would be more acceptable to the Khalsa, as for instance, Attar Singh Sindhanwalia, who lived at Thanesar in British territory.

Hira Singh kept himself informed of the goings-on at Bir Singh's *derah*. He wished to put a stop to them but failed to gain the support of the army against 'this God-inspired man.' He tried negotiating; then gave up the attempt in 1844,[2] when

---

1 Richmond to Thomson, 1 November 1843, No. 158, Punjab Government Archives.
2 British News-writer's Intelligence Reports, vide Gupta

reports of fraternization between Bir Singh and Attar Singh Sindhanwalia were confirmed. Among the people residing in the monastery were Jawahar Singh Nalwa son of the famous Hari Singh, Sardar Rattan Singh Gharjakhia, Diwan Basakha Singh and the Princes, Peshaura Singh and Kashmira Singh.

The news that Attar Singh, on the advice of the British, had accepted an invitation from Bhai Bir Singh and crossed the Sutlej was received in Lahore on 3 May. It spread in the city like wild-fire. Hira Singh made haste to summon the army *panchayats*, and explained to them the policy of the British government. He pointed out how, from time to time, the British had seduced the loyalty of the Sikh chiefs in order to gain dominance for themselves. 'The Sindhanwalia Sardars,' he is reported to have said, 'were thrust upon Maharaja Sher Singh, and you are aware of the tragedy that Lehna Singh and Ajit Singh wrought in the state. The stupid Jawahar Singh was then inveigled, and if some of you, who happened to be on the parade ground had not apprehended him, he would have escaped to British territory with the Maharaja. Suchet Singh had sent a huge amount of his savings in cash and bullion amounting to something like fifteen lakhs of rupees to Ferozepore, and would, with this money to fall back on, have been the next to stray from the path of loyalty to his sovereign, had he not lost his life. It is now Attar Singh, senior member of the Sindhanwalia family, who is stirring up strife for us by placing himself at the head of the disgruntled chiefs residing at Sarhali. He is sponsored by the British who desire to rule the country.[1] It is up to you to persuade Bhai Bir Singh to desist from association with these traitors, or else suffer the consequences of his unholy alliance; otherwise the sovereign character of your state will be sacrificed.'[2]

The Khalsa responded to Hira Singh's argument. On 5 May, a strong force moved out of Lahore; eleven infantry battalions with fifty guns, under Gulab Singh Calcutteea; 4000 cavalry

---

1 Lord Ellenborough, annoyed with the hasty action by Colonel Richmond in regard to Attar Singh, wrote to Queen Victoria on 10 June 1844, "it is much to be regretted that Uttar Singh should have been permitted to move from Thanesar to the Sutlej, with the known object of acting against the Lahore government. The error of the British Agent makes it impossible to protest against the violating of the strict letter of the treaty." Refererence probably to the posting of troops on the British side of the Sutlej.

2 Punjab Intelligence Reports, vide Gupta, p. 174.

## Hira Singh as Prime Minister of the Punjab

including 2,300 *ghorcharas*, with 300 swivels, under the command of the Dogra chief, Mian Labh Singh. One reaching Naurangabad (Sarhali) Labh Singh posted strong guards on the *ghats* and ferries on the left bank of the river to prevent Attar Singh from escaping across. A deputation of senior officers with Gulab Singh Calcutteea then went to Bhai Bir Singh to request him to retire from the conflict.

During the course of negotiations some statement by Gulab Singh Calcutteea angered Attar Singh who shot him down with his carbine. The Darbar troops instantly launched an attack. Princes Kashmira Singh and Peshaura Singh having deserted earlier to the other side, saved their lives. Attar Singh and Bhai Bir Singh were killed. A large number of peasants, who had come to help the Bhai, fled before the disciplined soldiers; many were drowned in their attempt to escape. The triumphant army returned to Lahore. Hira Singh accorded them a royal welcome by ordering a salute of guns from the citadel.

Their reception in the cantonment was very different. They were taunted with the epithet, *gurumar*, murderers of a guru; and when cholera broke out in their ranks, it was believed to be due to the curse of the Bhai. For all this Hira Singh and Jalla were held responsible. Hira Singh tried to appease them by liberal gifts of gold medals and ornaments;[1] he promised also, to build a *samadh* over the ashes of Bhai Bir Singh and grant a *jagir* worth five thousand per annum for the maintenance of the Sarhali gurdwara.[2]

One result of the Sarhali episode was the dismissal of Europeans from the service of the Darbar. It had long been suspected that Ventura and Avitable informed the British about the Lahore Darbar. The Khalsa troops at Sarhali had the opportunity of seeing for themselves that the insurrection had been fomented by the British with the assistance of well-placed informers. They were so outraged that they were willing to attack Ferozepore. Hira Singh, taking advantage of the anti-foreign temper of the army, discharged all the remaining Europeans. (Ventura

---

1 S.L. d. LV(III) p. 37 gives details; to colonels and cenerals, a pair of bangles each; commandants, one bangle each; company officers a gold necklace; each sepoy, one gold *butki* this being valued at five rupees in current silver coin.
2 See also Intelligence Reports 17-19 May, cited by Gupta, p. 191.

and Avitable had forestalled this move and departed soon after the death of Sher Singh).

Diplomatic relations between the British government and Hira Singh have to be viewed in the light of the animosity that had existed between his father and that government. This legacy continued to poison relations between the two governments in Hira Singh's time. Before his violent death, Suchet Singh had a sizeable amount of treasure in gold, silver and bullion, conveyed to Ferozepore (either because of the greater security of property in British India,[1] or, with a view to advancing some of it as an ingratiatory loan to the British during the Afghan war). In February 1842 Suchet Singh had made it clear to Colonel Lawrence that if and when the Punjab was invaded, he would stand aside, provided he was allowed to retain possession of his property.

The Ferozepore 'treasure' was stored in three huge copper vessels, each 'closed with lead on which the Raja's seal was affixed,' and buried in a house owned by the Dogra brothers.[2] When the news of Suchet Singh's death reached Ferozepore, his confidential agent Nihal Singh was discovered trying to remove it. Whereupon Captain Saunders Abbott, the Assistant Resident, took with him the Lahore vakil, Lala Ram Dayal, had the treasure dug up and taken intact to the British treasury. Abbott reported the matter to Colonel Richmond, and Ram Dayal to the Darbar. During the course of correspondence on this matter, Colonel Richmond made it clear that the treasure would be handed over to the Lahore government on a formal application being made. But when this was done he referred the papers to Lord Ellenborough in Calcutta. Ellenborough decided that the treasure should go to Suchet's heirs and not to the Darbar. The Darbar, in turn urged, that since it belonged to a subject of the Punjab, the decision should rest with its government and that it would be improper for Colonel Richmond to entertain any application for it. The matter was more complicated by the

---

[1] According to British news-writers from Lahore, a large number of citizens of the Punjab, left Lahore with hoarded wealth. In order to restrict this exodus the government of Hira Singh increased the guard on the *ghats* of the Sutlej.

[2] Raja Gulab Singh's monopoly of salt mines dated from Ranjit Singh's time, and he had built salt depots in various places. It was one of these that served as repository for Suchet Singh's treasure.

## Hira Singh as Prime Minister of the Punjab

fact that Colonel Richmond had written to Hira Singh, Gulab Singh and Suchet Singh's widow to ascertain their views.

Meanwhile Sir Henry Hardinge replaced Lord Ellenborough as Governor-General. Hira Singh, hoping for better results, had Dalip Singh write a personal letter to Lord Hardinge requesting that the property be handed over to him so that he might give it to those to whom it properly belonged. Since Suchet Singh's widow claimed it as entirely hers and her adopted son's; Hardinge referred the matter to his legal advisers. The decision arrived at was to the effect that it should be handed over to Dalip Singh provided all the claimants, including the widow acquiesced to this arrangement in writing. Colonel Richmond was instructed to explain this to the Maharaja and convey to Suchet Singh's would-be-heirs that unless they came forward with their claims the money would be handed over to Dalip Singh. Colonel Richmond received these instructions on 10 August, but took no action till the beginning of October. During these two months relations between Gulab Singh and Hira Singh deteriorated so that a written statement from either was not forthcoming, nor was the Khalsa government willing to concede that the property should go to the Dogra family: it preferred to treat it as forfeited to the Government since it belonged to one who had died without a male heir and in rebellion against his sovereign. The question became a constant source of irritation. The Darbar was forced to the conclusion that the British had no intention of parting with the treasure.[1]

Another issue between the two governments was in regard to the village Mauran which had once belonged in equal portions to the rulers of Nabha and Patiala. Dhana Singh Malwai, a distinguished officer of the Khalsa army under Ranjit Singh, requested the Maharaja that the village, to which he belonged, should be granted to him by way of *jagir*. Ranjit Singh agreed and asked the ruler of Nabha to transfer his share of the property to the Maharaja as a gift in consideration of an estate which the Maharajah would grant to Nabha's sister. This was arranged

---

[1] Eventually, as is formally shown on paper, the treasure was used as part-payment of the price of Kashmir, when it was alienated to Gulab Singh in 1846.

and Dhana Singh enjoyed undisputed possession until his death in May 1843. Davinder Singh, who succeeded Jaswant Singh to Nabha in 1840, was not happy with the arrangement and was eager to recover Mauran from Dhana Singh's son, Hukm Singh. He represented to the Agent of the Governor-General that he had obtained the consent of Maharaja Kharak Singh, (which afterwards was proved to be false) to resume Mauran. Clerk, in a somewhat ambiguous manner, wrote back to say that since Mauran appeared to belong to the Raja of Nabha, he might take it back. In August 1843, Davinder Singh seized the village, including Hukm Singh's personal property. The Darbar demanded restitution. The British produced a new argument to the effect that Jaswant Singh having been ruler of a dependent state should not have alienated the village to Ranjit Singh without the consent of the paramount (British) power. The original grant was therefore invalid and no satisfaction would be provided either to the Darbar or to Hukm Singh.[1]

The Sikh government had been justifiably offended by the attitude of the British in regard to Attar Singh. Hira Singh had lodged a strong protest with the British Agent at Ludhiana, and Colonel Richmond had been unable to provide an explanation for the fact that "Attar Singh traversed a distance of eighty *coss* through British territory without having been stopped even once in the course of his journey;" the Governor-General, himself incensed by this, shortly afterwards recalled Richmond from his post.

Factors which caused most uneasiness to the Sikh government was the movement of British troops, the building of additional barracks in cantonments at Ferozepore, Meerut, Ambala, Kasauli, Simla and Sabathu; purchase and storage of large quantities of wheat and other provisions. An unusual assembling of troops in Ferozepore was explained by the British as heading for Sindh, *via* the Sutlej. But Hira Singh was unconvinced. He arranged, during the first three months of 1844 that Khalsa regiments should move from Lahore to Mangat, thence to Kanha Kacha, and on to Luliani and Kasur. The British Agent re-

---

[1] Lepel Griffin, page 195, states "the decision of the British government irritated, in no small measure, the Sikh nation, and particularly so at the time when the Sikhs were in a feverish and excited state."

## Hira Singh as Prime Minister of the Punjab

monstrated with Hira Singh on a movement of 4000 horse and foot and sixteen pieces of cannon towards Kasur 'with doubtful intentions' and held out the threat that if a single soldier of the Lahore army crossed the Sutlej, 'the aggression will not be forgiven.' Hira Singh was not to be cowed by this bullying, and replied that when the British troops in Ferozepore left for Sindh, he would consider recalling his own troops from Kasur.

Meanwhile there was trouble in the frontier districts of the Punjab. Wherever it occurred, Gulab Singh's influence was clearly discernible; for it was in his nature to grasp every opportunity of furthering his own interests. He was in communication with the rebel chiefs of Darband, Pakhli and Zaida; and to Malik Fateh Khan Tiwana, who was the first openly to defy the Darbar, he offered assistance in money. This Tiwana Malik of Shahpur claimed a noble genealogy. His father, as head of clans had resisted the inroads of the Sikhs for a decade, only submitting to Ranjit Singh in 1819. The Maharaja was impressed by his soldierly bearing and fine horsemanship and conferred upon him a service *jagir* with the annual value of ten thousand rupees in lieu of sixty *sowars*. His son, Fateh Khan, also a gallant and good-looking soldier, won the favour of Dhian Singh, and was with him just before the latter was murdered; (however, as the Raja and his assassins entered the fort, he managed to remain outside.)[1] When Hira Singh learned about this, he began to suspect Fateh Khan of complicity in his father's murder; so that the Malik thought it best to escape from Lahore. Feeling unsafe in his home, Mitha Tiwana, he crossed the Indus and took refuge with the Bannuchi Pathans of Bannu and Tonk. The Darbar directed Diwan Lakhi Mal, Governor of Dera Ismail Khan, to march on Tonk and seize his person. Tonk was taken but the Malik escaped. Early in June 1844 he mustered the Waziri Pathans and started ravaging the countryside. He repulsed a small contingent of Sikh irregular horse sent against him. But towards the end of the month troops from Multan, Dera Ismail Khan (Mankera) and Lahore converged upon Mitha Tiwana, where Fateh Khan had arrived in the course of his predatory wanderings. He was trounced; Mitha Tiwana was

1 Lepel Griffin, p. 526.

sacked, and some of his people including his mother and son, captured. Fateh Khan himself escaped across the Indus. When trouble started in Hazara, he was quick to be on the scene. With moral and material support from Raja Gulab Singh whose relations with Hira Singh, were again strained, he continued to defy the Darbar. He remained at large till Hira Singh's death.

In August 1844, insurrection beginning in the uplands of Hazara spread towards Muzaffarabad on the borders of Kashmir and later to Baramula and Sopur in the valley of the Jhelum. At one stage the Muhammedan population of the entire region from Peshawar to the Jhelum was in a state of ferment. The anti-Sikh contagion spread to southern parts of the kingdom: Multan, Dera Ghazi Khan and Dera Ismail Khan. The sudden death of Diwan Sawan Mal removed the guarantee of peace and stability that his just administration had ensured in these districts. Sikh sovereignty had never before been so seriously challenged.

The trouble in Hazara was started by Sardar Habib-ullah Khan of Pakhli. He took advantage of the disorganised state of affairs at Lahore and attacked the Sikh garrison at Khori. Timely aid from Srinagar saved the situation. Habib-ullah Khan was killed. Two months later his son, having formed a league with some other Muslim chiefs of the valley, launched a crusade against the Sikhs. The allies took Khori and advanced towards Muzaffarabad, ejecting small Sikh garrisons from the forts on their way and captured Muzaffarabad. These successes encouraged the chiefs of Uri and Dobheta to join in the rebellion. The insurgents occupied Baramula and Sopur and were within striking distance of Srinagar, the chief city of the valley of the Jhelum. It had become a *jehad*, a holy war against the infidel Sikhs. Muslim troops in the service of the Governor of Kashmir, deserted and joined the rebels. Reports from the Governor, Sheikh Ghulam Mohi-ud-din, as quoted by Sohan Lal, were to the effect that the province of Kashmir, was almost lost to the Sikhs, *ez jauza-i-tassaruf Sarkarwala badar Khwahad raft*. Gulab Singh who could have sent help from Jammu made no attempt to do so. On the contrary, he was primarily responsible for circulating the rumour that the Sikh government was fast disintegrating.[1] The Darbar was thrown back on its own resources. Troops stationed in Peshawar were ordered to move to Muzaffarabad; and a body of 600 irregular cavalry to join them from positions in Hazara. The whole of the Jhelum valley and the bordering region of Muzaffarabad was, through the energy and resource of Hira Singh, reconquered (November 1844).

The financial resources of the state dwindled rapidly. The army and the nobility were the principal drains upon them. In the case of the army, numbers and salaries had persistently been raised. In the *Fauj-i-Ain* for instance, the total strength of all branches of the service, infantry, artillery and cavalry rose from 35,242 in 1839-40, to 51,452 in 1843-44, and its salary receipts from Rs. 4211,292 to Rs. 8730,108 per annum. Similar increase took place in the irregular cavalry. In 1843-44 the state was spending on its army a sum of Rs. 13336,528—nearly twice the amount Ranjit Singh used to pay.[2] Apart from this regular outlay there had been several occasions, within the short period of five years, when large quantities of cash, gold and silver were taken out of the state vaults for distribution as largesse by Chand Kaur, Sher Singh and Hira Singh.

*Jagirdars, rosinadars, and dharmarthwalas*, constituted another category of people who were a charge on the state. Between them they absorbed something like ninety-two lakhs of rupees per annum in the shape of revenue-free grants or assignments of revenue, (these assignments were made from time to time to appease civil and military officers or favourites of the rulers). During the troubled times that followed Ranjit Singh's death, many of the grantees extended their estates by usurping crown lands that adjoined their own; petty village officials were too easily induced not to bring such matters to the notice of the government. The actual amount of revenue which was thus diverted from the state treasury was therefore considerably more than Rs. 9200,000, that was officially estimated and sanctioned, as *Kharai-az-jama* in the rent rolls of the government.

---

[1] In April 1841, when General Mian Singh was killed by mutinous troops, and Sheikh Mohi-ud-din appointed governor, the Darbar specifically instructed Gulab Singh to help him if necessary, in restoring order.

The table on page 86 was compiled by the present writer from the original pay-rolls of the Khalsa army, and published in the catalogue of the Khalsa Darbar in 1919.

| Service | 1818-19 | | | 1838-39 | | | 1843-44 | | |
|---|---|---|---|---|---|---|---|---|---|
| | Strength | Salary p.m. | Per head | Strength | Salary p.m. | Per head | Strength | Salary p.m. | per head |
| | | Rs. | | | Rs. | | | Rs. | |
| Infantry | 7,748 | 60172 | 7.8 | 26,617 | 227660 | 8.5 | 37,791 | 483056 | 12.8 |
| Cavalry | 750 | 11723 | 15.6 | 4,090 | 90375 | 22 | 5,381 | 161660 | 30 |
| Artillery | 834 | 5840 | 7 | 4,535 | 32906 | 7.2 | 8,280 | 82793 | 9 |
| Total | 9,332 | 77735 | 8.32 | 35,242 | 350941 | 9.9 | 51,452 | 727509 | 14 |
| Irregular Cavalry | 3,577 | 1113782 | 311.3 | 10,795 | 3268711 | 302.7 | 14,383 | 4418840 | 307.2 |

This table was compiled by the present writer from the original pay-rolls of the Khalsa army, and published in the Catalogue of the Khalsa Darbar in 1919.

## Hira Singh as Prime Minister of the Punjab

No steps were taken to increase the income of the state. Revenue receipts became more irregular and arrears from governors and farmers of revenue (*ijardars*) such as Raja Gulab Singh, Diwan Sawan Mal and Sheikh Ghulam Mohi-ud-din, accumulated to the extent of more than a crore of rupees. To restore financial equilibrium it became urgent that taxes should be increased, expenditure on the army curtailed, and the feudal nobility induced to pay their dues. However, it was equally evident that an increase in the tax on land would be resisted as the amount charged under this head including a number of cesses, came to fifty per cent of the total yield. Enhancement of octroi duties and other minor charges, was not likely to make a substantial difference.[1] Retrenchment in the army was out of the question if it meant the docking of a soldier's pay. The most the government could dare to do was not to fill vacancies due to death or desertion and impose more stringent fines for absence from duty or any breach of discipline. The only resource that could then be explored was revenue-free grants. Hira Singh ordered a thorough investigation of the title deeds of *jagirdars*, and ordered every one of them to produce the original *patanama*, the deed granted him by the government. This perfectly just and reasonable measure created a furore among the nobility— not only because almost everyone concerned had encroached on land beyond what was granted, but also because of the choice of investigating officer who was no other than the obnoxious Pandit Jalla. His offensive manner towards the Sikh chiefs provided the excuse to refuse co-operation. Many of the dignitaries left Lahore beiging disgust. Bhai Ram Singh, Bhai Gobind Ram and Lehna Singh Majithia found the moment opportune for making pilgrimage to Hardwar or Banaras; others, such as Diwan Basakha Singh, Jawahar Singh Nalwa and Rattan Singh Gharjakhia sought refuge with Bhai Bir Singh. Among the few who were fined, or left with lawfully reduced estates were Sobha Singh Khalsia, Jamadar Khushal Singh, the Sahibzadas of Dera Baba Nanak and the widow of Maharaja Sher Singh.

Hira Singh had shown remarkable nerve and resource in dealing with a multitude of perilous situations,: Jawahar Singh's

[1] The income from salt, a state monopoly, was Rs. 1067,660.

designs of fleeing with the Maharaja to British territory; the revolt of the Princes, Peshaura Singh and Kashmira Singh; Suchet Singh's attempt to secure the Prime Ministership; the Attar Singh-Bir Singh alliance; general rebellion in the frontier districts and the bewildering problem that the position of the Khalsa army in the state had become. But his troubles were not at an end.

To celebrate the day of *Sankrant* 12 (December, 1844) Rani Jindan collected a number of articles including pieces of gold and silver to be given away in charity, as was customary with her on such occasions. Pandit Jalla questioned her right to give away so much wealth from the treasury. He is said to have used abusive language. The Rani, through her brothers, appealed to the Khalsa soldiers for protection. She reinforced the plea with promises of cash and salary increase. A few days before this Hira Singh had succeeded in angering the soldiers, by ordering the discharge of five hundred troopers. Appeals were made on their behalf by the army *panchayats*; the issue was still pending when the Queen-Mother made her plaint. Some of the Khalsa regiments moved out of cantonments to the open ground near the citadel. Once more they demanded the surrender of Pandit Jalla. This was refused. "In the early hours of the morning of 9th. Poh" (21 December) writes Sohan Lal, "Hira Singh and a party loaded with cash and jewellery on elephants stealthily left their residence. But they had hardly cleared the Taxali Gate, when they were noticed by a company of Sikh soldiers." The news was flashed to the military lines, and a body of 6,000 troopers led by Sham Singh Attariwala went in pursuit. They overtook the fugitives at a distance of thirteen miles. The Dogra minister and his friends put up a fight; but the odds were overwhelming. Among the slain were Hira Singh, Jalla, Mian Sohan Singh son of Gulab Singh, and Mian Labh Singh. Their severed heads were brought to Lahore as *troppes* and hung with chains on the branches of trees outside the Lohari gate,—*berun darwaza Lohari bar shakh az darakht awekhta sakhtand*; where they remained on public view for many days, a target for indignity and abuse.[1]

---

[1] The Nihangs and Akalis who revelled in such scenes, are said to have carried the head of Pandit Jalla, about the streets, demanding a few cowries, for a view of the exhibit.

## Hira Singh as Prime Minister of the Punjab

Moral values were indeed very much at a discount at this time.[1]

Major Broadfoot, Agent to the Governor-General, in a letter to Lord Ellenborough in England, on 17 January, wrote about the administration of Hira Singh and Pandit Jalla. "They had shown remarkable ability and courage, but the difficulties were insuperable. The great Sardars on the one hand and the disciplined army, or rather the drilled army, on the other, suffice severally to swallow up the revenue. Both together devour the country. Pandit Jalla tried by rigorous economy and punctual pay to keep the government going, while he reduced both the formidable bodies, using one against the other; but he left out of his calculations the mother of the nominal sovereign and she was suffered in contempt, to intrigue against him; or rather the task undertaken was impossible and both Sardars and army suddenly uniting, overthrew the Pandit and the Raja and revived anarchy."

---

[1] The young widow of Diwan Singh, who was killed in Hira Singh's company, prepared herself for *sati* as was the custom, in bridal array, and passed through the city thoroughfares being blessed, and giving blessing to the people. When she had actually mounted the pyre the soldiers fell upon her, 'tearing the rings with violence from her nose and ears,' jewels which had been intended for distribution to the poor. Major Broadfoot in his report observed, "she was burnt praying for the ruin of the Sikhs, who stood by laughing." Broadfoot, p. 245; S.L. d.IV(III) p. 69.

## Chapter 6
### THE LAST YEAR OF FREEDOM

THE army and a small clique of Sardars headed by Rani Jind Kaur and her brother succeeded in destroying Dogra hegemony in the Darbar. But they had no plan for putting a workable administration in its place; nor were the interests of the army, the chiefs and the Rani identical. The result was that instead of an improved situation, for some time there was virtually no government in the Punjab, no group strong enough to steer the vessel of the state away from anarchy. This state of affairs continued throughout 1845. Toward the end of the year, the Sardars and the Rani appeared to be united against the Khalsa army plotting to weaken or destroy it by tempting it to go to war against the British. Thus the day when Hira Singh Dogra was killed (21 December 1844) may be seen as the beginning of the end of the Sikh empire.

On returning to Lahore, Jawahar Singh went to Hira Singh Dogra's house and appropriated treasure, said to have been worth Rs. 3,000,000. He and his sister triumphed for two days. On the third, a grand Darbar was held at which the Sardars congratulated one another on 'obtaining deliverance from oppressive Dogra rule.' Jawahar Singh pressed his case for Prime Ministership. But neither the army, nor the chiefs were willing to accept the son of a kennel-keeper in this position. The proposal of Attar Singh Kalianwala was similarly rejected on the grounds that he was a *naherna*, barber, by caste.[1] Rani Jind Kaur, in any case, was in no hurry to fill the post of Chief Commander of the army which he had aspired to, having herself a different disposition at heart.

The atmosphere of uncertainty encouraged Peshaura Singh to try his chances of becoming chief adviser to the Darbar; with the elimination of the Dogras, any descendant of Ranjit

---

1 Broadfoot, p. 256. For the family history of Attar Singh, see Lepel Griffin, pp. 103-110.

## The Last Year of Freedom

Singh seemed likely to succeed. Peshaura Singh left Ludhiana with the cognisance of the British Agent. On arrival at Lahore on 1 January 1845, he was advised by Rani Jindan to accept a *jagir* worth Rs. 40,000 and live in peaceful retirement removed from the hazards of Lahore. She won over the army with the promise of an addition of half-a-rupee in the monthly salary; so that the *Panchayats* also advocated retirement to the Prince.

Meanwhile the government remained at a standstill. For routine administration a sort of working council was set up with Jind Kaur as president, her brother Jawahar Singh and Bhai Ram Singh as members, assisted by Bakhsi Bhagat Ram, Diwan Dina Nath and Fakir Nur-ud-din as senior secretaries. All military dispositions, were however, made under the sole authority of the army *panches*. The capital became the centre of turbulence and disorder; soldiers prowled in the streets maltreating the already terror-stricken citizens. Sikh chiefs, relatively secure in their feudal domains, ruled as irresponsible petty sovereigns.

Kohistan (the hilly districts of Hazara, Chhach and Attock) and the whole of the doab of Sindh Sagar from Kalabagh to Mithankot were in a state of ferment. Collectors of revenue were expelled and men of the war-loving tribes committed great excesses. Sheikh Mohi-ud-din, Governor of Kashmir, himself threatened to renounce allegiance to the Darbar in favour of the British as Gulab Singh had resolved to do three years earlier.

Gulab Singh's account with the Darbar was in arrears. His accumulated wealth had long been an object of envy to the Khalsa. He had appropriated the properties of his brother Suchet Singh and his nephew Hira Singh. His unpaid dues were estimated as amounting to something like a crore of rupees. The Khalsa therefore planned an expedition to the hills early in the year; their programme suited the Rani who was convinced that peace and quiet in the capital could only be achieved, if the major portion of the army were employed elsewhere. The account of the march presented by Sohan Lal makes shocking reading: the Khalsa soldier having, it seems, cast away all restraint, moral, religious or professional. Loot, rapine and senseless destruction of life became a common practice. "Nothing worse," the court diarist observes, "could be expected from a foreign invading army."[1]

The Rani despatched a small number of her own trusted Sardars and secretaries to negotiate with the Raja; among them were Sardar Fateh Singh Man, Diwan Rattan Chand Duggal, Sardar Sher Singh Attariwala and Baba Mian Singh Bedi. The Raja received them with great cordiality and entertained them lavishly for several days. With regard to the object of their visit he was non-committal suggesting alternately, submissiveness and defiance. At the same time he manoeuvred it, so as to receive a deputation from the army *panchayats* (the troops having arrived near Jammu) to play off one party against the other while keeping them strictly apart.[2] The first time he met the army representatives, Gulab Singh placed his sword and shield before them and supplicated with his palms joined. He made reference to the prosperity in Dhian Singh's time and the destitution after him; he made gracious acknowledgement of the benefits he and his family had received from the Khalsa; he warned them of the danger of letting the revenues be swallowed up by rapacious Sardars; he stated that whatever he and his family possessed, being derived from the Khalsa, was at the disposal of the Khalsa. He entertained them sumptuously for over a week and lavished gifts upon them. As a result both parties began to perceive the error of the Rani and her wastrel brother in the management of the state revenues. They forgot the mission on which they had been sent.

Negotiations were concluded on 28 February. Gulab Singh agreed to pay four lakhs as earnest of the full discharge of his obligations to the state. An altercation which took place between Sardar Fateh Singh and Wazir Bachna,[3] when the money was handed over, was ignored by Gulab Singh at the time. But he used it as a pretext for secretly instructing his men to waylay and murder both. When the party emerged from the belt of thorny bushes which surround Jammu, it was fired upon;

1 S.L. d.IV(III) p. 70.
2 During Jan. & Feb., 1845 he twice made overtures to the British.
3 Bachna was a jat of the Sheikhapura pargana, who managed the hill estates of Hira Singh under the supervision of Jalla. When the latter was transferred to Lahore in October, 1843, Bachna became general-manager, with the title of Wazir. After Hira Singh's death he was summoned to service in the Darbar. Lepel Griffin, p. 181.

## The Last Year of Freedom

Fateh Singh and Bachna were killed; Diwan Ganpat Ram who was on the same elephant, mortally wounded. The money was brought back to Jammu. Tact and more gifts enabled Gulab Singh to win a safe conduct from the soldiers. He decided to accompany them to Lahore personally to settle his accounts. He arrived at Shahdara on 4 April.

Jawahar Singh did not want Gulab Singh to come to Lahore. The fact that he had done so under the pledged escort of General Meva Singh and the Maniawala Brigade, made the Dogra all the more formidable. Jawahar Singh despatched some soldiers across the Ravi, hoping thereby to overawe the Raja. But Gulab Singh's supporters stood firm and 'prepared for battle'. This was averted by the intervention of Bhai Ram Singh and other dignitaries of the court sent by the Rani. During the night of the 4th, she sent a special messenger to Gulab Singh with a solemn assurance bearing the imprint of the palm of her hand dipped in saffron (*panja-i-zafran*) of her good wishes, and a guarantee of safety. Gulab Singh agreed to proceed to the city. Seated on an elephant, his face concealed, (*rue poshida*) he was ushered into Lahore on the morning of the 7th and lodged in the mansion of Prince Nau Nihal Singh. The Rani was evidently bent upon giving him a grand reception.[1] On the 8th, he was invited to the palace and introduced to the presence of the Maharaja and the Rani by Raja Lal Singh and Sardar Jawahar Singh (much against their peronal inclinations). Rani Jind Kaur, like many others of the Sikh nobility, believed that Gulab Singh was among the few who could restore stability to the kingdom and control the army. They went as far as to offer him the position of Wazir. But the Raja had his own shrewd instinct of the dangers entailed.[2] He refused politely and contented himself with making mischief between Jawahar Singh and Lal Singh. He also managed to persuade the government to accept Rs. 2,700,000, by way of arrears and extend the lease of his revenue-farms (with very slight modifications) for

---

[1] On the day of arrival the Raja was presented with a bag of money, by way of *Zayafat* (felicitation) Rs. 2,100, and an additional 250, for fruit, sweets and articles for the toilet, which made it, under rules of protocol, a very special *Zayafat*.

[2] "An Akali fanatic, could take the life of the Dogra Raja with applause and impunity." Cunningham, p. 268. A couple of shots were actually fired at Gulab Singh during his visit but missed their mark.

a period of two years. Early in July, he obtained leave to return to Jammu. "The Raja," Sohan Lal records, "covered his journey in unusually long marches, *munazil-i-tulana*, and heaved a deep sigh of relief on reaching home safe and sound after five months."[1]

About this time there was a severe outbreak of cholera in Lahore. The citizens regarded the epidemic as divine punishment for the acts of violence commited by the soldiery.[2] Business was suspended and the metropolis wore a veil of mourning. At one time there were as many as five to seven hundred deaths a day.

Rani Jind Kaur, having failed to persuade Gulab Singh to accept the Wazirat, decided the time had come to instal her brother Jawahar Singh in this position. Preoccupied with bereavement and fears which the epidemic brought in its train, neither the Sardars, nor the soldiers were in a mood to question the decision. The formal ceremony of installation was performed on Jeth 3 (14 May) ; when the courtiers assembled to present *nazrana* and *sawarna* to Jawahar Singh.

His appointment to the highest office in the state did not cause Jawahar Singh to mend his ways ; rather he took it as a licence to indulge himself more than ever in conviviality with undesirables and people of low origin, not exclusive of the palace servants. Commandant Bishan Singh, a Gaur Brahmin from North India, the adopted son of Jamadar Khushal Singh was one of his cronies. Bishen Singh had by his offensive manners incurred the displeasure of officers and men in two infantry units. When neither he nor Jawahar Singh would take notice of the soldiers' written complaints, they decided to take action; they dragged a piece of heavy artillery from the lines and forced their way into the fort towards Jawahar Singh's residence. They were only persuaded to stay their hands by the intercession of Raja Gulab Singh and Bhai Ram Singh.

In spite of all her efforts to propitiate Gulab Singh, the encouragement he had given to Peshaura Singh to press his claim against that of her son to the throne, rankled in Jind Kaur's mind.

---

1 S.L. d.IV(III) pp. 70-74; Broadfoot, pp. 282, 287, 291, 296.
2 On May 29, 2000 matchlocks and a vast quantity of golden bracelets were brought to the treasury; property of soldiers, who had died of cholera.

## The Last Year of Freedom

General Mehtab Singh was instructed by her to go to Sialkot and seize the estate of the Prince.[1] The latter put up a strong resistance and it was only on a fourth assault that the Prince was forced to retire within the fort. His followers proved incapable of standing up to the powerful artillery of the Lahore army. The Prince and his family were permitted to escape. They crossed the Sutlej to seek the help of the British.[2] No help was given by the British beyond the fact that the Prince was allowed to leave his family in British territory while he returned to the Punjab to roam in the Muslim-populated part of the country between the Jhelum and the Indus for about four weeks. By the middle of July, with the help of Pathan sympathisers, he surprised and took over the important, but weakly garrisoned fortress of Attock.[3] On July 17, he issued *parwanas* to Sardars zamindars and village elders, declaring his accession to the throne entered into correspondence with Dost Muhammad Khan of Kabul. This caused grave concern to Jawahar Singh who then cast about for an officer whom he could depend upon to send against the Prince ; if possible to finish him once and for all. His choice fell upon Chhattar Singh Attariwala whose daughter had recently been betrothed to Maharaja Dalip Singh. Chhattar Singh, much against his own wishes together with Fateh Khan Tiwana from Dera Ismail Khan, (who was instructed to muster all his available troops earlier) beleagured the fortress of Attock. The Prince had little chance of standing out against such a force. He accepted an assurance that if he accompanied Fateh Khan and Chhattar Singh to Lahore, he would be granted safe conduct and full consideration of his claim to his estate and other prerogatives. On 31 August, while preparing for the journey, he was taken off his guard, seized, thrown into a dungeon and strangled to death.

The leaders of the expedition sent this news to Lahore.

1 Mehtab Singh's brigade comprised 4 infantry battalions, one cavalry regiment and 25 guns, in all, 4814 men. vide pay-rolls Oct. 1845-Jan. 1846, Kh. D.R., v.I, p. 90.
2 It was reported that General Mehtab Singh was prohibited by the *panchayats* from molesting the prince, because he was Ranjit Singh's son, and also because they wished, if necessary, to use him as a counter against Dalip Singh.
3 The British news-writer of Lahore stated that when the troops got the news, they expressed admiration for the gallant enterprise and asserted that he must indeed be the son of Ranjit Singh.

Fearing the wrath of the Khalsa, Fateh Khan returned to Dera Ismail Khan, and Chhattar Singh sought temporary asylum in Raja Gulab Singh's territories. Jawahar Singh, not only dared to remain in the capital, but made the crime an occasion for rejoicing. "The ramparts of the fort," wrote Muhammad Latif, (p. 535) "thundered forth a salute and the city was illuminated at night."

This unseemly triumph served only to hasten Jawahar Singh's undoing. He was already distrusted by the Khalsa because of his attempt to escape with the young Maharaja into British territory; his manners were odious and unsuited to the position he had been given; he could claim neither rank nor personal stature, and his conduct in the matter of Peshaura Singh was deplored by all. Raja Gulab Singh saw his opportunity. He despatched a party of his most trusted Dogra sepoys under Mian Prithi Singh to stir up feeling against the Minister and bolster arguments with largesse.

The army *Panchayats* had by this time effectually assumed the power of government; they resolved, on 19 September, that Jawahar Singh must die as a traitor and communicated this decision to him and to the Rani. The Queen-Mother was told that she must hand over her brother, or else, she and the Maharaja might have to share the same fate. They avoided compliance and sent Fakir Nur-ud-din, Diwan Dina Nath and Attar Singh Kalianwala to negotiate. The two latter were detained by the Khalsa, while Nur-ud-din was sent back with the message that Jawahar Singh must present himself to the new government on the 21st; failing this, all the residents of the fort would be in peril of their lives. Four battalions of infantry were actually despatched from Mian Mir towards the city. Accordingly, the Rani, her son and Jawahar Singh started for **Mian Mir** on the afternoon of the 21st and arrived there soon after sunset. The Maharaja, his mother, and attendants were conducted to their tents and Jawahar Singh put to death, by sword and musket in the howdah of his elephant. The next morning his body was handed over to the Rani for cremation; and Diwan Dina Nath and Attar Singh Kalianwala, allowed to return with her to Lahore.

The army committees represented in the *Sarbat-Khalsa*, which

## The Last Year of Freedom

had thus manifested their power, revived the old democratic flavour of the Khalsa Commonwealth of pre-Ranjit Singh days ; their seal of authority was inscribed with the words *Panth Khalsa jeo*, and above this, the invocation *Akal Sahai* (God is our help). The names of Maharaja and Rani were dropped from official communications and the summons to appear before the Khalsa, which had been served upon them and Jawahar Singh was couched in peremptory terms. About this time also, the Khalsa resolved that the existing mode of administration with the assistance of senior secretaries of departments should continue until Dussehra, when the Khalsa would assemble and decide the future composition of the government ; that, in spite of Jawahar Singh's incitement the Khalsa would not commit any aggression on British territory but try to maintain peace ; If British troops should be moved from other positions, to reinforce the armies at Ferozepore or Ludhiana, the Khalsa would move towards the Sutlej ; otherwise each should keep its territory and its peace. This decision was conveyed to Diwan Dina Nath and Fakir Nur-ud-din for communication to all officers of the state and to the vakils stationed at British agencies.[1] A remarkable development that ensued upon the Khalsa's assumption of real authority in the state was an enforcement of very rigid discipline among the soldiers, which had for a long period, been in shocking abeyance.

Dussehra passed uneventfully. The appointment of either Gulab Singh or Tej Singh, as wazir was considered. But it was decided to leave the direction of affairs in the hands of the Rani, assisted by a council of secretaries, such as Diwan Dina Nath, Fakir Nur-ud-din and Bakshi Bhagat Ram, with the final say in matters of importance resting always with the Khalsa.

The Rani was far from being content. Her desire to avenge her brother death was given a bitter edge by the savagery perpetrated by the troops at the cremation. They snatched the jewels from widows in the act of *Sati* and Jindan had only

---

[1] Broadfoot's letter to Govt. of India, 26 September, 1845. Broadfoot, p. 348.

As an earnest of their own friendly intentions the new government apologised for Jawahar Singh's aggressive conduct towards the British Agent, and his genuine or pretended efforts to break the peaceful relations between the two governments. Broadfoot, p. 351.

been stayed by force from immolating herself and her son on the pyre. Her desire to see the army brought low continued to smoulder; she looked to the British for doing this as she had looked for assistance from them during Peshaura Singh's bid for power. When, after the death of Peshaura Singh the soldiers toyed with the idea of putting Sher Singh's son Sahdev Singh on the throne, her uneasiness was revived beyond all measure.

Early in the year both Jind Kaur and Gulab Singh, had out of their own reasons, made overtures to the British. Lord Hardinge's letters to Lord Ellenborough indicate that the Rani had proposed an alliance on the basis of accepting a subsidiary position; moreover, Hardinge indicated that the ruling party was willing 'to undertake the filthy job of prompting the Khalsa troops to commit a number of acts, direct and indirect, which might provide an ostensible cause for the British interference, provided these influential persons were permitted to retain their *jagirs*, their powers and their nationality, viz. the nominal rule of their Maharaja.'[1]

In January, while the Khalsa troops were marching to Jammu to collect the dues he owed the Darbar, Gulab Singh sent Bhai Ram Singh to ask for help from the British. On his return from Lahore he sent another special messenger to Major Broadfoot stating that from what he had seen he was convinced the war would break out in the coming winter. He proposed to muster against the Sikhs, inhabitants of the hills over whom he had complete control; to break off relations with Lahore and transfer allegiance to the British; to raise forty or fifty thousand armed men and destroy the Sikh army. Then the British might occupy Lahore without firing a shot. In return he asked for the enjoyment of his present possessions during his life, while Jammu and the neighbouring territories with an income of Rs. 1,200,000 a year, be guaranteed to him and his heirs for ever.[2]

The Rani and her chosen coterie of chiefs, who loved security and privilege more than honour or the independence of their

---

[1] Broadfoot, pp. 256, 267, 282 & 337. Whether this offer was made by the Rani and the chiefs of their own accord, or as result of subtle suggestion from Major Broadfoot, is not established; the major was capable of doing such things.

[2] Broadfoot, p. 330.

## The Last Year of Freedom

country, set about insidious propaganda to influence the Khalsa soldiers against the British, to the effect that 'regiment after regiment of red-coated English soldiers were coming up from Calcutta; that some of them were already in position to cross the Sutlej.' When passions had been roused sufficiently, a great council of army officers and Sardars was called in the Shalimar Gardens early in November, where the court was encamped on its way back from Amritsar. In an eloquent address, Diwan Dina Nath confirmed some of these reports. He reminded the Khalsa that the British had not returned Suchet Singh's treasure, nor restored Mauran village. He referred to reports that in the cis-Sutlej Sutlej states the high-handed British Agent was treating the Sikhs as if they were subjects of his government. He drew attention to the depleted state of the treasury—not a single rupee he said being forthcoming from Kashmir or Peshawar, whereas beyond the Sutlej lay flourishing cities, Delhi, Agra, Mathura and Banaras, waiting to be exploited. At the end of his oration, he offered the Rani's proposal, that Lal Singh be appointed wazir and Tej Singh commander of the armies, with unlimited authority in the event of hostilities. This was accepted without demur though neither Lal Singh nor Tej Singh had any distinction to recommend them.

Having thus prepared the troops for war, the Rani's junta unfolded other plans. The army was to be divided into seven divisions, each with an approximate strength of 8000 men. Of these one was to remain in Lahore; one to go to Peshawar; one towards Sindh; the remaining four, after crossing the Sutlej, were to proceed towards Ropar, Harike, Ludhiana and Ferozepore respectively. Each division was, severally, to engage the enemy and not attempt a concerted effort. The dubiousness of the entire plan was glossed over by religious sanction. The soldiers and sardars were invited to assemble at the shrine of Maharaja Ranjit Singh on the morning of the 19th, when Lal Singh and Tej Singh were formally installed in their new posts, and all present were required to lay their hands upon the scriptures to pledge fidelity to the government of Maharajah Dalip Singh, to his officers in the field, and the authority of the *panchayats* was suspended. The ceremony at the *Samadh* savoured of the ancient *yagnas* at which a beast to be sacrificed was first

## Sunset of the Sikh Empire

led for blessing to the altar of the High priest.

Sir Henry Hardinge was not anxious for precipitate war. His own preparations were not complete; and if Raja Gulab Singh were to implement what he had said, it meant the Punjab would be split in two, and therefore an easier proposition to handle. But the Raja's intentions wanted testing. He himself did not approve of any project in the interests of a few grasping sardars to maintain a puppet on the throne. And, on grounds of equity and moral justice, he could not be persuaded that the Sikhs had given him cause for war. To his Agent, Major Broadfoot, who was repeatedly urging the contrary, he replied as in a letter to Lord Ellenborough, dated 23 October, that in his view nothing had occurred "to justify the seizure of our friends' territory, who, in our adversity assisted us to retrieve our affairs." He advocated, for the present "abstinence from all interference or aid, by whomever solicited, defensive measures for the protection of our territory and destruction of those who violate it, must be our policy."[1]

He authorised Major Broadfoot to inform the Lahore Darbar that if Maharaja Dalip Singh "was deposed by violence the Governor-General would not recognise his successor." This served to allay Rani Jind Kaur's fears and confirm her view of the British as potential allies. Major Broadfoot, on his part, continued to keep in touch with Raja Gulab Singh, Bhai Ram Singh, and other members of the Punjab aristocracy who approached him.[2]

---

[1] Hardinge's letter to Lord Ellenborough is reported in full, Broadfoot, pp. 276 & 355.
Govt. to Broadfoot, January 1845. Broadfoot, p. 269.
[2] His biographer states that in his writings to Govt. Broadfoot was most discreet, either writing himself, or entrusting this to his immediate secretary R. Cust, and information received from 'the native gentlemen on delicate matters' was read and put into the fire, so that the names of his informants should not leak out.

## Chapter 7
### THE BEGINNING OF THE END

THAT war was inevitable had been generally believed both by the British and the Punjabis. Lord Ellenborough had, indeed, even fixed a date for its commencement, November 1945. He fully expected his successor to implement his policy, and maintained regular correspondence with him. Viewed in the perspective of history, this development is not surprising. Even the great Ranjit Singh had suffered more than one reverse at the hands of the British, and had to reckon with their expanding ambitions in setting his own course. In 1809, he was baulked of the project of incorporating the cis-Sutlej states into his kingdom. In 1835 he had to give up the idea of possessing Ferozepore, which three years later became a military cantonment for the British. He was forced to give up Shikarpur in favour of the Amirs of Sindh; and six years later suffer the British to swallow the Amirs and their country. In 1841-42 the Darbar was induced to recall its troops from little Tibet and give up newly acquired dominion in Lhasa, for no other reason than their startling success in that difficult terrain had alarmed the British.[1]

British expansion had come more and more to restrict that of the Sikh kingdom by building cordons around it of states either directly governed by the British or held in subordinate alliance. Following the line of the Sutlej on the Sikh kingdom's eastern boundary there were the British-protected Phulkian states and Muslim Bhawalpur; south and south-west lay Sindh, recently seized by the British; in the north-west, they had engaged in a long campaign to bring Afghanistan within their orbit of political influence, and even egged the Darbar to helping them.

Any doubt there may have been of British intentions was removed by their activities on the border; the building of new

---
[1] See also Proceedings of Historical Records Commission V. XXX, Part II, Paper by M. L. Ahluwalia.

cantonments; increasing the strength of garrisons; collection of military stores and provisions in various places, including Bassian, and placing in strategic positions, materials for pontoon bridges. Till 1838, the only British military station on the Sikh frontier was Ludhiana, its garrison not exceeding 3000 men and twelve guns. At the end of that year, a new cantonment was established at Ferozepore, and a division of British soldiers with twelve guns, maintained there even when the 'army of the Indus' departed for Kabul with Shah Shujah. So much in Lord Auckland's time. His successor, Lord Ellenborough (1842) founded a military station at Ambala, with smaller ones in its rear at Kasauli, Simla, and the Sabathu hills, climatically congenial for European troops and maintained in each a well-equipped force. He brought the strength of British garrisons on the Punjab frontier to 17,612 men and 66 guns. Within a year, Sir Henry Hardinge added to this 23,000 men and 28 pieces of cannon, distributed between Ludhiana, Ferozepore, Ambala, and Meerut. He also assembled 1100 picked horses and mules in stables at Mathura, and 500 elephants, 700 camels and large numbers of bullocks at convenient stations between Kanpur and the Sutlej. In September 1845, sixty large boats were delivered at Ferozepore, which would serve either as a flotilla or a bridge. These had been specially designed and built in Bombay, each fitted with a gun and two grappling irons with strong chains, and the capacity to carry 100 men. With them came a special detachment of soldiers to serve as guards under a European officer for each boat. The latter were provided at the request of Major Broadfoot who chose to behave as though a war was imminent and took upon himself to train and drill them under the very eyes of Sikh troops stationed in the cis-Sutlej territory. The Southern frontier was also menaced by Sir Charles Napier who after appropriating Sindh, held his troops in readiness to cross the ill-defined border into the Punjab.

It was absurd to maintain, as the British took pains to do, that these were 'measures adopted only to meet a contingent situation which might arise from the uncontrolled Khalsa army. The truth was expressed by Major Smith when he wrote : "we have for several years past, in fact ever since the death of Ranjit

## The Beginning of the End

Singh, been playing the fable of the shepherd boy and the wolf. The papers and the politicals have constantly being crying out, the Sikhs are coming.."[1] And so, the follies and excesses of the Sikh army, served as cover for very purposeful military preparations uncomfortably close to their frontiers.

A relatively minor, but lively, source of grievance for the Sikhs, was Major Broadfoot as Agent in Ludhiana. That he should have been appointed to that position considering his mainfest hostility towards the Sikhs which had made him most unpopular when he passed through the Punjab escorting the families of Shah Shujah and Zaman Shah in April 1841, was evidence in itself of Lord Ellenborough's determination to disregard civility in favour of military expediency in his dealings the Darbar.[2]

In his new office, one of Broadfoot first actions was to claim for his government the protectorate of all the cis-Sutlej estates. He refused to make distinctions between Nabha, Jind and Patiala, and those which had unequivocally accepted the sovereignty of the British and others under the Darbar. He declared even the latter to be 'liable to escheat on the death or deposition of Dalip Singh,'[3] (the Maharaja being at the moment ill, with smallpox). During the time of Ranjit Singh, British suzerainty over his cis-Sutlej possessions had never been claimed, and questions of jurisdiction that arose were dealt with by mutual understanding and good-will. The treaty of 1809 had touched only upon the subject that Ranjit Singh undertook not to send across the river any military force, except what was required for the internal administration of his own territory. This had, in no sense been obtained by the help of the British; therefore the suggestion of escheat in their favour could only rest on an unwarrantable assumption of their paramount authority. It was on some such assumption, and his own initiative, that

---

1 *Reigning Families of Lahore*, Introduction, p. XXIII.
2 Robert Cust called him "the prime mover, by many considered the cause of this war.". His actual appointment was made by Hardinge, but recommended by Ellenborough, who assured Broadfoot that Sir Henry "will carry out all my views. He is my confidential friend with whom I have communicated upon all public affairs for thirty years. I will not fail to make him acquainted with your merits and services." 17 June, 1844. Broadfoot, p. 208.
3 Cunningham, p. 280.

## Sunset of the Sikh Empire

Broadfoot intervened in a domestic quarrel among the Sodhis of Anandpur and placed the town and its adjoining villages under military pickets.[1]

Major Broadfoot went out of his way to irritate the people of the Punjab. In an effort to find some person to act as his *agent provocateur* in Lahore, he first thought of Genda Singh of Nabha. Genda Singh indignantly refused[2]—whereupon Broadfoot instructed the Raja of Nabha to 'prepare Genda Singh's son, who is a shrewd person' for the assignment, and so punish Genda Singh 'for his disobedience to the Sahib.'

In March 1845, Sardar Lal Singh *adalti*, a judge of the Lahore state, was crossing the Sutlej in the normal course of his duty with an escort of *sowars*, (horsemen) when they were challenged by Broadfoot on the ground that they had not asked his permission and ordered to return. Lal Singh failed to see why permission was required for crossing over to Darbar territory; nevertheless to avoid any untoward incident he agreed to turn back. As his boats were leaving the river-bank, the Major with his assistant Robert Cust and a force of '150 infantry and 300 sabres' reached the spot and managed to detain the last boat. All on board were seized and disarmed; in the scuffle, one of Lal Singh's men was shot; the rest were taken to a neighbouring village as prisoners. Broadfoot probably realised the illegality of this action. He cooked up the story that the men had not paid for provisions they had obtained on the trip, and when this was done, they were set free. George Campbell states with authority that the incident "was wholly unjustifiable. In a petty matter of supplies we never should have dreamed of interfering between a protected chief and his subject."[3]..And Robert Cust makes the admission that if Lal Singh had acted with less restraint, the shot that killed one of his following, "would have turned out to be the first shot of the Great Sikh War."[4]

---

1 In 1838 the British Agent was specifically instructed that the affairs of the Sodhis, and others of the priestly classes among the rulers, should be dealt with by Ranjit Singh, or a ruler of their own faith; see alsoC unningham, pp. 180-82.

2 Genda Singh was asked to keep "the Major informed of the state of affairs in Lahore, to spread hatred and discord in whatever way that could be done; to suggest the entry of the British; and to 'send us a genealogical table of the Sarkar of Lahore,'."

3 *Memoirs of George Campbell*, p. 77.

4 *Oriental and Linguistic Essays*. Robert N. Cust, p. 43.

## The Beginning of the End

However, at a time when the sentiments of the Khalsa were already inflamed by reports of the movement of British troops towards their frontier, Broadfoot sequestered two villages of the Darbar on the flimsy and ill-founded pretext that they were harbouring criminals from British territory.[1]

On about the 20th. of November British troops at Ambala and Meerut were instructed to hold themselves in readiness, and between the 2nd and 10th of December were actually on the move towards Ferozepore. Meanwhile Brigadier Wheeler, with about 5000 infantry, two regiments of cavalry and twelve field guns, left Ludhiana to converage on the same point.

The Governor-General arrived at Ambala on 2 December. The next day he severed diplomatic relations with the Darbar by dismissing its *Vakil* (representative) from his camp on the plea that the Darbar had not cared to explain the reason for movement of its troops. The *Vakil* had in fact, asked for explanations of Broadfoot's actions and for British military activities on the Punjab borders. On the 6th December, Sir Henry Hardinge himself, marched towards Ludhiana, A week later the Commander-in-Chief proceeded to join him.

On the 13th the Governor-General issued a proclamation declaring war on the Darbar. He annexed its cis-Sutlej territories, giving as reason, that on that day he had received news that the Khalsa army had crossed the Sutlej.[2]

The route taken by the British in their march to Ferozepore was, Ambala, Rajpura, Sirhind, Ludhiana, Rajkot, Bassian, Wadhni, Chirakh and Mudki, which they reached on 18 December, and where the first battle of the war was fought.

Sikh troops began to move on 24 November. Four brigades of the *fauj-i-ain*, under Tej Singh, after a fortnights leisurely march, arrived at Qadian between 9 and 11 December. Thence they took the road southwards through Jhangi and Nathianwala, to cross the Sutlej near Harike on the 12th.[3] A day was spent

---

1 Cunningham, p. 286.
2 Cust wrote "I rode behind the Governor-General and we sat under a tree, to await the infantry (Mudki). The G-G remarked 'will people in England consider this an actual invasion of our territory and a justification for war?'"
3 In the matter of dates, number of tr oops and movements we have followed the account by Diwan Ajodhia Nath in the *Waqai-Jang-i-Pherushahar*, compiled very shortly after the war and preserved in the Archives of the Panjab Government.

in selecting a camping ground and collecting such ferry boats as could be found. The embarkation of troops and war material, commenced on 13 December; it took 23 boats three days to get it all to the other side of the river. On the 16th, camp was pitched at Ludhiana in the Darbar's cis-Sutlej territory between Attari and the small stream of Sukhne.

The irregular cavalry under Lal Singh which was encamped at about a dozen points between Lahore, Padhana and Sursingwala also made towards Harike. Lal Singh was unwilling to cross the Sutlej but was forced to do so by his men. They encamped on the 16th at Mullanwalla from which they could easily communicate with the regular army. It was at Ludhiana that the Sikhs received news of the Governor-General's advance towards Ferozepore via Mudki. Since war had been formally declared and the cis-Sutlej estates annexed, Lal Singh was urged not to tarry at Mullanwala but to attack Ferozepore where the British garrison did not exceed 10,500 men; while the Sikh army consisted of 18,000 infantry, 16,000 *ghorcharas* and 85 guns.[1] But Lal Singh had not come to gain a victory over the British; his object was to solicit their good will and continue as minister in a dependent Punjab. He persuaded his men that they would win more credit by delaying action until they could encounter the main body of the enemy forces instead of the isolated garrison at Ferozepore. To the British, Lal Singh had already conveyed assurance of his friendly intentions through his confidential messenger, Shams-ud-din Qassuria, who told the Assistant Political Agent at Ferozepore (12 Dec.) that "both he and the Rani were the friends of the British and desired nothing more than that the Sikh army be destroyed."[2] He promised moreover, that he would keep back his irregular cavalry for two days after they had been required to join the regular forces. On the 16th he repeated the assurance that, in spite of their small number, no harm would come to the garrison at Ferozepore. Leaving one brigade of the regular army and a few *ghorcharas* something like six or seven thousand men with 20 field guns to watch over Ferozepore, he moved towards Mudki late on the afternoon of the

---

1 Ibid. also Journal of the Proceedings of the Historical Society, 1944, pp. 67-71; Kh. D.R., v. I, pp. 86-90; Lepel Griffin, p. 259.
2 Cunningham, p. 292.

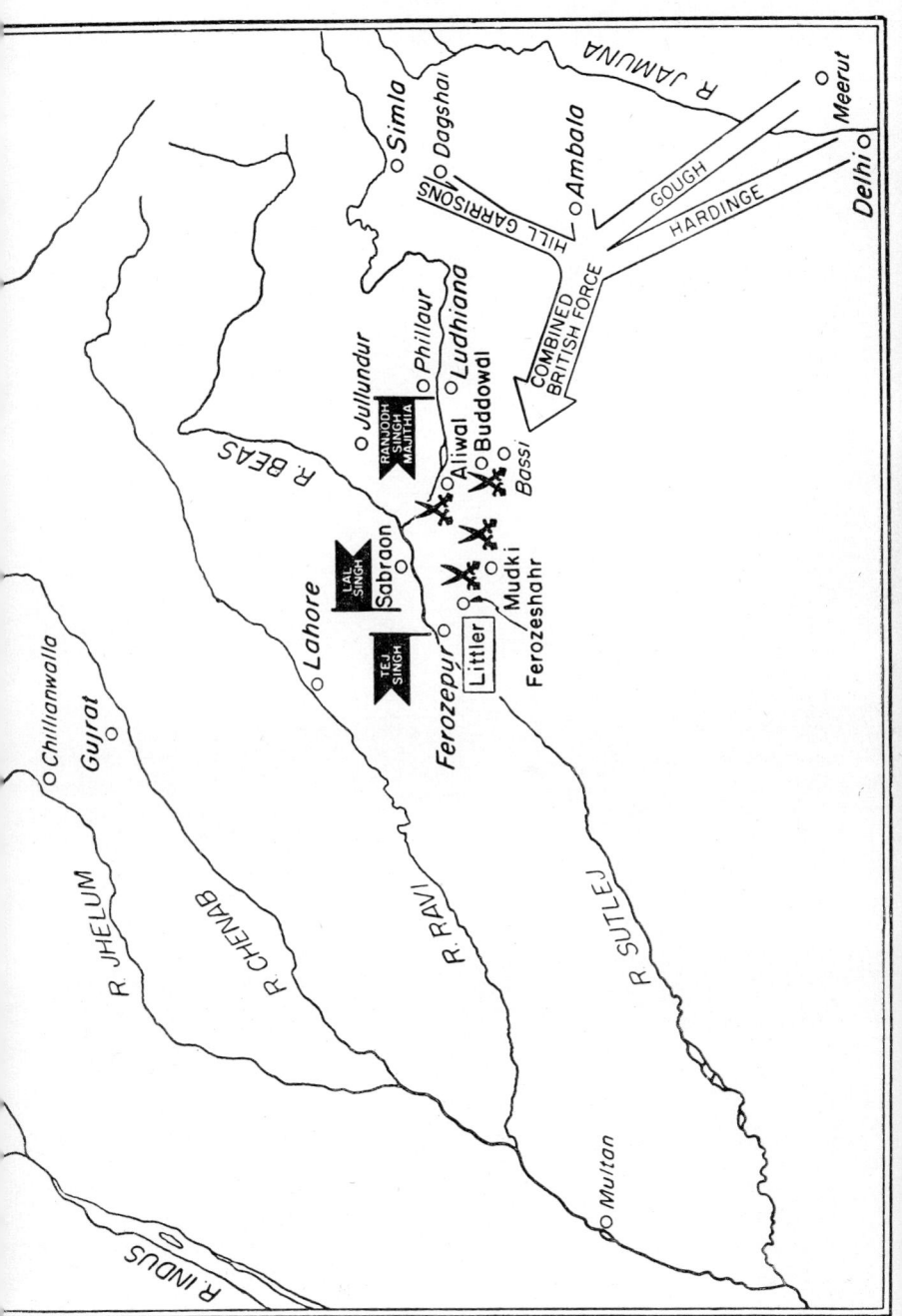

FIRST ANGLO-SIKH WAR 1845-1846

(*By courtesy of the Princeton University Press Drawn by Serbjeet Singh*)

## The Beginning of the End

17th. Sir John Littler, in command of Ferozepore emerged with only five thousand men, but the Khalsa did not meet the challenge.

During the course of their march, whether by design or accident, the troops lost their way. After a whole night's wandering, they arrived, not at Mudki but Pherushahr, in the early hours of the morning. It was here, that they got a message sent by Genda Singh, whose Nihang regiment had got to Mudki, announcing that the 'derah of the Nawab (Governor-General') had arrived there. Fatigued, after the previous night's adventure, the army started for Mudki, a distance of ten miles, to the south-east; the soldiers, despite Lal Singh, were eager for battle; any one of them, to use Cunningham's words, "would drag guns, lead camels, and load or unload boats with cheerful alacrity."[1]

Lal Singh marched from Pherushahr with only half the force on the false plea that Sardar Tej Singh might require the remainder in Lulliani. He reached Mudki about noon, and an hour or two later was faced by Sir Hugh Gough's force of about a thousand men of all arms with forty guns. In between the two armies was a level plain which offered no serious impediment. Lal Singh opened the attack; and having committed his men, disappeared from the field. The fighting lasted for about a hundred minutes during which, in the words of the British Commander-in-Chief, 'the Sikhs fought as if they had everything at stake.' At one moment a cavalry regiment charged upon the enemy with such force as to cause confusion 'men lost their heads and began firing right and left upon their own men.' It took the timely intervention of General Havelock with two European regiments to retrieve this situation. With darkness the fighting ceased, the Sikhs having lost 17 guns; of their dead and wounded there is no record. British losses in men and officers, considering the brevity of the action, were heavy; 215 killed, including Sir Robert Sale,[2] Sir Joseph McGaskill and two aides of the Governor-General; and 657 wounded.

The battle of Mudki served to dispel a notion that had gained credence with the British that the Sikhs were no great force to be

1 Hardinge, R.I.S. p. 86.
2 On his way from Simla, a collection of swords that had been presented to Sale, for former services, was stolen, which was regarded as an omen. Broadfoot's biographer quoting from the *Calcutta Review*, no IX, v. VI, Broadfoot, p. 358.

reckoned with.¹ They realised that they could not inflict the crushing defeat upon them that they hoped for without reinforcements. The Khalsa were therefore able to retire unmolested to Pherushahr. There was no movement of troops on the 19th or 20th, though both at Ferozepore and Mudki the adversaries remained at very close range of each other.

Sir Henry Hardinge was a prudent soldier. He ordered Sir John Littler to bring assistance from Ferozepore, and sent all his available transport to meet European troops coming from the hills to speed their arrival. These reached Mudki on the evening of the 19th, where they were able to rest for twenty-four hours while awaiting the force from Ferozepore.² Lord Hardinge decided also that he must take part personally in the fighting and courteously offered his services as second-in-command to Sir Hugh Gough, waiving his prerogative as Governor-General, to the chief command.³

Sir John Littler left Ferozepore on the morning of the 21st with 5000 infantry, 2 regiments of cavalry and twenty-one guns. Relying on the assurances given by Lal Singh and Tej Singh, he left his strategic post very poorly defended in spite of the fact that an army of 20,000 trained Sikhs was hovering at a distance of only six miles.⁴ At about 1.30 p.m. he joined the main British force, raising the number to 17,000 men, with 69 guns.

The Sikh army on the field at Pherushahr consisted of 12 battalions of infantry, 4 regiments of cavalry and 50 guns of the *Fauj-i-ain* and some fifteen thousand irregular horse, the total amounting to twenty-five or thirty thousand.⁵ They entrenched themselves in a formation about a mile long and half a mile deep. The soldiers had used the respite, to the best of their ability, throwing up earthworks, with no guidance either from their senior

1 It was this that moved Lord Auckland to offer Sher Singh a mere 12,000 men to subdue the Khalsa; General Pollock to assert that the Sikhs would prove incapable of dealing with Afghans; and Hardinge, from his Agent's reports, to think of the Lahore army as 'a mere rabble.'

2 When Gough insisted on an immediate attack on Pherushahr, Hardinge replied "No Sir, I must exercise my civil powers as G-G and forbid the attack until Littler's force has come up." Viscount Hardinge in Hardinge, R.I.S. p. 90.

3 Lord Cornwallis and Lord Hastings of Moira had exercised this right.

4 Hardinge to Ellenborough, 30 Dec., "it was evident that no attack would be made on Ferozepore." Broadfoot, p. 411-12.

5 This includes the number still at Ludhiana during the main battle, J.P.H.S. 1944, pp. 67-70; Kh. D.R. v. I, pp. 87-90.

## The Beginning of the End

officers or expert technicians ; this information was conveyed to the enemy by Lal Singh's emissary Shams-ud-din.[1]

Although it was the afternoon of the shortest day of the year, when his dispositions for attack were complete, Sir Hugh Gough was so anxious to strike that he gave orders for storming the Sikh entrenchments at 3.30 p.m. Sir Hugh, himself led the right, Sir Henry Hardinge the centre and Sir John Littler the left wing of the assailing force. As the British army came in sight, the Sikh gunners opened fire. Undeterred by the storm of shot the British continued to advance. Their siegne guns were brought into play, checking the Sikhs, so that some of the foot soldiers were able to leap over the mud entrenchments and grapple with the Sikh gunners ; infantry of the *Fauj-i-khas* came forward to the rescue and poured in such quick volleys of musketry firing that within ten minutes two hundred of the English soldiers were killed or crippled, and Littler with his soldiers retired for the moment. Sir Harry Smith in trying to take another position in the Sikh lines was also repulsed, but not before the elite *Fauj-i-khas* had been severely mauled. British cavalry, led by Sir Walter Gilbert and General Wallance showed tremendous daring, and at one point seized a couple of batteries, losing 270 men in the exploit ; they continued their assault until nighfall. The British now found themselves in a grave posision. Half their number under Littler and Harry Smith were outside the Sikh entrenchments, but the other half within, unable to advance. At one stage some of their officers advocated retreat to Ferozepore. This timid counsel was spurned by the two war veterans in command. However, it is clear from the Governor-General's letters, that he was acutely aware of the delicacy of his position. He had no reserve of troops, while the Sikhs had Tej Singh close at hand. And in case it should be necessary to retreat to Ambala or Delhi, the march through 160 miles of Sikh territory lying between the Sutlej and the Jamuna, would be extremely hazardous and provide an opportunity for the whole of upper India to rise

---

1 He went to visit Major Broadfoot on the 18th. and the 21st. He came of a Pathan family which had retired from Kasur to Mamdot with Nawab Qutb-ud-din Khan when the latter was made to surrender Kasur to Ranjit Singh (1807). As Lal Singh's emissary he was regarded by the British as 'a safe man' and rewarded by them after the war, with Rs. 5000, and a pension of Rs. 2500 per annum.

against British power. He visited one regiment after another of the tired soldiers, using the formula : "we must fight it out boys! Attack vigorously in the morning, beat the enemy or die honourably in the field. For his own part, he handed over to his civilian son a few precious objects, a watch, a sword and some medals and decorations, and sent instructions to Sir Frederick Currie to destroy all his secret papers in case of accident.

At this point indeed, the Sikhs might have won had they been possessed of a worthy leader. Lal Singh had spent the day of battle hidden in a ditch; and at night stole away to Amritsar.[1]

Before dawn, Gough and Hardinge re-formed their troops and summoned Smith and Littler from their camps. Without waiting for them, however, they decided to take advantage of the dimness before sunrise and make an immediate attempt to dislodge the Sikhs. Refusing to be daunted by heavy artillery, their infantry stormed the enemy positions at bayonet point, while the dragoons rode into and through the Sikh encampment almost without hindrance. The Khalsa who had exhibited such courage a few hours earlier was soon in full retreat, leaving in the field their dead and wounded, besides 73 pieces of cannon, stores, camp equipment and ammunition.

Meanwhile Tej Singh was pretending to guard Ferozepore (a manifest absurdity, since Sir John Littler had left it in broad daylight on 21 December). Under pressure from the Khalsa during the night of the 21st he did eventually make a move, but arrived between 9 and 10 in the morning when Lal Singh's army was already in flight. He might have won the day against the British force which was exhausted and famished. But all he did was to make a feint attack and withdraw at the very moment when the British had exhausted their last round of ammunition.[2]

In the words of Colonel Malleson, the battle of Pherushahr, "was a battle gained after it had been lost, and then regained after its success once more had been imperilled." A contemporary Panjabi poet described it as first won then lost by the Sikhs. Trotter in his *Life of Nicholsan* says, "three days later, (then Mudki) began at Pherushahr that long, changeful and bloody

---

1 Lepel Griffin, p. 359.
2 Gough to his son 16 January 1846. Rait, v. I p. 28.

## The Beginning of the End

fight, on which, for many hours the fate of India may be said to have hung." "Another such action," General Havelock observed, "will shake the Empire." British losses amounted to 2200, killed or wounded ; ammunition ran short, and they had only a few siege guns with them, the Sikhs were thus enabled to re-cross the river into their own country. Sir Henry Hardinge's estimate of Khalsa casualties was 4000.[1]

The theatre of war shifted to the upper Sutlej between Ferozepore and Ludhiana. Opposite Ludhiana on the right bank of the river, the Sikhs had a military post at Phillaur ; its peacetime strength had seldom exceeded one thousand men. Now that the British garrison had moved to Bassian to guard the provisions depot there, the Khalsa pressed for an increase in strength of the Phillaur garrison ; a force of ten thousand men with sixty pieces of artillery was therefore despatched under Sardar Ranjodh Singh Majithia. Although it crossed the Sutlej on the 17th, Majithia failed to take advantage of the fact that the main part of the British force was concentrated at Mudki, and the country was wide open for a kind of offensive the Sikhs were trained in: a small body of irregular horse with light camel swivels let loose on the country from Ambala to Delhi would have created panic and compelled a diversion of forces from Mudki. Instead, the British were given time to detail Sir Harry Smith to move towards the relief of Ludhiana and at the same time offer protection to convoys of guns, ammunition and treasure that were on the way from Delhi. Ranjodh Singh and Harry Smith came face to face near Buddowal where a brief skirmish ended in victory for the Sikhs. But Ranjodh Singh did not follow this up, contenting himself with appropriation of baggage and transport cattle. Meanwhile a regiment of lancers under Colonel Cureton came to the assistance of Harry Smith, so that he was able to get in touch with Ludhiana.[2]

Ranjodh Singh Majithia resumed his march and was joined by a brigade of four battalions, raising the strength of his force to 15,000 men. Sir Harry Smith, being reinforced by a division

---

[1] Broadfoot, p. 414. There is no statement about this in the Sikh records
[2] For Ranjodh Singh's conduct see Cunningham, p. 303:306; Lepel Griffin, p. 88. The latter states "though no traitor to the Sikh govt. as Lal Singh and Tej Singh were, he was as bad and contemptible a general as they were. Like them, he was the last to enter the fight and the first to run away."

commanded by Brigadier Wheeler prepared, (28 January) to give battle. A fiercely contested encounter took place at Aliwal, where the Sikh soldiers gave evidence, once more of their devotion to their cause. Their infantry engaged in many a desperate hand to hand encounter with British cavalry. Colonel Malleson wrote, "they knelt to receive the dashing charge of the British Lancers and their Indian comrades ; but as these approached, they instinctively rose and delivered their fire. Beneath the charge that followed, they did not yield, nor was it till they had three times been ridden over, that they gave way. After the battle it was found that the ground was more thickly strewn with the bodies of the victorious horsemen than of the beaten infantry."[1] The English pushed their advantage to the utmost, forced the enemy to re-cross the Sutlej, and seized more than fifty of their guns (22-23 January).

The decisive battle of the campaign was fought at Sabraon on 10 February. The Ferozepore front had remained quiet after Pherushahr ; the British having learned something of their adversaries, 'toughness'. Reinforcements of men and officers of known repute were called for from all over British India and the resourceful magistrate of Delhi, John Lawrence, was asked to supply ammunition from the local magazine without delay. When all this had been done the British resumed their offensive. That the Sikhs remained quiescent during this period, was not due to unreadiness among the troops, but because the Darbar in Lahore, was engaged in tortuous negotiations. Lal Singh and Tej Singh having discredited themselves with the army, the Queen-Mother determined on counsel from Gulab Singh and once more offered him the wazirat. He, eager as ever to exploit the helplessness of the Darbar, replied that he would only consider the invitation if it came in writing, from the *Sarbat Khalsa*. Time was, therefore, lost in getting the invitation signed and sealed by two representatives of each brigade and delivered in Jammu.

Thus, once more, the Khalsa was inveigled into entrusting supreme authority to one who was not a Sikh ; who moreover

---

[1] Malleson, p. 369. Captain Hambley of the Kings Lancers, said about the Sikhs in this battle, "although beaten they were not dismayed, and though their leader was the first to fly and quit the field, their courage never quailed." *General of a Cavalry Officer*, pp. 149-50.

was not likely to have forgiven the brutal treatment of members of his family at the hands of the Khalsa, and who was known to have negotiated with the enemy.[1] In doing so they passed over another of the Rani's candidates for supreme authority, Sham Singh Attariwala, who was a proved soldier and a man of great integrity.[2] When Gulab Singh arrived in Lahore, he immediately assumed the role of elder statesman and reproached the Khalsa for having engaged in hostilities with such a powerful neighbour without adequate planning or leaders of their own choice. He then opened negotiations on behalf of the Darbar with the British who knew something of his potentialities for good and for mischief, (but had reason to be grateful to him for not joining the war). The Agent posted at Ludhiana at this time was no other than an old friend, Henry Lawrence ; the Dogra had entered into correspondence with him at the commencement of the Sikh war, tendering his allegiance, in return for a guarantee of his possessions. Lawrence in a letter dated 3 February 1846, stated that the British appreciated his wisdom in not having taken up arms against them, and that his interests would be taken into consideration.

The British had no wish to prolong the war. The Raja was told that they would be prepared to recognise the present Sikh sovereign provided the Khalsa army was disbanded and re-formed at a reduced strength. Gulab Singh did not dare accept any proposal that adversely affected the Khalsa and explained the difficulties of the Darbar in this respect giving it to be understood, however, that he would render every assistance that lay in his power to implement any plan the British might have for the state of Lahore. The parties then came to an understanding, according to Captain Cunningham, that "the Sikh army should be attacked by the British, and when beaten it should be abandoned by its own government, and further, that the passage of the Sutlej should be unopposed and the road

---

1 Bhai Ram Singh had carried a message from him to Hardinge in December 1845, saying that he was ready to treat, and would carry out whatever orders might be given by the British govt. Hardinge, R.I.S. p. 81.

2 When the Rani entrusted Lal Singh and Tej Singh with authority, Sham Singh retired to his estate in Attari, in disgust. After Pherushahr, the Rani begged him to return, and taunted him when he refused with being afraid to die. See Lepel Griffin, pp. 63-65.

to the capital laid open to the victors. Under circumstances of such discreet policy and shameless treason the battle of Sabraon was fought."[1]

It was now up to Gulab Singh to persuade the Khalsa to fight. Persuasion was not necessary: the Khalsa were only too impatient to grapple with the enemy. By the close of the first week of February, the Sikh army had constructed formidable entrenchments on the British bank of the river near Sabraon. Their batteries were placed as high as the stature of a man and protected by deep trenches. These defensive works extended for about two and a half miles and were connected with the right bank of the river by a bridge of boats. Some twenty to twenty-five thousand men, and seventy guns were placed behind these entrenchments. Nevertheless, the Darbar courtiers were determined to see the Khalsa beaten. Lal Singh was re-imposed on the army. Two days before the battle, the traitor sent Shams-ud-din to Major Lawrence with detailed information regarding the dispositions of the Sikh army.[2] The weakest point of the Sikh defence, was the right flank where the loose sand made it impossible to throw up high parapets or place heavy guns ; it was to be protected by *ghorcharas* and light camel guns which only fired balls one or two pounds in weight ; moreover the command of this wing was reserved by Lal Singh for himself. On the basis of intelligence provided no doubt, by Shams-ud-din, Cunningham writes "..it was arranged that the whole of the heavy ordinance should be planted in masses opposite particular points of the enemy entrenchments, and that when the Sikhs had been shaken by a continuous storm of shot and shell, the right or weakest point of their position should be assaulted in line by the strongest of the three investing divisions, which together mustered nearly fifteen thousand men."[3]

The British army advanced to take up its position before dawn on 10 February. With daybreak British guns were arranged in an extended semi-circle so as to embrace within their range almost the entire line of Sikh fortifications. They opened

---

1 Henry Lawrence, R.I.S. p. 65.
2 Governor-General to the Secret Committee, 18 Feb. 1846. Parliamentary Papers.
3 Cunningham, p. 312; Lord Hardinge, R.I.S. pp. 115-16.

## The Beginning of the End

ned the assault. The heavy cannonading continued for three hours. The Sikhs stood manfully by their guns returning 'flash for flash, and fire for fire.' The Governor-General and Commander-in-Chief, then agreed that musketry and bayonet charges would yield better results.[1] Accordingly, the left wing of the British infantry under the command of Sir Robert Dick marched in unwavering line against the Sikh right. When they came within three hundred yards of the Sikh batteries, deadly fire from the heavy guns together with well-directed quick volleys from musketry and light *zamburaks,* deflected and drove them back. However, they reformed their ranks and renewed the attack with still greater vigour. Robert Dick and the brigadiers, Stacey and Wilkinson, joined in the assault to cheer their men, who charged with fury, leaping ditches to swarm up the ramparts and seize the enemies' guns: but the Sikhs would not yield. Hand to hand encounters ensued with the Sikh infantry advancing in all directions. A large number of British soldiers were killed and Dick himself mortally wounded. Then Sir Robert Thackwell's cavalry brigade came along and rode over all obstacles to secure Dick's objective.[2]

Meanwhile Sir Harry Smith and Sir Walter Gilbert had led their divisions against the centre and left of the Sikh lines. They too were repulsed and compelled to withdraw in confusion before the Sikh's murderous fire. Sir Henry Hardinge rode up in person and gave the men the command to rally. "No sooner were the words uttered", wrote Viscount Charles Hardinge, "than Colonel Wood, his aide-de-camp, galloped to the centre of the line, seizing the colours from the hands of the ensign, and carried them to the front."[3] The men who joined him stormed the Sikh breastworks and engaged in hand to hand fighting, so desperate on both sides, that the trenches were soon filled with dead and dying. Eventually, the somewhat comingled

---

[1] the two met and 'held a few words of converse about 9'o'clock.' *Calcutta Review,* v. VIII, July-December 1847.
[2] Sir Hugh Gough, in his despatches bestows fulsome praise on Thackwell who had personally led his dragoons at this crucial moment.
[3] Hardinge, R.I.S. p. 117; Hardinge had been so severely bruised by a fall from his horse on 28 January, that he was almost a cripple during the rest of the campaign; he came to the field of Sabraon in his carriage, and mounted his horse only when the guns opened fire, *Calcutta Review,* July-December 1847.

ranks of Smith's and Gilbert's ranks succeeded in forcing their way through the defenses, into the interior of the Sikh camp; here too they encountered tough resistance at every step. Sir Lepel Griffin in *The Punjab Chiefs*, describes many heroic acts performed on this day by the Sikhs. Sham Singh of Attari covered himself with glory. On the morning of the battle, "the white-bearded Sham Singh, dressed himself in white, and having mounted his white horse, addressed the men, begging them as true sons of the Khalsa, to die rather than turn their backs on the enemy. During the first part of the battle he was everywhere present, urging the Sikhs to fight bravely, and it was not till he saw that all was lost, that he spurred forward against the 50th regiment, waving his sword and calling on his men to follow him. Some fifty of them obeyed the call, but were driven back into the river, and Sham Singh fell dead from his horse pierced with seven balls.[1]"

The Sikh's valour was of little avail against the British onslaught. They were driven to the river, where they found their vital bridge of boats had been blown up by Tej Singh who had fled at the first assault of the enemy. While trying to swim the river, perhaps to fight again, British horse-artillery galloping close upon their heels, poured a relentless fire of grape and canister shot, killing more than five thousand in a brief orgy of savagery bearing comparison with the actions of Changez Khan and Timur.[2]

British losses amounted to 320 killed and 2083 wounded; Lord Gough's assessment of Sikh losses was 8000 men and officers, killed in battle, drowned or disabled. Sikh official records provide no precise information on this score.[3]

---

[1] After the battle when his servants obtained permission from Sir Hugh Gough to search for his body, it was found where the dead lay thickest; The night before Tej Singh had counselled him to fly with him, but was refused with scorn. Lepel Griffin, pp. 63-64.

[2] As against attempts to explain away these disgraceful episodes, W. Edwards, a civilian attached to the Governor-General's camp and conversant with secret documents, states "the Sikhs made a gallant and desperate resistance, but were driven towards the river ... their bridge of boats ... by Tej Singh and Lal Singh had by previous consent been broken down. *Reminiscences of a Bengal Civilian*, pp. 99 & 100; Hugh Gough to Sir Robert Peel "were it not from a deep conviction that my country's good required the sacrifice, I could have wept to witness the fearful slaughter of so devoted a body of men." Quoted in Rait, v. II, p. 108.

[3] Heirs of 2,861 men killed during the campaign were later granted a charitable allowance, but this is no indication of the actual number.

## The Beginning of the End

By the afternoon of 10 February, not a single Sikh soldier in arms remained on the British side of the Sutlej. The same night a couple of British divisions pushed across the river into Punjab territory and by the 13th their entire force had crossed to encamp at Kasur, 38 miles from Lahore. Pathan chiefs of Kasur who had been deprived by Ranjit Singh of their estates forty years earlier, came with presents to welcome the conquering Governor-General. Two days later a deputation of select dignitaries of the Lahore Darbar led by Gulab Singh Dogra arrived to negotiate terms of peace.[1] Certain matters having been arranged, the deputation was sent back, with as little ceremony as it had been received; to further humiliate it, the delegation was informed that the young Maharaja and chiefs who had remained at Lahore, must present themselves in person at the Governor-General's camp. The place fixed for the meeting was the village of Luliani on the road to Lahore. On 18 February a brief meeting took place, where all ceremony customary on such occasions was omitted, and the Maharaja and his escort were made 'to put on the mien of humiliation.' The Maharaja was led through the gate of the citadel by a couple of English cavalry regiments and then conducted to the palace by the dignitaries of his own court.[2] The impression the British desired to convey was that the kingdom had been restored to Dalip Singh by the generosity of the Governor-General.

Lord Hardinge addressed himself to the task of setting up a stable and a pliant government at Lahore.[3] The Khalsa were made to vacate the citadel and its immediate vicinity. These were occupied by British and the Muhammedan Najib battalions in the service of the Darbar. Sikh troops were ordered to move across the river and camp at Shahadara and no Sikh soldier was to enter the city without a permit. Increments in pay extorted from Sher Singh, Hira Singh and Jawahar Singh, were cancelled and pay fixed at the rate prevalent under Ranjit Singh. The Doab of Bist Jalandhar, now being ceded to the

---

1 Gulab Singh was armed with a solemn declaration signed by the Darbar, and the *Panches*, to show they would abide by such terms as he could obtain. Allen & Co. 1846, V. II, p. 358.
2 Annual Register, pp. 355-56.
3 He issued a proclamation on 18 Feb., that no harm would come to citizens.

## Sunset of the Sikh Empire

British, all who came from that region were automatically regarded as discharged from service of the Lahore state. They were paid their arrears and ordered to quit Lahore territory.[1]

The soldiers who had fought so valiantly posed a major problem. About 20,000 of them though vanquished were not without fight. Some were encamped at Raiwind, half-way between Lahore and Ferozepore ; a few thousands near Amritsar . In addition, there were strong garrisons at Peshawar, Multan and various points in Kangra. European troops had suffered considerably in the campaign ; and the season was advancing into summer. The British-Indian treasury was depleted. The idea of an immediate annexation of the Punjab had to be deferred. But Lord Hardinge was determined to make the state so weak that its eventual absorption into the British empire would present no major problem. His views were stated in a letter he addressed to his secret committee : "A diminution of strength of such a war-like nation on our weakest frontier, seems to me imperatively required. I have therefore, determined to take a strong and fertile district between the Sutlej and Beas. This will cover Ludhiana, and will bring us within a few miles of Amritsar, with our backs to the hills. In a military sense it will be very important ; it will weaken the Sikhs and punish them in the eyes of Asia.[2] I shall demand one million and a half in money, as compensation ; and if I can arrange to make Gulab Singh and the hill tribes independent, including Cashmere, I shall have weakened the war-like republic. Its army must be disbanded and reorganised. The numbers of the artillery must be limited. The Maharaja himself must present the keys of Govindgarh and Lahore, where the terms must be dictated and signed."[3]

Treaties that were concluded between the British and the Darbar, and separately, with Gulab Singh, show that Lord Hardinge outstepped his original design. Writing to the Agent at Lahore, in October 1846, he observed, "....by the treaty of Lahore (March 1846) the Punjab was never intended to be an independent state. By the clause I added, the Chief of the

1 S.L. d. V, p. 1.
2 To bring home to the public, their victory, 250 cannons captured from the Sikhs were paraded through every station from Ferozepore to Calcutta.
3 Hardinge, R.I.S. pp. 122-24.

## The Beginning of the End

state can neither make war nor peace, nor exchange nor sell an acre of territory, nor admit a European officer, nor refuse us a thoroughfare through its territories, nor in fact, perform any act (except in its own internal administration) without our permission. In fact the native prince is in fetters and under our protection, and must do our bidding."[1]

The treaty made with the Darbar on 9 March, was a blend of 'confiscatory, retributive and repressive clauses ; in it, the splitting of Ranjit Singh's compact empire, a part each for the British, for Gulab Singh and the Darbar, was already foreshadowed ; and the army reduced to one-third of its strength. A supplementary treaty (March 11) suggests that arrangement for an adequate British force in Lahore for the protection of the Maharaja, and the services of an experienced political officer to help in reconstructing the government, was made entirely at the instance of the Darbar; in fact, the British having secured certain political, territorial and financial advantages in the state, it had become imperative for them to have some political staff, backed by an armed force in Lahore, but the Darbar, aware of its acts of treachery towards the Khalsa was only too willing to be manoeuvred into demanding protection.[2]

The facts in regard to the treaty with Gulab Singh Dogra (16 March) are somewhat obscure. One version is that as the Lahore Darbar was unable to pay the war indemnity demanded by the British, or to furnish an acceptable security; Raja Gulab Singh came forward with an offer of Rs. 7,500,000, if all the hill territory between the Beas and the Indus, were made into an independent state under his rule. Sohan Lal provides a more complex story : that three of the senior officials of the Darbar, Bhai Ram Singh, Khalifa Nur-ud-din and Raja Lal Singh waited upon the Governor-General on 28 February, to discuss the penal clauses of the treaty to be drafted. They were told that all guns that had been used against them were to be confiscated and that, since the Lahore government could not guarantee the indemnity asked for, they should surrender the whole of the Kohis-

---

1 Governor-General to Sir Henry Lawrence, 23 October, 1846, quoted by Edwardes and Merivale, p. 417.
2 The Maharaja's request was addressed to Henry Lawrence and passed on to Sir Frederick Currie who returned it with amendments to be incorporated in the text. Allen & Co. 1846, v. II, p. 370.

tan territory and Kashmir. The representatives of the Darbar then withdrew to confer with the cabinet and the Queen-Mother ; it was decided to try and pay the full amount rather than concede territory; Diwan Sawan Mal was to contribute Rs. 4,500,000 Gulab Singh 1,700,000, Misr Rallia Ram 1,700,000, Shaikh Imam-ud-din, 1,700,000, Tek Chand 300,000, and the Queen-mother from the Lahore treasury 5,000,000. Diwan Dina Nath, went accordingly with a message to the effect that the indemnity would be paid in cash. But the British insisted on their pound of flesh in the shape of the territory asserting that the Darbar had offered this.[1] The British spokesman is reported to have put the matter coarsely, saying that it did not become the Darbar to wish to retain that which had been spewed up.[2]

The fact is that Hardinge, wishing to reduce the territory and power of the Lahore Darbar, had found a trend to vacillation[3] in its counsels, and in Gulab Singh's attitudes, a means of furthering his own policies. The stipulated indemnity was never fully realised as a result of the arrangement with him, and Cunningham was to pronounce it 'hardly worth the British name and greatness.' But Hardinge was firm about the necessity, in a letter to Lord Ellenborough he stated : "Gulab Singh had purposely kept aloof. Were we to abandon our own policy and to treat the only man who had not lifted up arms against us with indifference as he came to our headquarters especially deputed to confer with us by the Darbar, as one who had not joined in their unprovoked invasion ? His forbearance was rewarded, because his forbearance was in accordance with an intended policy...."[4] The arrangement with Gulab Singh, whether or not it preceded negotiations with the Darbar officials was in keeping with the long-term project envisaged by Lord Ellenborough, and implemented by his successor.

1 The Rani had done so perhaps, in order to checkmate Gulab Singh; now instead, it appeared that the British were proposing to create a new state of Jammu & Kashmir for Gulab Singh's benefit. S.L. d. V. pp. 2-3; Pannikar pp. 98-99; Cunningham, p. 319.

2 S.L. d. V. p. 2; *Dar-i-kaffaz dahan me ayed bas labidan an Munasib nest.*

3 Of the stipulated indemnity a quarter was waived in lieu of a portion of the hill territory that the British decided to appropriate; and 15 lakhs was considered to have been liquidated in the form of the treasure Suchet Singh had left in Ferozepore which was now decided to have been inherited by Gulab Singh.

4 Hardinge, R.I.S. pp. 135-36; Pannikar, p. 101.

PLATE 6     THE SECOND LAHORE DURBAR OF 26 DECEMBER, 1846

("By courtesy of the Victoria and Albert Museum and Mrs. A.E. Anson Taken from W.G. Archer's Paintings of The Sikhs")

## Chapter 8
### THE KINGDOM OF LAHORE BECOMES THE STATE OF LAHORE

YOUNG Dalip Singh was recognised by the British as Maharaja, with his mother, Jind Kaur as regent. Lal Singh was confirmed in the position of wazir, and Tej Singh as head of the State army (as reward for their services to the British cause during the war). The Governor-General had agreed, as the new government was nervous about the wrath of the Khalsa, to appoint Henry Lawrence to Lahore to give 'advice and guidance' and to maintain a British military force in the capital until such time as the Sikh army was disbanded and re-organised: it was suggested that this task would be complete by the end of 1846.[1] In regard to these arrangements, McGregor, in his *History of the Sikhs*, states: "In appearance, there is a King, a Prime Minister and an army, but one and all are dependent upon British power. The capital of the country is not garrisoned by the Sikhs. It is entirely in the hands of the paramount power, whose soldiers are lent for a time to preserve the semblance of a government, but in reality to keep possession of the advantages already gained, until the season of the year shall enable the Governor-General to annex the whole, to the British possessions, if such a step be deemed necessary."[2]

Subsequent events show very clearly a settled policy on the part of the British to produce a deep and lasting impression of their power. On the morning of 21 April, a herd of cows being driven outside the city to graze encroached upon the ground of a British artillery barrack. The sentry struck out at the animals and injured some of them. When news of this spread in the city the Hindus closed their shops as a mark of protest and crowds assembled to listen to the plaint of the owners of the cows. Henry Lawrence, McGregor and Edwardes, went out to try and pacify the people, but "hardly had we gone to the

1 Lord Hardinge, R.I.S. p. 126.
2 Quoted by Viscount Charles Hardinge, p. 127.

house of the second owner of the cows," Lawrence wrote, "when disturbance started. Our attendants scuffled with a crowd of Brahmins and Khutrees, and brick-bats from adjoining houses were thrown upon us."[1] Edwardes was hit on the head. Lal Singh and Sher Singh were summoned and ordered to apprehend the offenders. When they did not comply immediately, Henry Lawrence, with an escort of Muhammedan infantry, went to the spot in person and arrested a number of men. The Maharaja, with a number of leading courtiers called upon the British Agent to try and appease his wrath, but to no avail. In a letter to Currie, Lawrence reported that he ordered the houses from which the brickbats were thrown, to be razed to the ground ; and further, that the faces of two of the owners having been blackened, they were fettered and placed in public view to act as a deterrent.[2] The court chronicler adds : "on Friday, the 14th Baisakh, under orders signed and sealed by Raja Lal Singh, the Brahmin who was under arrest and had confessed his guilt, was sent to the scaffold ; name, Rulia Misar, sub-caste Dutt, resident of Lange Mandi.[3] The citizens of Lahore had not witnessed a hanging for more than fifty years. About these punitive measures, Lawrence merely stated to his government, "this will make some impression on the minds of the people of Lahore,"[4] (as indeed it did, for later, when Lal Singh was dismissed from office and banished and the Queen-Mother removed from Lahore to Sheikhupura, not a shop was closed in the city, and no word of protest uttered in the streets.)

The fort and town of Kangra and some hilly territory between the Sutlej and Beas were ceded to the British by the treaty of Lahore. Sunder Singh Ailadar, in command of some 300 men in the fort, when asked to vacate, replied that he would open the gates to no one except the Maharaja of Lahore. Officers of the Darbar, such as Ranjodh Singh Majithia, Diwan Devi Sahai, Misar Rup Lal and Diwan Dina Nath were in turn sent to persuade the garrison to deliver up possession of the fort but met with the same answer.

1 Lawrence to Currie (Foreign & Political Department), 21-22 April, 1846, quoted by Edwardes and Merivale, pp. 391-92.
2 P.G.R. Lawrence to Currie 22 April, 1846; Jagmohan, p. 40.
3 S.L. d. V. p. 30; Jagmohan, p. 40.
4 Ibid. Lawrence to Currie.

## The Kingdom of Lahore becomes the State of Lahore

The fort of Kangra, which 'breathed this proud defiance' as described by Bosworth-Smith in his *Life of John Lawrence*, "stands on a precipitous and isolated rock, four hundred feet high, and is connected with the main range of hills only by a narrow neck of land twenty yards wide ; this neck is defended by strong walls built up against the solid rock which had been scarped for the purpose, and a winding passage through seven different gateways gives access to the fortress." The route to be followed therefore, for heavy artillery and ammunition lay along the river Beas, but this too was found to be beset by natural difficulties. A young British officer, Harry Lumsden, with the help of a local labour gang succeeded in discovering a possible route, and engineers were set to work to construct an emergency road for the guns. This was accomplished within a week after which elephants were brought into use to drag the heavy guns to the gate of the fort. Three senior members of the garrison, who were persuaded to visit the camp of Henry Lawrence to discuss terms, were allowed to witness the work in progress—two large elephants, surely and majestically, pulling an eighteen pound gun, with a third pushing from behind ; and another such formation following.... When the last gun had been placed on the plateau, the deputation from the fort was given leave. Within an hour the white flag went up ; the men defiled out and, one by one, threw down their arms and made their way quietly to the plains. (18 May 1846).

By the treaty of Amritsar the province of Kashmir and the estates of Jammu and Kohistan were transferred to Gulab Singh. The implementation of these clauses was left to the Lahore Darbar. By now the eyes of the traitorous Darbaris were wide open. Rani Jindan and Lal Singh made heavy weather of the transfer ; they encouraged the local zemindars and *jagirdars* of Kohistan to create disturbances ; by way of keeping up an appearance of good faith they ordered the governor at Jasrota to spare no pains to bring the zamindars to book, but if he failed, to retire to a safer position. On the basis of this cryptic message, Misar Rup Lal, the governor, retired leaving arms, ammunition and provisions within the fort. These were seized by the rebels. The spirit of revolt spread. It took all of Gulab Singh's energy and resources to acquire possession of

Punch, Bhadarwah, Sumruth, Ramnagar and Jasrota.

Revolt in Kashmir presented an even more menacing aspect. Ghulam Mohi-ud-din, who had been governor, was succeeded, upon his death in 1844, by his son Shaikh Imam-ud-din. Both father and son had amassed private fortunes during their tenures as collectors of revenue in Jullundhur ; they were among the worst defaulters in payment of revenues to the state. The balance due as a result of their stewardship of Jullundhur amounted to forty-five lakhs. With the decline of the government in Lahore, the idea of independence always attractive, became more plausible. The chiefs of the valley surrounding the hills of Uri, Muzaffarabad, Rajauri and Kurna were only too ready to help him if he used this as an opportunity for reviving Muslim domination of the region. One of his wives too, 'bigoted in the Mohammedan faith' was in favour of such a scheme. He played with the idea of obtaining support from the British by an offer of ready money.[1] His father had offered allegiance to them despite his sworn allegiance to the Lahore Darbar. Now that relations between the British and the Sikhs had radically altered, he might succeed in obtaining terms for himself, as good as those obtained by Gulab Singh.[2] At the same time Lal Singh, piqued by the windfall in the fortunes of Gulab Singh, did all he could to encourage the Shaikh to resist the occupation of the province. He issued a *parwana* from the Darbar exhorting the soldiers from Lahore to remain loyal to the governor. The latter, therefore, felt in a very strong position in disregarding any order from the Darbar or the British Agent to deliver up the province to its new ruler.

On 30 August, he defeated the troops of Raja Gulab Singh in battle. The commander to the Dogra army, Wazir Lakhpat Rai was killed, and his colleague, Wazir Ratan Singh, forced to seek asylum in the fort of Hari Parbat.

Lord Hardinge took a grave view of the matter, particularly, as with the advent of winter, military operations in the valley would become difficult. Under orders from Calcutta, the Lahore Darbar was roused to action. The landed property of the

---

[1] *Calcutta Review*, July 1847. pp. 248-49; Edwardes & Merivale, p. 396.
[2] Gulab Singh's rise to power had excited the ambition of others; Tej Singh is reported to have offered twenty-five lakhs for a province of his own, Cunningham, p. 319.

## The Kingdom of Lahore becomes the State of Lahore

Shaikh in Jullundhur and Hoshiarpur, was confiscated and his tenants taken into custody. A large force from Lahore was ordered to move towards Kashmir. Sir John Littler also marched towards Jammu to hold the province against insurgents and to be in readiness to proceed to Kashmir if necessary. Sir Henry Lawrence supported by a British force from Jullundhur. under Brigadier Wheeler, arrived in Kashmir on 21 October. Thoroughly alarmed by these measures, Imam-ud-din tendered his submission to Captain Herbert Edwardes on 31 October, 1846.

Captain Edwardes was a young and energetic officer. When he learned that the Shaikh had been authorised in his action by Lal Singh, he despatched confidential agents to assure him safe conduct and the release of his people from confinement, provided he gave up his rebellious scheme and presented himself at the British camp within two days to provide evidence of Lal Singh's complicity. The Shaikh agreed to do this and joined Edwardes at Thana, He was introduced to Henry Lawrence to whom he gave the documents which exposed the minister's perfidy. A week later Gulab Singh was installed on the *masnad* and Henry Lawrence returned to Lahore (29 November).[1]

Arrangements were then begun for bringing Lal Singh to trial for his role in the Kashmir débâcle. Sir Frederick Currie was sent from Calcutta to hold an enquiry.[2] A ceremony for the giving and receiving of gifts between the two states was performed at a special meeting of the Darbar.[3] On 3 December, the court of enquiry commenced its sittings with Sir Frederick Currie as president, Lt.-Colonel Lawrence, Sir John Littler, Mr. John Lawrence, and Lt.-Colonel Goldie as members. Dignitaries of the Darbars, including Attar Singh Kalianwala, Sher Singh Attariwala, Tej Singh, Diwan Dina Nath and Khalifa Nur-ud-din were present. Lal Singh and Imam-ud-din were summoned before the court. Three letters which the former had signed, two to Imam-ud-din and one to the Darbar soldiers

---

1 Gulab Singh entered Srinagar on 9 November, having spent the previous night with Henry Lawrence at Rampur. Edwardes & Merivale, p. 400.

2 For a fuller account of the trial see *Trial of Lal Singh* by Sethi; S.L. d. V. pp. 8-18.

3 When Lal Singh offered Currie 1,100 gold *butkis* as *ziyafat*, the latter espostulated at its being more than the customary 700, and was told "the friendship has become twice as deep as before."

in Kashmir were produced. The evidence was found conclusive. Lal Singh was held to be unworthy of the wazirat both by the Darbar and the British government. He was therefore deprived of his office and ordered to leave the Punjab. After a week's detention in Lahore, he was conducted to Ferozepore, thence to Agra and Dehra Dun.[1]

After the sentence had been read to Lal Singh, Sir Henry Lawrence summoned Bakshi Mohar Singh, the minister's personal clerk and ordered him to surrender the seal of office. The failure of the Rani Jindan-Lal Singh government was a foregone conclusion : it never commanded respect in any quarter. As early as 30 March, Hardinge had written to Henry Lawrence, "when I consider the character of the Rani, her minister Lal Singh, and the absence of any man of master-mind among the Sikhs, I think the probability is adverse to the continuance of a Sikh Government."[2] "The history of Lal Singh," Sir Lepel Griffin was to write, "is the history of the Panjab, during three years. But there was no significant event in either which may be worth noting. There was perhaps no single honest and able man in the whole Court of Lahore, and just a few may be distinguished as men of integrity from the rest of the crowd, who left the country for the time being, in sheer disgust. Raja Lal Singh rose to power by the exercise of arts which in a civilised community would have sent him to the scaffold."

After Lal Singh's dismissal, the powers of government were invested in a council of four, Tej Singh, Sher Singh Attariwala, Diwan Dina Nath and Khalifa Nur-ud-din. A circular, was sent to all government officers in the muffasil, to this effect, and that no *parwana* was to be considered valid unless it bore the seal of all four councillors. This government, however was not intended to last long ; the Governor-General was at the time engaged in shaping an alternative form of administration and was consulting his home government on the subject. His

[1] Captain Hodson, one of his guards wrote "I was sent both days to bring him to the tents where the proceedings were being held, and when he was deposed, I was commissioned to accompany him to his honourable confinement. I and two other English officers were all sent to take him away, put him down at his sponging-house, and ride away without so much as a stone being thrown at us." In 1865, Lepel Griffin found Lal Singh still residing at Dehra Dun on a pension of Rs. 12,000. L.G., p. 597.

[2] Hardinge to Lawrence, quoted by Edwardes & Merivale, p. 385.

despatch dated 19 September runs as follows : "It is impossible to place any confidence in the professions of the Maharani or the Vizier that the advice of a British Agent would be followed if our garrison were to be permitted to remain ; the British government would in such a case, be a party to the oppression of all classes of the people. Again, if the troops are withdrawn we are warned that the country will be plunged into a state of anarchy, and the destruction of all government will ensue. Neither of these results would be consistent with the humanity or sincerity of our policy, and they will be opposed to our interests."[1]

"The other course, which may be open to the British Government to take, and which has constantly occupied my attention since September 3, would be to carry on the Government at Lahore in the name of the Maharaja, during his minority, or for a more limited time, placing a British Minister at the head of the government, assisted by a Native Council, composed of the ablest and most influential chiefs. This course, however, could not be adopted, even if the offer to surrender the Regency were made by the Maharani, unless her Highness's solicitations were cordially and publicly assented to by the great majority of the chiefs."

"If therefore, the chiefs should not join the Regent and the Darbar in calling upon the British government to act as the guardian of the young prince during his minority, and to conduct the administration, no attempt would be made to carry such a measure into execution. I should, in that case, scrupulously adhere to the terms of the agreement. Those terms could not be suspended, even temporarily, without some such public act as that of assembling all the chiefs who have an interest in the state through the lands they hold from the Maharaja ; and in any such

---

[1] John Lawrence to Sir Frederick Currie, 9 September: "... if the British forces are removed the country would become the focus of intrigues and sedition. Their presence has notoriously kept Multan loyal, and preserved Peshawar. The revenue is now daily embezzled and receipts are certainly unequal to expenditure. The army costs seventy lacs of rupees a year, while income is ninety lacs at the highest. Such a state of things cannot last. What will happen after the departure? It will not be politic and it will not be just, I think, to leave the country ... we should have a free hand in the government of the country, and should reserve the disbursement of revenues and the appointment of officers in our own hands."

proceeding the proposal must originate with the Lahore, and not the British authorities."[1]

"If therefore, the proposal of the Regent and the Darbar should lead to an offer to carry on the Lahore government by a British Minister, during the minority of the Maharaja, and the proposal should be confirmed by the influential chiefs publicly convoked for the deliberation of such a measure, I should be disposed to give the experiment a favourable consideration."[2]

Henry and John Lawrence were assiduous in implementing Hardinge's policy. On the one hand, they sought to exacerbate a feeling of helplessness that prevailed in the Lahore Darbar, and emphasised the fact that the time agreed upon for the withdrawal of British troops was at hand ; on the other, they set themselves to foster in the minds of the individual Sardars, hopes of obtaining favour with the British if they remained 'loyal'. They were given to understand that in their doing so, lay the only chance of retaining their estates and privileges. This would serve in the words of Lord Hardinge "as powerful stimulus to ensure their adhesion to the conditions imposed." As indeed it turned out to be.[3]

The Rani's good-will was not so easily to be gained. As soon as the Governor-General's proposals came up for consideration in the Darbar (9 December) she made a counter-proposal, that she be formally recognised as head of the government, and be lent by the British two regiments of infantry, one of cavalry and a battery of artillery. This was not acceptable to the British, nor did they encourage the Sardars to fall in with it. Irate debate in the council "was renewed morning and evening eliciting strange philipics and recriminations, and even abuse, within the palace, and usually ending in the Sardars rising and withdrawing in a body, saying that the Rani wished to bring ruin on her son and all the Khalsa; that she might act as she pleased, but for their

---

[1] Hardinge to Currie, 10 Dec,: "the coyness of the Darbar and the Sardars is very natural but it is very important that the proposal should originate with them, and . . . our reluctance to undertake a heavy responsibility must be set forth . . . " Currie's Correspondence.

[2] Quoted in Sir Henry Lawrence, by Innis, R.I.S. pp. 76-77.

[3] S.L. d. V, p. 14. In reply to a question from John Lawrence the Sardars said "*Ki padshahi Maharaja Bahadur qaim-o-mustaqil bashad; wa mayan rizaq ba khurem em muddaa mayan ast,*" (the rule of the Maharaja should continue, and so also our own estates and emoluments).

## The Kingdom of Lahore becomes the State of Lahore

part, the palace was no place for respectable men, and that they would cross the Sutlej with the British troops..."¹

Lord Hardinge was encamped at Bhyrowal, a few marches from Lahore, and there planned an elaborate charade to stimulate the Darbar into decision. He began to send instructions to Currie on 12 December, with a view to creating an impression of military arrangements afoot. He wrote ; "I send this by express to desire that the Regiment of Native infantry, the 2 guns and the Irregular Cavalry, escorting Lal Singh may not return to Lahore....these troops will cross the Sutlej and encamp at Ferozepore till further orders, and the troops ordered from Ferozepore to Kasoor will be countermanded....my object is to give the Lahore Darbar a hint that the garrison is on the move.. it also authorises you to send another regiment of native infantry from Lahore to Ferozepore, there to encamp till further orders and not to be relieved by any other regiment from Ferozepore.. H.M. 80th regiment will receive orders to march to Meerut at any moment. H.M. 10th at Ferozepore are ready to relieve them but will not move till ordered, nor will it transpire that they are intended to relieve the 80th. These announcements will be made to accelerate the Darbar's decision."²..

Two days later he wrote "..this day (14 December) and tomorrow will enable you to form a pretty accurate judgement of the progress you are likely to make. I authorise you to desire Sir John Littler (in command of the British garrison at Lahore) to move all the troops out of Lahore by the end of a week, on the day you may judge to be the most expedient, encamping them as near as may be convenient, to the citadel. If this hint should be unnecessary by the temper of the chiefs to assent to our views, it will not be made...."³

Lord Hardinge's stratagem was effective. The Sardars sent messages to Lawrence pledging their support to the Governor-General's scheme. Henry Lawrence, keeping in view the Rani's counter-proposal, wished matters to be arranged in a constitutional manner. An assembly of people with more than fifty Sardars among them was to decide the future administrative

1 Edwardes & Merivale pp. 406-409.
2 Hardinge to Currie, 12 December 1846, 11 a.m., Camp Bhyrowal. Currie's Correspondence, pp. 14-16.
3 Ibid. 14 December, p. 16.

## Sunset of the Sikh Empire

set-up of the state during the minority of the ruler. This meeting was held in Henry Lawrence's tent on 15 December, and "was more fully attended than any state meeting I have yet seen at Lahore ; the momentous importance of the occasion to the Khalsa having, in addition to the Ministers and principal Sardars drawn many petty chiefs, officers, and yeomen to the spot. An Akali, in the full costume of his order, with high blue turban, wreathed with steel quites and crescents, was quite a new figure in this deliberative assembly, and showed that all ranks took an interest in the business of the day."[1] Sir Frederick Currie then explained to the members of the impromptu constituent assembly, clause by clause, the terms on which the Governor-General would consent to keep the British troops in the Punjab; and at the same time, place at their service, a senior British officer to advise in matters of administration. They were then left to discuss the matter among themselves,[2] while Currie and Lawrence went to another tent. After a while a deputation of six Sardars arrived, asking by way of change in the Governor-General's proposal, only that the amount required in return for the loan of British troops, Rs. 2,600,000, be reduced. After an amicable talk this was done and the sum fixed at Rs. 2,200,000. Currie then sent an express letter to the Governor-General at Bhyrowal, informing him that agreement had been reached, to which the reply was immediate and most gracious : "the result deserves my most unqualified approbation, and I shall be happy to record another instance of the approved ability, zeal, temper and judgement you have shown, aided by the local experience, reputation and well-established influence of Lt.-Colonel Lawrence. It is quite impossible to have brought this affair to a more satisfactory conclusion."

"Your intimate knowledge of my sentiments and the concurrence of our views in Panjab politics, have enabled you most successfully, to realise all the objects I had in view, not only in the substance of the arrangements made, but in the form of the

---

1 Edwardes and Merivale, p. 407.
2 Diwan Dina Nath expressed a wish that they might adjourn in order to ask the opinion of the Rani but was silenced by Sir Frederick Currie who said: "the Governor-General is not asking the opinion of the Queen-mother, but of the Sardars, who are the pillars of the state." Edwardes & Merivale, p. 408.

PLATE 7

JAWAHAR SINGH
*Maternal Uncle of*
MAHARAJA DALIP SINGH

proceedings, for you have conducted this matter so judiciously that the truth and sincerity of our policy cannot be brought into doubt, or the honour of the British government suffer any impeachment. This Hindoo state has another opportunity afforded to it of re-establishing its government and at the same time, of securing the tranquillity of this frontier, and, I hope of all India."

"The moral effect of the Sikh chiefs entreating the British government to become the guardian of the prince, by the continuance of a British garrison at Lahore, and our consent to undertake the responsible charge, must be felt throughout Asia in raising the reputation and extending the influence of the British character."

"Personally I may regret that it has not been my fate to plant a British standard on the banks of the Indus. I have taken the less ambitious course, and I am consoled by the reflexion that I have acted right for the interests of England and India."

"I have seen John Lawrence. He seems to be of the opinion that the new arrangement might be signed by the Maharaja coming to this camp and seeking me, followed by my paying him a friendly visit at Amritsar or Lahore. I would prefer this course because I should like, with Sir John Littler and Lawrence to visit the works at Lahore, and make an arrangement better calculated to keep the sepoys and town's people separated... In the long run depend upon it, the town people will like us the better, the more we are kept separate and distinct from them."[1]

The agreement, consisting of eleven articles was finally ratified by Sir Henry Hardinge and Maharaja Dalip Singh when the latter was induced to visit the Governor-General at Bhyrowal on 24 December, 1846. By it the Regency Council was doubled in size by the addition of Sardar Attar Singh Kalianwala, Shamsher Singh Sindhanwalia, Ranjodh Singh Majithia and Bhai Nidhan Singh. The eight councillors were mentioned by name and it was stipulated that no change be made without the consent of the British Resident acting under the orders of the Governor-General. Article 6 stated that the British Resident assisted by an efficient staff "shall have the full authority to direct and control the duties of every department ; the allowance of the Maharani was fixed at one lakh and fifty thousand, and the arrangement was to continue till 4 September 1854, when Maharaja Dalip Singh should attain the age of sixteen.

The preamble of the treaty as the Governor-General had so ardently desired, emphasised the point that the British government had taken over the administration, and agreed to keep their troops in the country at the request of the chiefs of the state made of their own free will (*baraza-o-raghbat-i-khudd*). The British resident backed by an army then, 'virtually became the successor of Ranjit Singh on the throne of Lahore.' Writing about the salute of guns which greeted the Maharaja on his arrival at Bhyrowal, Captain Trotter remarked : "..to any listener gifted with statesmanlike forecast, the salute must have sounded like the boom of minute guns over the grave of a once powerful nation. With the best of intentions India's most peaceful viceroy had now gone more than half-way, to annexing one more independent kingdom to an empire already over-grown."

The Maharani, having been outwitted by British statesmanship, remained an embarrassment. Sir Frederick Currie in his personal correspondence with the Governor-General recommended that she be removed from Lahore; but the latter replied ; "there is an objection to separate her from her son on the grounds of her political intrigues counteracting the measures of the new government, as it may be said that she is punished in anticipation of any political offence she has committed."[1]

A couple of months later Sir Henry Lawrence found, in what came to be known as the Prema Plot, an excuse to request his government for the removal of the Maharani from the capital. Prema, an old military retainer of Raja Gulab Singh, had been a recipient of a charitable allowance from the Darbar. The allowance ceased when Gulab Singh became independent ruler of Jammu and Kashmir. With several other discontented men and officers of the army, Prema secretly plotted to murder the British Resident and Tej Singh when they attended a fête at the Shalimar gardens. This was discovered, a number of persons were arrested and brought to trial before a court consisting of senior members of the council of regency and three British officers.

---

1 Hardinge to Currie, 16 December 1846. Currie's Correspondence, p. 19.

## The Kingdom of Lahore becomes the State of Lahore

The evidence was largely hearsay; no incriminating documents of any significance were produced by the prosecutors, and the Maharani only appeared in the picture because her *munshi*, Buta Singh, was alleged to have met Prema once or twice. The Governor-General was not satisfied that evidence had been provided to justify the expulsion of the Queen-Mother.[1]

Six months later, Rani Jindan did manage to give offence. The Resident, desiring to confer titles of honour on certain Sardars who had rendered services to the British during the war, arranged that the ceremonial awards should be made by the Maharaja on the morning of 7 August, at the exact moment fixed by the court astrologer, and the *takhtgah* (stand of the throne) beautifully decorated for the occasion. When the time came the Maharaja refused to apply the *qashqa* (saffron mark) on the forehead of Tej Singh. In Hardinge's words: "the Rani, indignant that her enemies should be honoured, tutored the boy that he should affront the Chiefs in the public Darbar when he had to dip his finger in the saffron paste and anoint their foreheads. He resolutely played his part, put his little hands behind him, sat back in his chair, and one of the priests performed the ceremony. In the evening she would not allow the prince to be dressed up to see the display of fireworks."[2] When the matter came up before the Council the day after the incident, the Resident and the Regency agreed that the Maharaja had acted under the influence of his mother; the Council recommended that Amir Baksh, Har Dayal, Jiwan Singh, Hira Singh and a maid-servant named Mangala, who were considered to constitute 'a mischievous little group', be removed from her service and sent away from Lahore;[3] that the Rani's personal movements be restricted within the four walls of the palace (*Rani dar hijab buda bashad*): and she be stopped from giving audience so freely and frequently to people of her choice.

The Resident considered that this would be construed more as a warning than a punishment. He told the Council that it would be in the interests of the tranquillity of the State, the

---
1 For a fuller account of the Prema Plot see Sir Henry Lawrence to Eliot, September 1847. P.G.R.
2 Hardinge to Currie, Simla, 10 August. Currie's Correspondence, p. 141.
3 The destination suggested for Amir Baksh and the others, were frontier towns like Dehra Ismail Khan, Peshawar, Hazara and Dalipgarh.

smooth running of administration, and the satisfactory upbringing of the Maharajah, if the Rani were to leave Lahore. He over-ruled the Council and obtained the sanction of his government to send Rani Jind Kaur to live in the fort of Sheikhupura, and reduce her allowance from 150,000 to 48,000 rupees per annum. Sir Henry Lawrence treated the matter as 'top-secret', not sharing his confidence even with the Regency Council till arrangements regarding escort and conveyance were complete, and the hour fixed for the departure. He made sure also, that the boy-Maharaja, should be out on an excursion at that time and so obviate any possibility of an embarrassing scene.[1]

Thereafter Rani Jindan had no part whatever in the administration of the country, nor was she allowed much opportunity of seeing her son. But the Resident was not at ease as long as she was in the Punjab. In March 1848, Sir Frederick Currie, who was then Resident, received a report from Major Wheeler that certain persons were attempting to corrupt the soldiers under his command. Precautions were taken and secret agents set to work. But nothing much transpired. With the insurrection in Multan in April, however, the Resident's suspicions were quickened and he appointed Major Lumsden of the Guides Corps to investigate the matter. On the receipt of certain new information, Lumsden, Hodson and Cocks, made a surprise raid on the residence of Commandant Kahan Singh in the city and seized his person. Certain of his associates were rounded up the next day and tried for attempting to subvert the loyalty of the troops. Kahan Singh and Ganga Ram were hanged (*bar dar kashidand*) ; a third, Tulsi Ram was sentenced to life imprisonment (*daim-ul-habas*) ; in the case of another, Gulaba, the sentence was suspended (*multavi*), when he turned approver.[2] Ganga Ram had been in the service of the Rani, and it was alleged that the tempting bribes he offered the sepoys were of her providing. The Rani's private papers were subsequently searched,

---

[1] S.L. d. V. p. 78-9; Hardinge to Currie, Simla, 23 August 1847: "I received a letter from L (Lawrence) last night in reply to a memo of mine, 16 August, authorising the removal of the Rani from Lahore, which was agreed upon by the Darbar and H.H. was removed with her female attendants at 9 O'clock at night on the 19th, the Prince having ridden to Shalimar Gardens at 6 o'clock, there to remain, which is occasionally the custom. She submitted fairly well . . ."

[2] S.L. d. V. pp. 99-102.

but neither there, nor from any other source was any proof of her guilt, to be found. The Rani challenged her would-be accusers and demanded a regular trial. But the Resident preferred to drop the matter on the grounds that 'a formal trial of Maharaja Ranjit Singh's widow would be most unpopular and hurtful to the people.' And yet he wished to give a semblance of constitutional proceeding to his decision to be rid of her. He summoned the members of the Regency Council to his residence-cum-office in the Anarkali building and obtained their approval of the Rani's banishment from the Punjab and a further reduction in her allowance from forty-eight lakhs to twelve. The Councillors, according to the court chronicler, "gave their approval and each one individually signed and sealed, without demur the order of banishment drawn up by the Resident (*mavahir khud ha babat muqadama baza bar kagaz navishta sahiban sabat kardand*). A party of four senior officials of the court, led by Khalifa Nur-ud-din with one regiment of cavalry was despatched to Sheikhupura to escort the Maharani. She was led into the belief that she was being taken back to Lahore, and gladly accompanied them. When the party reached the suburbs of Lahore, instead of entering the city, it took the road to Ferozepore. Near Kahna Kacha, Nur-ud-din made over charge of the person of the Rani to a mounted escort of Major Wheeler's irregulars who had been sent to receive her.[1]

The Resident, meanwhile, had not been inactive in the matter of reorganising the administration. The Lahore treasury was almost empty; it had to meet the British demand for twenty two lakhs per annum for the maintenance of the thousand-armed men in the capital. The new government had to devise economy in expenditure and tap fresh sources of income. The standing army of the State, which was a heavy charge on revenue was, by the treaty of March 1846, to be reduced so as not to exceed 25 battalions of infantry and 12,000 cavalry. It was arranged, therefore, that every day a number of soldiers should be paid arrears in salary and discharged.[2] At the same time the

---

1 Ibid. Dalhousie to Currie, 28 May, 1848; Trotter, *Hodson of Hodson's Horse*, p. 52.
2 Henry Lawrence to the Foreign Secretary 3 July, 1847, reported a saving of Rs. 30,00,000, during the preceding six months, from retrenchment in the army and other institutions. P.G.R. book 175.

scale of pay for those who were to be retained in service, was cut down to the level that prevailed in Ranjit Singh's time. Sir Henry Lawrence hoped to reconcile the soldiers to this by granting certain compensatory benefits. The practice of levying *kasrat*, a cut of six or eight per cent, which belonged more to the system of the Mughals than the Sikhs, was abolished. Leave rules, *ain-i-rukhsat-o-raza*, were made more lenient; regular monthly payment, which had not been customary with the Darbar was to become the rule, and extra allowance known as *bhatta*, one rupee for each soldier per month, when on the move or in camp.[1]

The Darbar had no organised judiciary nor a codified system of law. The *Kardar* (collector) of each district had been wont to administer justice in so far as this was beyond the capacity of local *panchayats*. The *panchayats* of the early nineteenth-century Punjab were noted for their effectiveness and integrity, but with the instability of the central government after Ranjit Singh's death, there was a diminution of their authority, and too often, disputes in the villages came to be resolved with the aid of sabres or cudgels. Henry Lawrence established appellate courts in each of the four areas to deal with cases the Kardar or panchayat had not been able to settle. This was an innovation as previously there had been no intermediate authority between the District Collector and the Maharaja. For the guidance of the judges a manual embodying unwritten laws and customs was prepared by a conclave of fifty headmen especially invited from villages scattered about the country. Revenue suits, however, were not within the jurisdiction of the new courts. In regard to revenue matters, Henry Lawrence was anxious to render the Collector, 'as innocuous as possible.'[2] He appointed a number of British officers 'to help and advise' Indian governors and collectors, electing men for this purpose, whose loyalty and devotion he was sure of. "Never was a man more willingly, more ably and more heartily served," wrote Mrs. Edwardes, the wife of one of the assistants.[3] To the outlying districts

---

[1] For a fuller account see an article by the present author in the *Journal of Indian History*, V. XIV, part 3.

[2] John Lawrence described the Kardars as 'the official locusts of the land' because they so often withheld dues from the state, while they continued to despoil the peasantry.

[3] *Life and Letters of Edwardes*, by Mrs. Edwardes, pp. 57-58.

were appointed, Herbert Edwardes to Bannu, James Abbot, Hazara, Herbert, Attock and George Lawrence, Peshawar. Others of these selected young men were John Nicholson, Lt. Hodson, Lt. Lake, Harry Lumsden, Reynall Taylor, Lewin Bowring and Henry Cocks. They were instructed to "re-settle the country, assess lightly, make the people happy and instill confidence into them as to the good intentions of the British." They were also to collect information regarding the resources of the district under their charge, and report freely to the Resident. Besides this privilege of direct access over the head of the native governor, or the Council of Regency, they were vested with wide discretionary powers. Every one of them in time came to exercise his authority in a manner which took for granted that the Punjab had passed into the hands of the British, and that he at his headquarters was the representative of his government. An inveterate 'superiority complex' characterises the weekly reports submitted to the Resident.[1] Herbert Edwardes, addressing the people of Bannu on one occasion said, "I offer you liberty, and not only offer it, but guarantee it so long as the Sikh treaty with the British lasts. Only pay of your own free-will into any treasury you like, an annual tribute of Rs. 40,000, and no army shall again enter your valley, no Sikh show his face within your boundaries, you shall be left with the undisputed enjoyment of your own country and your own laws." Towards Diwan Daulat Rai, the governor of the province, Edwardes' behaviour was arrogant and rude, and it was on his recommendation that the Diwan was removed from his post and Commandant Cortland installed in his place; in like manner George Lawrence brought it about that Autar Singh, governor of Peshawar, should be dismissed and replaced by Gulab Singh Povindia, who he found more amiable. It was occurrences of this nature that sowed the seeds of dissension.

The banishment of Jind Kaur was one of the last acts of public importance of Henry Lawrence in his capacity of Resident. He went to Simla in August being in a poor state of health, to return in November on a brief visit before sailing for England

---

[1] These 'political diaries' were preserved in the Record Office of the undivided Punjab till 1947. Extracts from them were published under the title, Punjab Government Records, vols. III-VI.

on furlough, on the same boat as the Governor-General. He had got on well with the Sikh nobility and the peasants; he had the kind of imagination which might have served to avert trouble. Realising fully the wounded pride of the Khalsa, "like a prudent physician" his biographer averred, "he endeavoured to apply balm."

Sir Henry's brother, John, became acting Resident until such time as Sir Frederick Currie should be available to take up the post. Like his brother, John Lawrence was devoted to duty and had sympathy for the common man. Prosperous peasantry, he believed, would be 'the bulwark of the country, rather than the Sardars, so many parasites let loose upon the poor tillers of the soil.' Land and customs reform were the first subjects to engage his attention. He had already achieved a summary settlement of the land in Kangra, Hoshiarpur and Jullundhur, and hoped to employ the same principles in his new position.

His view was that the fifty per cent of gross produce, which the state exacted as its share, was exorbitant and the further unauthorised taxes, which collectors were wont to levy, made the burden insufferable; that these evils could only be abolished if regular records were available. He ordered a summary settlement to be made, as had been done in the Jullundhur division, under British officers, who had been appointed assistants to Henry Lawrence. These men had no previous experience in revenue matters, nor was any reliable data of land measurement available to them, so they took as guide the collection figures of the past few years in the Darbar account books, and all owing abatements on various counts fixed a sum, *juma*, for each village. An old practice of dividing the produce by *batai* or *kankut*, which had afforded scope for the collector or revenue farmer, to defraud the ryot, was abolished, and the Kardars were henceforth required to give receipts for the amounts obtained from zamindars and enter this in a register which was maintained in the village as a permanent record of all such transactions. These changes had beneficial effect on the lot of the peasants. Nevertheless, many of them found the rigid enforcement of the rule that all payments be made in cash difficult to fulfil and were often induced to leave some their land uncultivated. At the same

## The Kingdom of Lahore becomes the State of Lahore

time, landlords almost every one of whom had encroached on land beyond the area strictly given by *jagir* deed, were resentful of the record of rights, and of Lawrence's unceremonious ways in regard to them.[1]

Under the prevailing system, almost every article of trade was subject to state duty. John Lawrence summarily exempted daily necessities such as corn, ghee and fuel. He gave to the Department of Customs *Chaukiyat*, an entirely new shape. Transit and town duties were abolished so that tradesmen should be freed of the 'extortion and insolence of the petty officers of the Customs Department.' Only import and export duties were to be retained ; for this purpose three customs frontiers were established, the eastern one to be marked by the courses of the Sutlej and the Beas ; one along the Indus for trade with the north and one along the north-west frontier. The newly constituted department was placed in the charge of Misr Ralia Ram, who chose his son, Sahib Dayal, to work with him. John Lawrence, in his report to government on this matter said that the loss to the treasury would amount to Rs. 223,000 per annum, but this was more than compensated by the relief it brought to the poor.

His reforming hand touched upon many subjects. Working hours in public offices came to be fixed and officials required to observe them. For the guidance of law courts, rules and procedure were formulated which developed into Civil and Criminal Procedure Codes ; a beginning was made towards the establishment of a public postal system. John Lawrence concerned himself also with the eradication of social practices which he held to be evil. Under his instruction the Resident's assistants as they moved from place to place would assemble people of the locality, and invite them to take a pledge, to educate the masses. They were often asked to report by way of slogan, "thou shall not kill thy daughters ; thou shalt not burn thy widows; thou shalt not bury thy lepers."

All such activities, social, administrative and economic : British officers busily going to and fro with parties of land

---

[1] When Rai Bhaj Singh, the Darbar vakil, came to him in the morning with papers for signature he was wont to say "*aj kya naya daga hai*"(what new villainy today?) Bosworth Smith, *Life of Lawrence* Vol. I, p. 242.

surveyors, carrying measuring chains, telescopes and other paraphernalia, changed the complexion of things and there must have been many who regretted what appeared like the passing of the familiar Sikh Raj. Sir Frederick Currie, in a letter addressed to his government on 6 April, after he became Resident wrote about the changes he found; "all these measures taken to improve the system of administration by John Lawrence have a result of transferring administration of the country from the hands of the Darbar to our own to a much greater extent than was contemplated when the introduction of the new arrangement was determined ; and conduct of all details, even the most minute in every department, except that of accounts, devolves on the Resident. I could wish that our interference with these details had been less, but it is impossible to recede...."[1] With reference to the same matter, John Trevaskis wrote ; "Having thus sown the wind, John Lawrence proceeded on furlough leaving his successor, Currie to reap the whirlwind."[2]

1 Weekly Proceedings, no. 32, P.G.R.
2 Trevaskis, *The Land of the Five Rivers*, pp. 210-11.

## Chapter 9
### RISING AT MULTAN AND THE FIRST SIEGE

The province of Multan was one of the largest administrative units of Ranjit Singh's empire : its governor was required to pay a sum of Rs. 2,700,000 per annum to the state; a balance of 1,200,00 was expected to cover the costs of management and the governor's personal emoluments. It was made up of three distinct territories, the trans-Indus which included Dera Ismail Khan, Sanghar and Dera Ghazi Khan ; Sindh Sagar Doab, between the Indus and Chenab, Kalabagh and Mankera ; and the territory which lay between the rivers Chenab, Ravi and Sutlej. Diwan Sawan Mal held charge of this province for twenty-four years (1821-44) during which it flourished and its people were content. On his death in September 1844, his son Mul Raj succeeded him, having himself served as collector in two important districts, Shujabad and Jhang ; in both places he had won the unqualified approval of his exacting father. Unfortunately for him, he succeeded at the time when the central government was in the hands of Hira Singh, who bore in regard to him, a long-standing enmity. Hira Singh demanded of a heavy *nazrana* (offering on succession) amounting to thirty lakhs. Mul Raj lodged a protest and bided his time without making payment. After Hira Singh's fall, the matter of the succession fee was taken up by Lal Singh, who, without waiting for a reply from Mul Raj, despatched a powerful force from Lahore to collect arrears of payment and the succession fee. Lal Singh's troops were repulsed near Jhang. Henry Lawrence decided to intervene and summoned Mul Raj to Lahore to discuss the matter (October 1846). Mul Raj agreed to pay twenty lakhs for arrears and succession fee, to pay a higher revenue, and to allow one-third of his territory to be formed into a separate sub-division, Jhang. It was a hard bargain, but Mul Raj was grateful to be able to continue in office in spite of Lal Singh's designs.

Soon after he met with other difficulties. John Lawrence, as acting Resident exempted certain articles of common use from duty ; merchants of Multan insisted that the new system should apply to them. This was unacceptable to Mul Raj, as it meant a large loss of revenue. He was further embarrassed by Lawrence's innovation whereby appeals against decisions of provincial courts could be made to the Darbar; he did not expect his own judgements to be fairly dealt with while Lal Singh was Chief Minister; in fact, in a number of cases his judgements had been set aside and as a result his prestige suffered. In negotiating with the Darbar, he contended with reason, that the agreement he had entered into did not bind him to accept the new octroi rules, nor to send up cases to Lahore. When he discovered that the Resident was adamant on the subject of a uniform administrative system throughout the Sikh kingdom, he decided to resign. He wrote to Henry Lawrence about this on 21 November, 1847, and a week later presented himself at Lahore. Henry Lawrence had left on furlough ; he was interviewed therefore, by John Lawrence, who agreed to relieve him of his duties in March 1848. At his request, he was assured that his resignation would be kept secret even from members of the Council. He returned to Multan in the last week of December.[1]

The new Resident, Sir Frederick Currie, arrived in Lahore on 6 March and John Lawrence left for Jullundhur on 3 April.[2] Currie did not feel he was under any obligation to treat Mul Raj's resignation as secret, nor to honour him with a *jagir* on his retirement. This being agreed upon by the Council, they suggested as candidates for the governorship, a choice of Shamsher Singh Sindhanwalia and Kahan Singh Man ; the latter, being considered by the Resident more amenable to advice and guidance was selected and given the promise of an annual salary of Rs. 30,000 ; Mr. Vans Agnew was appointed political adviser with Lt. Anderson as assistant. These three with their retinue set out by river on 5 April, while their main escort of 1500 men and six guns went by land. The party reached Multan on the 18th

---

1 Currie to Elliot, makes reference to a memorandum of Lawrence's dated 6 April, explaining his reasons for this arrangement; that the Resident had so much to do, it would be better if Mul Raj continued in office for a time. After that the government would be able to select an able British Executive Officer. Of course, he should be accompanied by a Sikh Chief in command of the Darbar troops. Parliamentary Papers, 1847-48.

2 Lawrence was detained in Lahore because of the birth of a son on 17 March.

and took up residence in the Idgah, a spacious, well-fortified building outside the city walls. Next day Mul Raj showed them over the fort and handed over the keys to Kahan Singh. They arranged to leave in charge one company of soldiers from their escort. After explaining the situation to the old garrison, the British officers accompanied by Mul Raj and Kahan Singh set out to return to their camp. The four officers were riding abreast. As the small cavalcade emerged out of the Sikki Gate of the fort to cross the narrow drawbridge, a certain Amir Chand attacked Mr. Agnew with his spear. Agnew fell off his horse.[1] Mul Raj, fearing for his own life galloped off to his residence, leaving word with his chief, Bhagwan Das, to seize Amir Chand and bring him to his garden-house. News of the incident spread to the fort. Men of the old garrison came pouring out and set upon Anderson who had also ridden off, leaving Agnew for dead. Meanwhile Kahan Singh and Mul Raj's brother-in-law, Ram Rang, extricated Mr. Agnew from the crowd, put him on an elephant and took him to his own camp at the Idgah. They picked up Anderson on the way. Agnew, who was not severely wounded, sent a note to Mul Raj asking him to come to the Idgah at 11 a.m. Soon after, the two companies of soldiers, who had been left in the fort, were turned out and came to the Idgah. Agnew sensed danger and sent express letters to Major Herbert Edwardes and General Cortlandt at Bannu and a report to the Resident at Lahore.

On receiving Agnew's note, Mul Raj and Ram Rang started out for the Idgah. They had only gone a few paces when they were assaulted by the mutinous troops; Mul Raj was pulled off from the saddle and taken back to be confined in his house. He managed to send a confidential agent, Tulsi Ram, to the Idgah and acquaint the British officers of the helplessness of his position. He informed them that the entire garrison, Hindu and Mohammedan, was in rebellion, and advised them look to their own safety. Thereupon, Agnew placed his six guns in position. Nothing of importance occurred at the Idgah during the night of the 19th.

---

1 It was stated in evidence later, that Amir Chand was provoked by Kesho Ram, a peon of Lt. Anderson's, who, as Agnew passed, gave him a push and said "why do you not salute when a Sardar is passing?"

At Aam Khas, Mul Raj's residence, soldiers continued to pour in. Towards the evening of the 19th they succeeded, in persuading Mul Raj to lead their revolt.[1] Mul Raj's family and their valuable possessions were removed to the fort and the next morning manifestos were issued in his name exhorting the people to strike for freedom. Guns from the fort and the Aam Khas opened fire upon the Idgah. The fire was returned. Soon after troops in the Idgah escorting the British officers from Lahore, began to show symptoms of disaffection. In the evening they went over to Mul Raj's side almost in a body. As the news of this desertion spread, the rabble of the city headed by 'a misshapen monster, Godar Singh Mazhabi, forced their way into the Idgah and brutally murdered Agnew and Anderson.[2] On receiving the first report from Agnew on 21 April, Sir Frederick Currie made arrangements for the despatch of troops from Lahore. Sardar Shamsher Singh Sindhanwalia, Raja Sher Singh Attariwala and Diwan Dina Nath left on the 24th with the troops made available. A small British movable column was to follow a little later. Before it could leave, news about the murder and the desertion of the escorting troops were received. Currie had reason to doubt the integrity of the Darbar troops and the wisdom of despatching them to Multan. Moreover, he did not want to engage the British soldiers on a campaign in the desert in the heat of summer. An express message was sent to recall the three members of the Council and they were told that the Darbar must put down the rebellion with its own resources. The Darbar chronicler avers further that the Resident conveyed to them that if they failed to do so, the British government would send its own troops to take possession of Multan. The Sardars were nonplussed by this attitude. Since the Darbar was paying twenty-two lakhs per annum to maintain a strong British force in the country, they could not understand why it was not being sent to Multan. But he was adamant ; his argu-

---

[1] A contemporary ballad in Punjabi by Hakim Chand relates that when he was vacillating, Mul Raj's mother dubbed him a coward; she castigated him bitterly for having given up the government of a province, which his father had held for a quarter of a century; it may have been this that moved him to join the revolt

[2] Godar Singh's fingers were crippled and crooked. Trial of Mul Raj, Appendix IV.

ment was that of the strong against the weak. He also suspected the Sardars of treachery.[1]

What Henry Lawrence would have done in such circumstances may be judged by the action he took in Kangra and Kashmir. "If Henry Lawrence's health had not forced him to leave for England, the same quick perception of what was necessary, the same inimitable faculty for dealing with individuals and his love of precipitate and bold action, might well have kept peace in 1848 not only at Multan but throughout the Punjab."[2] John Lawrence had no doubts about the action required. In letters to Currie, Millot and Brigadier Wheeler, he wrote, "I very much fear now that any troops of the Darbar marching on Multan will do as Kahan Singh's escort have done. Despite the heat and advanced season of the year, I would counsel action. Otherwise you will have emeutes as you fear, in Bannu, Hazara and Peshawar. The officers, willing or not must go with the soldiers to give their lives.... I see great objection to this course, but I see a greater one in delay. The Darbar neither can do, nor will do anything. I never saw them do anything. The initiative must in all cases come from us." To Sir Henry Elliot he wrote, "Currie seems inclined to leave it to the Durbar and not to march troops on Multan....the season, no doubt is terribly bad for moving troops, but the alternative seems worse. The lives of none of our officers in Bannu, Peshawar and Hazara will be safe if speedy retribution does not fall on these scoundrels. It was touch and go in the Kashmir affairs two years ago. It was then a question whether the Shaikh surrendered if the troops of the Lahore Durbar went over to him. If we do nothing the whole of the disbanded

---

[1] S.L. d. V. pp. 95-97; he states that when the news-sheet from Multan was read out in the Darbar, Currie's immediate question was in regard to Kahan Singh's having escaped unhurt while the British officers were injured; Currie's letter to Dalhousie, 25 April 1848 P.G.R. p. 178; Currie's letter to Dalhousie, May 17, "I can't quite make out what Kahan Singh's conduct has been." Currie's Cor. p. 58...

[2] Morrison, *Lawrence of Lucknow*, p. 166; When he heard the news from Lucknow Lawrence got the rest of his leave cancelled and landed at Bombay in December 1848. He went to Lahore, via Multan, where he halted for two days in the first week of January, hoping to conciliate Mul Raj, but there he received a letter from Currie, "There are strong rumours current that if you should arrive anywhere near Multan .. Diwan Mul Raj means to surrender to you. I have no doubt whatever that you would not receive him".

soldiery of the Maharaja will flock down and make common cause with the mutineers."[1]

But Currie and Dalhousie, who assumed that the outbreak at Multan was a premeditated movement of the Khalsa, wished to watch developments, to see the flame of rebellion spread, so as to warrant the dispatch of a full-fledged British invading army for its conquest. As early as January 1845, Currie wrote to Major Broadfoot, "....we must not have a Muhammedan power on this side of Attock. The Rajputs of the hills could not hold the Punjab, and if it cannot be Sikh, it must, I suppose, be British."

The Commander-in-Chief and his senior staff recessing in Simla, endorsed the view of the Resident that the summer season was unsuitable for campaigning by British soldiers near Multan. The Governor-General wrote to Currie on 15 May, "you have acted with prudence and discretion in pausing before you engaged, and in now finally determining not to engage the British troops in such a district as Multan, and at such a season in the year, in operations on such an extensive scale on which they must have been conducted....when the period shall have passed during which military operations are impracticable, I shall consider it my duty to put forth if necessary, the whole power that the government of India can command for the purpose of inflicting signal and severe punishment on those guilty of this outrage and of exacting from the state of Lahore that national reparation which it is my firm determination to obtain. This is not merely a question between the Government of India and Diwan Mul Raj of Multan. The servants of the Company have been murdered while employed in the interest of the state of Lahore, by one of its chief servants, have been treacherously betrayed to their death by the desertion of the troops of Lahore. The Government of Lahore has failed and still fails, and I fear, aways will fail, to punish the murderers and suppress the treason. We must do this for ourselves. In due time we will do so, but I will hold the state of Lahore answerable for such reparation for

---

[1] Lord Dalhousie tried to make sure of this, "it would be valuable to all of us," he wrote, "to have the means of proving as you reported, and have since repeated, that an outbreak was contemplated before, and that Mul Raj and Multan were merely the opportunity for the outbreak, and not the causes of the general insurrection in the Punjab." Currie's Correspondence, pp. 78-80 & 122 & 135.

all this hereafter, as the Government of the Honourable Company may think it fitting or right to command." In fact, that Governor-General had set for his guidance the principle, "in the exercise of a wise and sound policy the British Government is bound not to put aside or neglect such rightful opportunities of acquiring territories or revenues as may, from time to time, present themselves."

These long-term designs, fully accepted also by the Commander-in-Chief and the Resident, were not a secret. The consequent delaying tactics, evoked bitter criticism from some of the more outspoken British officers : "....we are not to do anything against Multan till after the rains, which I consider is a great mistake....should the people once take it into their heads that we cannot act in the hot weather, we shall have lots of summer campaigns."

Lt. Herbert Edwardes, to his colleague, Major Hodson, wrote on 24 May, "you express a hope in your letter that the British Government will act for itself and not prop a fallen dynasty. In other words, you hope we shall seize the opportunity to annex the Punjab. For this I cannot agree with you, for I think, for all that has yet happened, it would be both unjust and inexpedient. The treaty we have made with the Sikh government and people, cannot be forfeited by the treachery of a Gurkha regiment in Multan, the rebellion of a discharged *Kardar*, or the treasonable intrigues of the Queen-mother, who has no connection with the Sikh government of her son."[1] On 9 June, he wrote to Currie "....you are certainly running a great and unnecessary risk in waiting for the cold weather, and giving the Sikhs the temptation to rise, when by a mere march the rebellion would now be settled....I am afraid considerable mischief has been done by the idea of annexation getting abroad."[2] Lumsden, another young officer, writing to a senior, characterised the decision for

---

1 *Hodson of Hodson's Horse*, p. 55.
2 Edwardes was reprimanded for this. Dalhousie to Currie, Currie's correspondence: "It would be a friendly act," wrote the Governor-General, "if you, or some of his well wishers would point out to him that for an assistant to the Resident to transmit to his government a volunteer opinion that they would be guilty of a breach of faith of they adopt a particular policy which the Govt. of India, Her Majesty's ministers and the Secret Committee all contemplate as probable, is hardly discreet, quite unbecoming and altogether unnecessary."

delay as : "a resolution to have a grand *shikar* in the cold weather headed by himself" (the Governor-General). Henry Lawrence said in one of his letters, "as sweeping war in the following winter, and the conquest of the Punjab, formed the real aim of the new government."[1]

The conduct of events, as it turned out, serves to reveal very clearly the deviousness of the policy at work. After Edwardes and Cortlandt had scored a victory over Mul Raj's troops at Sudasam on 1 July and the fall of Multan seemed within sight, Dalhousie fearing to be baulked of a plausible excuse for setting aside the treaty with the Sikhs, sent a letter (14 July) marked private to Currie : "Suppose that either through fear of Lt. Edwardes' army or from internal dissensions, the fort of Multan should fall and the insurgent force should disperse, our policy would be greatly more doubtful and more perplexing. The punishment of the criminal will be secured either way, not so the reparation we have declared our intention of exacting. At present the state of Lahore is a flagrant offender against the British Government ; crime has been committed against us, and the Darbar has declared they cannot give us justice on the criminal because its troops will not obey its orders. But if the Diwan's force shall now surrender or fly, they surrender or fly before General Cortlandt and Lt. Edwardes commanding the troops of the Darbar, in which case, the Darbar will have obeyed our call and will have acted against the rebel, to his end."

"I am aware in your letters you have regarded all that have been done by the force I have named as done by *you* and not by the Darbar, most justly, so far as the *reality* of the thing is concerned. But the Darbar will contend that General Cortlandt's are their troops, the new Pathan levies (under Edwardes) are made in their name, enlisted under their colours, and paid with their money. And if there were any ambiguity about it, Lt. Edwardes in his letter of the 21st has effectively removed it, for he has there, officially informed the Bahawalpur General that the two corps are fighting for the Maharaja, for the restoration of the Maharaja's rights and that the guns captured from the rebels, belong neither to him, nor to the British, but to the Maharaja."

1 Marshman, Part II, p. 658; *Sir Henry Lawrence* by Innes, p. 93.

"If then, Lt. Edwardes' troops, although in company with the troops of Bahawalpur, shall take Multan and Mul Raj, in that case our demand for reparation will be open to argument, and as it seems to me, we shall have to confine ourselves to the request of payment of our little bill, on behalf of the Nawab and ourselves."

Having decided to postpone major operations till the cold weather, Currie had to decide on a strategy for the intervening time. He arranged with the Darbar early in May to despatch four armies to Multan by different routes. One under the command of Sher Singh Attariwala, Shamsher Singh Sindhanwalia and Attar Singh Kalianwala, had orders to move along the river Ravi and occupy Mul Raj's territory between Lahore and Tulamba; they were not to proceed, however, beyond Tulamba till further instructions. This division was about 5000 strong with 10 horse artillery guns and 20 mortars and composed principally of the *ghorcharas* and one battalion of trained infantry. The second division under Shaikh Imam-ud-din, was to march along the Sutlej and occupy Multan territory up to the district of Mailse, and to advance no further than Ludden. Imam-ud-din's force was composed of 2000 newly recruited Muslim soldiers and two guns. Jawahar Mal Dutt of the artillery was instructed to take command of a third army and move it from its headquarters at Mankera; it comprised one infantry battalion, one regiment of cavalry and a troop of horse artillery. He was to recruit on the way to Multan another 2000 men, largely Muslim, from the Sindh Sagar Doab; he was to occupy the parts of Multan lying in the upper Doab. The fourth army, which was to converge upon Multan, was to be supplied by the Nawab of Bahawalpur, a devoted ally of the British. He was requested to provide as large a force as he could spare and to occupy Mul Raj's territory between the rivers, Chenab, Indus and Sutlej, as far as he was able keeping in touch with Lt. Herbert Edwardes. Edwardes and Cortlandt were to try to occupy the whole of the trans-Indus territory under Mul Raj. Edwardes had permission to cross the Indus if and when it was expedient to do so in order to co-operate with the Bahawalpur troops, but not to cross the Chenab and proceed to Multan. Currie's immediate objective was to quell the rebellion in the province of Multan but to leave the credit of occupying the citadel for British troops in the winter. "the great object", he wrote to Lt. Edwardes on 10 June, "is to confine the Multan rebellion within the smallest compass, till we can put the final extinguisher on it, by capturing the fort. To do this, the best plan undoubtedly, is to shut Mul Raj up in his fort till the British force arrives there...." He also added "yours and Bahawalpur's are the only forces that can be relied upon in the offensive operations."

The Resident's orders to occupy the trans-Indus territory did not reach Edwardes till 19 May. But he had already started preparations on receipt of Mr. Agnew's letter on 22 April. After a day's march from his camp at Dera Fateh Khan, he crossed the Indus on the night of the 24th, and encamped at Leiah, a district where a number of powerful Pathan families lived. Edwardes' force consisted of one Sikh infantry battalion (*Fateh Paltan*) and Pathan levies with a few guns, the total not more than 1500 men; he hoped to rouse the local Pathans in joining him, in the hope of throwing off the yoke of the 'infidel Sikhs.' On 26 April, he wrote to the Resident from Leiah : "the Pathan gentry of the Doab are beginning to come in, among others, Nassar Khan Badozye, who fighting on behalf of Mul Raj, gave Lal Singh's detachment such a thrashing two years ago." After a week's halt, Edwardes re-crossed the Indus to await the arrival of General Cortlandt—who joined him on May 4.[1] Reports reached him that Mul Raj was advancing from Multan, and there was the danger of the *Fateh Paltan* going over to his side. Moreover orders from the Resident, not to cross the Indus till further instructions were received on 19 May. But Edwardes and Cortlandt took advantage of the enforced delay to seize the districts of Sanghar, Dera Ghazi Khan and Hurrand from the officers of Mul Raj.

In these district, there were three strong fortresses, Mangrota, Ghazi Khan and Hurrand. The sentiments of the Pathans and Bilochis who predominated were entirely inimical to the Sikh Raj. Edwardes exploited these sentiments to his advantage. Having tried and failed in an attempt to subdue Chetan Mal

---

[1] Cortlandt joined the infantry of the Lahore Darbar in 1832, on a salary of Rs. 500/- per month; his wife being provided with a small stipend. In 1842, an allowance was sanctioned for their child. *Maharaja Ranjit Singh*, by the present author, p. 102.

the governor of Mangrota, he enlisted the aid of the Muslim Bilochi chief, Mitha Khan, pointing out to him the wisdom of gaining favour with the British, the future rulers of the Punjab. Mitha Khan was not entirely persuaded, and while he called out his tribesmen to make a display of friendship with the British, he was not anxious to commit himself in open conflict. Instead, he sent a confidential agent to Chetan Mal advising him to retire from his weakly garrisoned position at Mangrota. Chetan Mal saw wisdom in this and in joining his nephew Longa Mal, governor of Dera Ghazi Khan, so that with their combined forces they might make a stand against the enemy. In the early hours of the morning of 11 May, Mitha Khan was able to hand over the keys of the fort, his messenger shouting as he came, "the Hindu has run away."[1]

Ten days later, another Bilochi Chief offered his services to Edwardes for the purpose of seizing the fort of Dera Ghazi Khan, where Chetan Mal and Longa Mal were entrenched. Kaura Khan's first attempt failed. He withdrew after losing fifty men, his own nephew being among the slain. Next day (21 May) the whole of Kaura Khan's tribe, the Khosas, were on the move, and their attack proved irresistible. Chetan Mal was killed and Longa Mal made captive. Kaura Khan was honoured and rewarded; the loyalty of the Khosas was thus secured for the future. "They followed me afterwards," Edwardes wrote, "to the war with four hundred Biloch horsemen of their own tribe, and shared with me many months of hard fighting, without any other recompense than their food."[2]

Against Hurrand, Edwardes tried a similar technique. He reported to the Resident on 27 May, "the brother of one of the officers in the fort is in my service, and I have this day, sent him with an open *parwana* to the *Kardar*, Mohkam Chand, to come in with all his officers; and a secret *parwana* to his Pathan officers to overcome him, and the Sikhs if they refuse to come in and consider themselves my servants for the future. As the fort is strong and has two heavy guns in it, I am rather anxious about

---

[1] Edwardes, V. II, pp. 210-12.
[2] Kaura Khan was awarded the title 'Ali Jah' and a rich *Khilaat*. Besides the jagir he held from the Lahore Darbar, with an income of Rs. 1,000, he was allotted a pension of Rs. 1200 by the Govt. of India. Edwardes, V. II, pp. 248-51.

the success of this manoeuvre ; but Kaura Khan has gained such honour in these parts by his victory over Longa Mal, I am tolerably confident that the Pathans will be glad of the opportunity of similarly distinguishing themselves against the Hindu rebels." On 6 June, he informed the Resident that "one hundred Pathan sowars of the garrsion have engaged to come over, but are unwilling to turn upon the rest of the garrison." Edwardes' hopes were not fulfilled in this case. Mohkam Chand remained steadfast in his loyalty to Mul Raj. The siege dragged on. In the middle of August, command of the besieging force was handed over to Sardar Nassar Khan Popalzai, in whose fidelity Edwardes had faith, and Edwardes and Cortlandt moved to the bank of the Indus in order to join the Bahawalpur force which was on its way. The *Fateh Paltan* which was suspected of having sympathy with Mul Raj, was left behind with Nassar Khan.

Edwardes continued in his endeavours to win over the Pathan chiefs, whom he described as "free from the infection of treachery, and bold villains, ready to risk their own throats and cut those of any one else." Whereas about Mohkam Chand he opined : "this morning (2 June) the *Kardar* sent in his answer which stated that Diwan Mul Raj made him *Kardar*, and either Diwan Mul Raj or Maharaja Dalip Singh must order him to give up the fort. If Mohkam Chand was taken alive I would hang him." No doubt, affected by Edwardes' communication, the Resident on 9 June, conveying to Lt. Lake, his appointment as Political Agent to Bahawalpur stated : "....your duty will be to join the headquarters of the Bahawalpur troops and to give advice, which will be implicitly followed in directing the movements of the troops, and the operations which are to be undertaken for carrying out the objects of the government....it is not 'probable' that any opportunity will be given you of getting possession of the fort of Multan, but such a circumstance is not impossible. Bahawal Khan has great influence with the Pathans in the service of Dewan Mul Raj ; there is believed to be a strong feeling of jealousy and dislike between the Pathan and Sikh portions of his army, and the former may rise on the latter at any moment, in which case the city would most likely be plundered, the force break up, and the occupation of the fort by the nearest force might then be accomplished...."

## Rising at Multan and First Siege

Mul Raj, having failed to give any help to his officers in the trans-Indus area, determined to make a stand in the territory between the Indus and Chenab which was now threatened by Edwardes. The latter established an advance camp on the Indus and moved as far as Khangarh on the right bank of the Chenab. Here he halted awaiting support from Nawab Bahawal Khan. The Nawab's force, 8,500 horse and foot, with 30 camel swivels and 11 guns, commanded by Fateh Khan Ghori,[1] crossed the Sutlej on 31 May. After a fortnight of leisurely marching, they encamped fifteen miles south of Shujabad, a substantially fortified town within Mul Raj's domain. The Diwan had despatched a force of 8,000 with ten pieces of cannon under Ram Rang to attack the Bahawalpuris before they were reinforced by Edwardes' and Cortlandt's armies. Ram Rang arrived at Shujahabad on 16 June, and took up a position three miles south of the town. Edwardes received intelligence of Ram Rang's intentions on the 15th and with characteristic vigour set about requisitioning all available boats at the Khangarh ferry to transport his troops across the Chenab. In a letter dated 15 June, he wrote to Currie : "I have written to Mustapha Khan in Multan that now is the time for him and his friends to desert Mul Raj and to go over to Peer Ibrahim Khan (of Bahawalpur) or to the *kumarkote* previous to the fight. Also, to Ram Rang, the commander of the rebel force, I have written to say that I presume he accepted the command, in order to give himself an opportunity of coming over to us with his nephew Har Bhagwan Dass, as it is no secret that his loyalty got him the wounds from which he is still suffering. Should he come over, I have assured him of every kindness. Either one of the other or these desertions would dampen the ardour of the rebels considerably."[2]

Edwardes and Cortlandt between them had a force of 6,500 horse and foot, 30 camel swivels and 10 guns ; a large proportion of the men were Bilochis and Pathans, recently recruited by

[1] Edwardes described Fateh Khan Ghori as "a little old man, in dirty clothes and with nothing but a skull-cap on his head sitting under a tree, with a rosary in his hand, the beads of which he was rapidly telling and muttering in a peevish helpless manner 'ul humdooliallah' while his army was engaged in action." Edwardes V. II, p. 385.

[2] It was conveyed to Ram Rang that the help he had rendered to Mr. Agnew, in his dire emergency, proved him to be a friend of the British, and would be rewarded if he now complied.

Edwardes. To get this force with all its paraphernalia of horses, draught cattle, guns, ammunition boxes across the river with the 47 boats, that had been commandeered, was no easy task. On the morning of 17 June, Edwardes' army was closer to the Bahawalpur force than Ram Rang's in terms of distance, but with the three-mile wide Chenab intervening. Edwardes stated later that Ram Rang was in a position to crush the Bahawalpur troops, mostly irregulars, who had never seen a round of shot fired and were led by a senile octogenarian. During the early stages of the fighting the Bahawalpur force was almost beaten. But it rallied with the arrival of Edwardes and his 3,000 Pathans who had been able to cross the river. He was unable to do more than stave off the attackers until Cortlandt joined him in the afternoon. "Those seven hours," he wrote "I shall never forget if I live seven centuries." When Cortlandt's guns arrived, ninety minutes of non-stop artillery fire and a dashing charge of two Pathan levies turned the scales against Ram Rang. The Multanis were driven from the field leaving behind eight guns and a considerable amount of camp equipment. Much as he wished to do so, Edwardes was unable to pursue the fleeing Ram Rang for want of cavalry.

Mul Raj attributed the failure of his army to the treachery of his Pathan soldiers. Edwardes corroborates this; "they (the Pathans) showed none of that hot-headed gallantry for which their race is distinguished; and having no heart in the cause, left the brunt of the fighting to the Sikhs, who suffered in consequence out of all proportion." Whether Ram Rang's failure to follow up his initial advantage had anything to do with Edwardes' subversive offer is not stated.

Edwardes and Cortlandt, with their Bahawalpur allies then moved in the direction of Multan. On 28 June they reached Surajkund, six miles away from the walled city, where they were joined by Lt. Lake, an engineer who was commanding Bahawalpuri troops in place of Fateh Khan Ghori. Shaikh Imam-ud-din 'the pardoned leader of the Kashmir rebellion' also arrived with his contingent of 4,000 Muslim soldiers to assist his friend and benefactor, Major Edwardes. The total strength of the army facing Mul Raj, was 19,000 horse and foot with 22 guns and 30 *zamburas*.

## Rising at Multan and First Siege

Mul Raj was determined to lead his troops in person. On the morning of 1 July, he took up position on the plains of Sudosam with 1,100 men and a park of ten guns about two miles away from the enemy. It was mid-day on 1 July, a very trying time of the year, when he chose to go into action.[1]

The Multani army showed tremendous courage and resolution; though heavily outnumbered, its gunners engaged in an artillery duel with those of Lt. Lake. Edwardes recorded: "it was impossible for them long to sustain the superior fire of twenty two, which were brought into action on our side, though justice requires me to pay the tribute of admiration to the obstinacy with which Mul Raj's artillerymen stood their ground."[2]

A chance cannon shot from one of the British batteries hit the howdah of Mul Raj's elephant. Mul Raj fell; but rose immediately to continue the battle. His momentary absence from view caused some panic, which Lt. Quin, a daring young man on the personal staff of General Cortlandt, took swift advantage of making a charge with two infantry battalions. The assailants continued the pursuit for some distance. "Almost under the walls of Multan," Edwardes wrote to his government, "I halted our fatigued troops and the failing daylight not permitting us to ascertain whether we were under the fire of the fort, I thought it best to return to our camp."[3]

Mul Raj lost an opportunity in allowing his enemy to approach so close to Multan. The terrain along the main road to Shujahabad was intersected by broad deep ravines only to be crossed by improvised bridges made up of unhewn logs, straw and mud. Again, between Surajkund and the city of Multan lay an immense canal, *Wali Muhammad kā nālā*, 30 feet wide and twenty deep, the only pucca bridge being under the control of the Diwan. "The most highly disciplined army," Edwardes observed "could hardly fail to be thrown by these deep and irregular *nullahs* into confusion. One only marvels why Mul Raj did not turn his local knowledge of the terrain to account and attack the approaching army among these dykes."

---

1 Mul Raj, it was rumoured, was insistent on engaging in battle at this particular time as Bhai Maharaj Singh, after consulting the stars, had said it was auspicious for him.
2 Edwardes, V. II, p. 446.
3 Ibid. p. 448.

Edwardes was unable to push his advantage further; the town and citadel of Multan were strongly fortified and he had no siege guns with him. He urged upon the Resident that "the supreme need of the hour was for the British to take the field with an adequate number of guns and other siege material," and that the period of three months which was yet to elapse before the British army took the field according to the official programme, was too long a time to keep his forces so near to those of Mul Raj.

His repeated requests seem to have carried conviction with the Resident. Currie directed General Whish to collect his troops from Lahore and Ferozepore and advance upon Multan. Whish's force set out in two columns, one leaving Lahore along the Sutlej river route two days later. About 8,000 men, including 2,000 British soldiers, and 45 guns arrived at Multan on 19 August, the siege train taking another two weeks in transit. Raja Sher Singh, Sardar Shamsher Singh and Attar Singh Kalianwala with 5,000 men, 12 guns and 115 swivels had meanwhile joined Edwardes.

General Whish's march was slow; he took 39 days to cover a distance of 220 miles between Ferozepore and Multan. Mul Raj had time to improve the defences of the town and the citadel. Outside the twenty-foot ditch that surrounded the city he raised an enormous rampart of mud. Two to three thousand of the Diwan's selected soldiers were posted in the fort, while ten thousand were posted in entrenched positions to defend the town.

General Whish directed his first efforts in the field of psychological warfare. On 4 September, he issued a proclamation as follows:

"I invite both (town-people and garrison) to an unconditional surrender within twenty-four hours after the firing of a royal salute, at sunrise tomorrow, in honour of her Most Gracious Majesty, the Queen of Great Britain, and her ally, the Maharaja Dalip Singh.

I shall, otherwise, in obedience to the orders of the supreme Government of India, commence hostilities on a scale that must ensure early destruction to the rebel traitor and his adherents, who having begun their resistance to lawful authority with a most cowardly act of treachery and murder, seek to uphold their unrighteous cause, by an appeal to religion, which everyone must know to be sheer hypocrisy.

If the town be surrendered to me, as above suggested, private property will be respected; and the garrison of the fort will be permitted to withdraw unmolested, on giving up Diwan Mul Raj and his immediate associates, and laying down their arms at one of the eastern gates of the town and fort, respectively."

"Given under my hand and seal this 4th day of September, 1848." Signed, Major-General W.S. Whish, C.B., commanding the army before Multan.

On the 7th the attack was opened and continued for two days. Mul Raj's men fought back. A night attack failed badly and having suffered considerable losses, General Whish withdrew his forces for a time. Fighting was resumed on the 12th with greater intensity. Two days of hard knocks, given and received, enabled the British to gain some ground and bring their heavy batteries to within 1,200 to 600 yards of the town. At this critical juncture Raja Sher Singh, in response to the wishes of his father, and the importunities of his troops, decided to withdraw his support from the British. Early on 14 September, he gave orders to break up the camp of five thousand veteran Sikhs and move *en masse* to join Mul Raj. This sudden defection made it imprudent to continue with the siege. Troops and a considerable quantity of ammunition and camp equipment had to be left behind.

General Whish retired to Surajkund to await reinforcements. Meanwhile Sher Singh left Multan on 9 October and marched unmolested northwards, inciting the Punjab chiefs and disbanded soldiers of the Khalsa army to insurrection, They began to muster under the banner of Attari. Mul Raj was given time to recover strength and to rebuild his defences.

## Chapter 10
THE HAZARA EPISODE AND THE DEFECTION OF SHER SINGH

HAVING followed the course of events in Multan from the day of the occurrence at the drawbridge over the ditch (19 April) to the day of the 'defection' of Raja Sher Singh (14 September) and the subsequent suspending of hostilities on that front, we now take up the story of the trouble which, in the meanwhile, was brewing at Hazara and in other frontier districts of Bannu and Peshawar and eventually led to the Second Anglo-Sikh War.

Sardar Chattar Singh, Governor of Hazara, came from the well-known family of the Sikh chiefs of Attari. His daughter, Tej Kaur, was betrothed to the boy Maharaja Dalip Singh in August 1843. His eldest son, Sher Singh, was created 'Raja' and was nominated by the Resident to serve on the Council of Regency of the State early in 1847.

The Political Adviser at Hazara was Major James Abbott, a man of truculent nature, and utterly unsuited for the delicate duty assigned to him. From the day he took charge, Abbott's endeavour was to reduce the authority of the Sikh Governor, and to bring himself into prominence. He made use of the opportunity which the outbreak at Multan afforded him. He began to treat with suspicion every action of Sardar Chattar Singh. In his weekly reports to the Resident, he presented Chattar Singh as a sympathiser of the rebels. He shifted his own residence to Sherwan in the midst of the Pathan population at a distance of some 30 miles from Haripur, the headquarters of Sardar Chattar Singh. Like Herbert Edwardes in Bannu, Abbott had built up his influence with the Pathan chiefs of the highlands and turned to account their hostile sentiments towards their Sikh masters.

Abbott's attitude towards Chattar Singh was the major factor in the crisis that followed. On receiving reports from his spies that the Darbar forces stationed in Pakhli were in a state of excite-

## The Hazara Episode and the Defection of Sher Singh

ment and might some day leave Hazara to join the insurgents at Multan and that Chattar Singh might also accompany them. Abbott proceeded to raise Pathan levies as a counterpoise to the troops of the Lahore state and incited them. "I assembled the chiefs of Hazara", he writes," and explained what had happened, called upon them, by the memory of their murdered parents, friends and relatives to rise and aid me in destroying the Sikh forces in detail."[1] The Pathans readily responded to his call, assembled in great numbers, and moved towards the town of Haripur. It was later discovered that Abbott had received vastly exaggerated reports from his agents.

The governor, Chattar Singh, as a measure of precaution directed detachments of Darbar troops stationed in and about the town to encamp near the walls of the fort so that they would be protected by the mounted ramparts. Everyone complied with the orders of the governor except the artillery commandant Col. Canora, an American in Sikh service.[2] He would, he said, take his orders from Major Abbott. He was told that the Major was residing at Sherwan and was not aware of the peril, and by the time message was sent to him and the answer received, the insurgents might seize the battery. On finding him obdurate, Chattar Singh ordered an infantry company to take Canora's gun by force. Whereupon the American commandant stood between the gun with a lighted portfire in his hand and said that he would fire upon the first man who came near. When the infantry company advanced, Canora ordered his Havildar to fire. On his refusal to do so, Canora cut him down and himself applied the match to one of the loaded guns. Luckily, the gun misfired. He was overpowered and slain (10 August).[3] The matter was reported to the Resident by Abbott. Sardar Chattar Singh was removed from his office and his jagir was confiscated.

In view of the facts and the Resident's conviction that it was not Chattar Singh but Abbott who was at fault, it is difficult to understand the orders to which the Resident put his signature. In his letter to Abbott dated 19 August, he (Currie) observes,

---

1 Abbott's letter to Currie, 17 August, 1847, P.G.R.
2 The pay rolls of the Khalsa army show that Col. Canora joined service some time in 1840, on a salary of Rs. 4/- per diem. Vol. I. p. 65.
3 Abbott to Currie 13 August, 1848 and also Currie to Gough 15 August, P.G.R. ; also Lahore Political Diaries Vol. IV. pp. 222-25.

"It is clear that whatever may have been the intention of the Pakhli brigade, no overt act of rebellion was committed by them till the initiative was taken by you by calling out the armed peassantry and surrounding the brigade in its cantonment.... I have given you no authority to raise levies, and organise paid bands of soldiers to meet an emergency. It is much, I think, to be lamented that you have judged of the purposes and feelings and fidelity of the *Nazim* and the troops from the reports of spies and informers very probably interested in misrepresenting the real state of affair. None of the accounts that have yet been made available justifies you in calling the death of the Commandant Canora 'a murder', nor in asserting that it was premeditated by Sardar Chattar Singh."[1] Sir Frederick Currie while reporting the matter to the Foreign Department also expressed an opinion that Abbott's statements were not worthy of much credence. "Sardar Chattar Singh", he writes, "was an old and infirm man, the father-in-law of the Maharajah, with more at stake than almost any man in the Punjab, and that he should have taken the leading part in the affairs of the kind described by Captain Abbott, is altogether incredible."[2]

The report of Captain Nicholson whom the Resident had directed to proceed from Peshawar for investigation of the matter shows also that the initial fault did not lie with Chattar Singh. Though Nicholson, too, while proposing, a penalty for the 'misconduct of Chattar Singh' upheld the view (of Abbott) that the Sardar's office and estate should not to be restored to him. All that Nicholson could guarantee the Sardar, on behalf of the Resident, was his 'life and *izzat*', if he surrendered himself. But beyond this Nicholson was not prepared to give any assurance. Not even the assurance that if the Sardar succeeded in clearing himself, the penalties imposed upon him would be remitted.

---

1 Currie to Abbott dated 19 August 1848 ; also J.M.P. 108.
2 Currie to Sir Henry Elliot Foriegn Deptt., dated 19 August P.G.R. When examined in context of facts relating to the family of Sardar Chattar Singh, Sir Frederick Currie's view appeals to reason. Chattar Singh was descended from the junior branch of the House of the Chiefs of Attari. During the reign of Ranjit Singh, the Sardar and his sons took no prominent part in the politics of the Lahore Darbar. The present position of the family was due to the nearness of their relation with Maharaja Dalip Singh and the good-will of Sir Henry Lawrence. If anything, good relations with the British.

## The Hazara Episode and the Defection of Sher Singh

When we examine Sir Frederick Currie's views regarding the conduct of Sardar Chattar Singh as stated in some of his communications addressed to his Government and to Major Abbott, and the orders which he eventually passed in this case, it appeared as if he had abandoned all considerations of justice and equity. The only plausible explanation is that under the stern rule of Lord Dalhousie, no officer dare do things his own way. Regarding the troubles in the Punjab, Dalhousie believed that the rising in Multan and the trouble in Hazara had proceeded from a common source viz. an organised conspiracy of the Khalsa against the British. He had resolved, therefore, to adopt extreme measures to put down this rising, finish with the kingdom of the Sikhs and punish both Mul Raj and Chattar Singh. In one of his letters to Currie dated 16 September, he gave a clear inkling of his intention when he said, "Chattar Singh deserved to be smitten ; I can see no room for doubt."[1] Perhaps this explains why Currie's hands were tied in the Hazara case.

After what had happened, there were only two courses open to Chattar Singh, viz. either to make an abject submission to the British Resident or openly challenge his authority. The old feudal baron of Ranjit Singh chose the latter and more honourable course. On the morning of the 20th day of August, so goes the tradition in the family of the Chiefs of Attari, the aged warrior called for the Granth, offered his prayers, and on the conclusion of a brief ceremony took the vow that "from this moment, this head is devoted to God and these arms to the service of the Khalsa". The party then moved into the open ground of the Government House at Haripur where the saffron flag of the Panth was unfurled and preparations for war were taken in hand.

When Chattar Singh decided to go to war, did he calculate his chances of success or failure? What were the resources military, material and moral he was hoping to draw upon? His immediate surroundings were not favourable : quite the contrary. Hazara was far away from the home-districts of the Khalsa viz. Lahore and Amritsar. Its population as well as those of the adjoining districts of Peshawar, Bannu, and the Derajat was

---

1 Currie's, p. 97.

overwhelmingly Muhammadan. They were ready at the first opportunity to throw off the yoke of the 'infidel Sikhs'.

Of his family members, only his youngest son, Avtar Singh happened to be at Rawalpindi within easy reach. His eldest son, Raja Sher Singh, with a division of the Darbar troops was fighting for the British at Multan in co-operation with Edwardes and Cortlandt. His second son, Gulab Singh, was serving on the Council of Regency during the absence of his brother Sher Singh. Immediately on the receipt of the news of the Sardar's revolt, Gulab Singh was placed under arrest and detained in the Lahore fort under orders of the Resident.[1] Chattar Singh's sons were consequently not in a position to render him assistance. Nor did the Sardar expect any help or even sympathy from the members of the Regency Council as they were completely kept under the thumb of Sir Frederick Currie. It was with their active co-operation that Currie was able to establish a reign of terror in the Punjab.[2] The properties of Diwan Mul Raj and those who had joined him were confiscated and their families and relatives were harassed and placed under surveillance.[3] Under these circumstances, Chattar Singh did not expect open or active help from the Sikh nobility, except from those few who would be prepared to stake their all for the sake of their own and their country's freedom.

The Khalsa army was the one element to which the Chief of Attari could turn for support. The Khalsa were not happy with the Resident-ridden rule of their government; they resented reduction in their scale of pay and smarted under the overbearing attitude of the British officers. The disbanded soldiery were another source from which Chattar Singh could draw strength. They were trained in European methods of war by the late Maharaja Ranjit Singh. They had fought against the British in the last war and were well acquainted with their methods of fighting. They had been discharged from service only recently and under pressure from the British government. They needed little persuasion, therefore, to join in a crusade against the British. They

---

1 S.L.D. V. p. 127.
2 Dalhousie to Currie dated 28 November. "Whatever you do, pray you make sure of the persons of those chiefs you have. It will be well to hold them in terrorism". Currie's p. 124.
3 S.L.D. V. pp. 129-30.

## The Hazara Episode and the Defection of Sher Singh

were scattered all over in villages and small towns of the Punjab.

Nearer Hazara, the seat of trouble, Peshawar, Bannu and Tonk, ten regiments of infantry, three of cavalry and about 20 guns of the regular state artillery were stationed. Besides these there were smaller garrisons at Attock, Pakhli, Naushehra and Hassan Abdal which were included within the jurisdiction of Chattar Singh as Governor of Hazara. These accounted for another two to three thousand trained men of all arms. If he could bring all these troops over to his side Sardar Chattar Singh might have strength enough to cross swords with the British.

The immediate task before the 'rebel Sardar', therefore, was to secure the co-operation of the Darbar troops posted in the trans-Indus districts of the State. Anti-British propaganda among the disbanded Khalsa soldiers was already being done by Bhai Maharaja Singh and others since the beginning of the outbreak at Multan. Secret emissaries were accordingly despatched by Chattar Singh in all directions: Peshawar, Bannu, Derajat, Hassan Abdal and Rawalpindi. He also sent his confidential men to Raja Gulab Singh of Jammu, Amir Dost Muhammad of Kabul and his brother Sultan Muhammad who was residing in Peshawar, requesting help in liberating the Punjab from the 'oppression of the Farhangi'.

We now turn to the reasons for the defection of Sher Singh: he has been much maligned by English historians. It was after twenty-two days of the receipt of the first message from his father that Sher Singh left the British camp with five thousand men (14 September). We also know that during these three intervening weeks, his father had sent him repeated meassages to come to his aid; but he did not do so. Two points, therefore, must need be determined—firstly whether it was at the bidding of his father that Sher Singh deserted the British or were there other equally compelling reasons which precipitated this action? And secondly, when did he actually resolve to turn against the British? Although it is impossible to be positive about people's motives, in this particular case, Major Edwardes' communications render our task comparatively easier. They throw sufficient light on the subject and help us in resolving the issue.

*Sunset of the Sikh Empire*

Major Herbert Edwardes and Raja Sher Singh had come to know each other well. They used to meet and talk as friends very often during the ten weeks they were together in the field at Multan. "The Raja and myself", Edwardes tells us, "are on the best of terms ; we discuss Sardar Chattar Singh's conduct as if he was not his father and I never disguise any bad news I hear of him".[1] Edwardes was thus, in a position, to get the news at first hand. We can, therefore, depend upon his communications to Sir Frederick Currie. On examining the data available in these papers, we come to the same conclusion today, to which Major Edwards had arrived a hundred and twenty years ago viz. that Sher Singh decided to part company with the British at some time between the 12th and 13th September ; and that in spite of his father's repeated biddings to join him, he had never seriously entertained the idea before this. This view also finds support from Sher Singh's own letter which he wrote to his brother Gulab Singh (Lahore), on 13 September. An English translation of this letter, taken from Parliamentary papers, p. 359. is reproduced by Edwardes in his book, Vol. II, pp. 608-09. It reads :

"......You have frequently written to me to remain firm in my fidelity to Captain Edwardes and to act in all things according to his instructions. I have in no wise deviated from this counsel. The Singh Sahib (Sardar Chattar Singh) has several times written to me that he constantly obeyed Captain Abbott's directions, but that officer, acting according to the suggestions of the people of Hazarah, has treated him most unjustly, and caused him much grief and trouble ; and that he has also exerted himself to destroy and disperse the Khalsa troops. The Singh Sahib writes to me, that I had nothing to do with the treaty with the English ; and that, if I wish to preserve my existence, and the religion of our country, I must act accordingly, and join him.

"Hitherto, Captain Edwardes has treated me with great kindness but, within the last week, his feelings towards me have changed. I *resolved, therefore, yesterday* to join the Singh Sahib, and devote myself to the cause of our religion."

---

1 Edwardes to Resident dated 4 September 1848 noted on p. 591, Vol. II.

## The Hazara Episode and the Defection of Sher Singh

"If you have any regard to the directions of the Singh Sahib or my advice, prepare immediately on the receipt of this, to join the Singh Sahib or to go to Jammu, or any other place you may think fit. If you disregard my advice, act as you please ; but remember that it is incumbent upon sons to obey the instructions of their father for life is short. Do not wait for any other letter. God is between us. If we live we shall meet, if not, God wills it".

Enclosed in the above letter there was another note on a separate page which runs as under :

"The matter is this :—I shall enter the fort of Multan with my troops on the Ist Asuj (14 September), if you are with me and the Singh Sahib, make your escape as you best can ; if you are not with us, act as you think fit. It is useless to write more ; make arrangements regarding our family as the Singh Sahib has directed you. Delay not an instant".

On another page (Vol. II, p. 610-11), Edwardes refers to the conversation which he incidentally had had with the Sher Singh some fourteen months after this event (November 1849). This lends further support to the view expressed above. This conversation he had with his old friend in the presence of Mr. Henry Lawrence and Dr. Login, the Superintendent of the Palace. In reply to Edwardes' question as to the precise reasons for his going over to Mul Raj, Sher Singh is stated to have thown up his hands : "My evil destiny. It all took place in one night.[1] My mind was distressed by the Sikh force being ordered away from Multan. More pressing letters than ever came in the very next day from my father, imploring me to join the movement ; and I wrote off to Mul Raj for the first time, to say that I would march to him next day morning". This is also corroborated by the statement which Mul Raj's priest and private secretary, Misr Kuljas Rai, made before Herbert Edwardes when the latter was appointed to try the Misr as an accomplice with

---

[1] Much later after the war was over, Sher Singh was suspected though erroneously to have entered into conspiracy with some of the chiefs of the late Khalsa army who were still in hiding. He was brought from Attari and interned within the Lahore fort. For his pro-British leanings, Sher Singh was reviled in Mul Raj's camp as 'Sheikh Singh', and in his new camp he was nicknamed as Mussalman. Edwardes, Vol. II, p. 590.

the Diwan. "Amongst other questions", writes Edwardes, "I asked him (Kuljas Rai), how long Raja Sher Singh had been in correspondence with Mul Raj before going over ? He replied that the Raja never wrote but one letter to the Diwan all the time he was at Multan, and that was the night before he came over. We were astonished ; for though we knew, all the Raja's soldiers were our friends, we believed the Rajah himself was our enemy. What has been stated above leaves no room for doubt that Sher Singh's mind was made up suddenly sometime on the 12th or 13th September."

The obvious reason for this violent reversal of his feelings regarding the British was the order of the British General which was served on the Sikh troops on evening of the 11 September to quit Multan. What precisely had made him and his colleagues suspect the fidelity of these troops is not stated in clear terms. They had been in the field for ten weeks ; but nothing untoward happened during this time which should have conveyed doubts about the honesty of their intentions. At the same time we cannot say that the fears of General Whish were altogether unfounded or imaginary. When he started from Lahore, the Resident had given him to understand that the Chiefs (Sardars) were loyal but their troops were not. He even went to the extent of giving him authority to annihilate these troops in a couple of hours, if they committed themselves to any treacherous proceedings. Major Edwardes too had communicated to the General an adverse opinion regarding the loyalty of these troops.[1]

Now that General Whish with the British troops was expected to arrive in Multan on 18 August and that he wanted to encamp the at Seetal Ki Mari, it was considered highly imprudent, from military point of view to let the Sikh division stay in their present position at Suraj Kund. If the Sikh camp continued at Suraj Kund, the situation of the four military camps would be somewhat like this : Mulraj's troops encamping outside the walled city of Multan ; Lake and Edwardes with their troops encamping

[1] See Currie to Dalhousie dated October 1848. P.G.R. : also Parliamentary papers, 1848-49, p. 251. The Khalsa army as a whole (and not particularly this division at Multan) was not happy with the British controlled Darbar of Lahore. They would welcome any opportunity which was likely to restore the Khalsa Raj.

at the Tibbi mount in front of Mulraj's ; Sher Singh's Sikh troops in the rear of Edwardes at a distance of three miles ; and General Whish at Seetal Ki Mari in the rear of Sher Singh. In other words, Mul Raj, Lake and Edwardes, Sher Singh and Whish would be more in the alternating order in respect of their camps. This was considered to be fraught with danger. Sher Singh and his two colleagues were accordingly, persuaded though not without some argument, to agree to exchange positions with Edwardes' and Lake's troops. This was carried out on the 16th-17th August. But as the change was abrupt and in the event of the arrival of a strong British army it naturally gave rise to a feeling of distrust in the minds of the Khalsa soldiery ; and more especially for the reason that Lake and Edwarde's force was almost entirely made up of Mussalman soldiers whom the British General was now wanting to keep nearer his own troops (in preference to the Sikh troops). Their misgivings were deepened when the Sikh troops, while changing positions, noticed that Edwarde's troops were marching in regular battle order, though there was no occasion for such demonstration. Again, on 4 September, when General Whish sent warning to the garrison in Multan to surrender, he did so, not in the name of the Maharaja, the actual sovereign of the Punjab, but in that of Her Majesty, the 'Queen of England'. This shows how the minds of the responsible British officers were working. Three days later when the siege actually began[1], Sher Singh's men discovered that they were not given any share in the fighting. This further confirmed their belief that the British officers reposed no confidence in them and they (Sikhs) were not wanted there.

Then on the night of 11 September they were abruptly told to quit Multan. This news created a commotion in the Khalsa camp. Taken in the context of the treatment meted out to them during the last four weeks, Raja Sher Singh's fidelity also gave way. On the morning of the 14th, he broke camp and moved *en masse* to join Mul Raj.

---

[1] Referring to the incident, Edwardes states in his book "Our anxiety must have been great respecting the issue for, I remember that we marched to meet the Raja in order of battle *and halted in firm array* to let him and his troops go by".

## Sunset of the Sikh Empire

The reasons for the growing apprehension of the British were the news which their spies brought them, the frequent visits of Sardar Chattar Singh's messengers from Hazara to his son Raja Sher Singh, and the messages from Mul Raj conveyed to men and officers of this force through their local friends. The reports sent by the spies were not dependable. They picked up bazaar and camp gossip and passed it on as confidential, taking care, however, to get their report substantiated by the domestic servants of the European officers with whom they (the spies) used to mix freely. Mul Raj's message though plain was cunningly worded so as to seduce the simple-minded Sikh soldier stating that Multan was only a province of the Khalsa Kingdom and he (Mul Raj) was the servant of the *Sarkar Khalsa* and not a rebel against the authority of Maharaja Dalip Singh. It further assured Sikh soldiers that they could come to the town (Multan) and make purchases whenever they wanted without let or hindrance. But the Diwan's tactics could not succeed as Sher Singh and his colleagues were keeping a vigilant eye on their camp. Here and there a sepoy or two, slipped away from the camp and joined Mul Raj, but no desertions from the Khalsa army took place on a scale worthy of notice.[1] One solitary case where an attempt to do so was brought to light was that of Sardar Sujan Singh Ahluwalia and his two companions of the irregular cavalry. They were court-martialled and punished.[2]

Sher Singh replied to his father's communication by advising moderation. He requested Major Edwardes to exercise his personal influence with the Resident to relieve Chattar Singh of his duties at Hazara but with honour due to an old Sardar.

---

[1] A few of Diwan Mul Raj's secret emissaries who were caught or apprehended were openly disgraced and put on an ass with their faces blackened and sent back to the Diwan. 'Edwardes, Vol. II, p. 549.

[2] The case against Sujan Singh and his companions was that they helped in distributing copies of Mul Raj's manifesto. (Major Edwardes is inclined to believe that Sujan Singh was actuated in his conduct more by a feeling of wounded pride and personal revenge than any genuine sympathy with the cause of Mul Raj), In March 1847, Sardar Sujan Singh with his troops or irregular horse accompanied Major Edwardes to Bannu along with other troops, Sujan Singh's Mahaot, one day cut off green fodder for his chief's riding elephant. On receiving the complaint from the Pathan, owner of the field, Major Edwardes ordered the Mahaot to be tied up to the triangles and flogged in the presence of men and officers. The Sardar's pride was wounded. Edwardes, Vol. I, p. 20. Jhanda Singh was ordered 7 years imprisonment and Darbar Singh for life.

## The Hazara Episode and the Defection of Sher Singh

The question of disarming the Sikh troops was also considered but it was ruled out as unfeasible because of the position they then occupied. Nor was there any reason for taking that extreme measure. At the same time, it cannot be denied that the Khalsa army, had become so notoriously lacking in discipline that its own officers were never sure that their commands would be obeyed. Under the circumstances, the British could argue that to let this force of 5000 veteran soldiers stay in the camp during the siege was extremely risky.

The immediate circumstances which seem to have increased General Whish's apprehension was the repulse which his attacking parties had met during the night of 9 September. That night, Edwardes reported to the Resident, the attack was hastily planned and badly conducted. The attacking troops suffered considerable loss in killed and wounded before they could be withdrawn. The fighting had to be suspended for the two following days. This exposed the weakness of the besieging forces. The decision to remove the Sikhs from the field at the same time as the renewal of the siege operations on the 12th was not without significance. General Whish was unnerved; his fears of the Sikhs assumed magnified proportions.

Sher Singh's two senior colleagues, Sardar Shamsher Singh Sidhanwalia and Sardar Attar Singh Kalianwala, were not prepared to run the risk of losing their *jagirs* by deserting the British. As soon as Attar Singh noticed the general stir in the camp, he rode off to seek protection from Major Edwardes. His son, Lal Singh, joined him three weeks later. Kehar Singh Sindhanwalia following the example of Attar Singh also fled to Edwardes' camp on the 14th. But his uncle, Sardar Shamsher Singh, while getting ready to escape was surrounded by his men and prevented from doing so. He managed to steal away on the following night.[1] Among others of lesser note who deserted Raja Sher Singh may be mentioned the names of Nidhan Singh Sindhanwalia and Kirpal Singh Malvai. Those who remained with

[1] Edwardes writes, "Sardar Attar Singh fled at the very moment of defection and was the first man to bring me the news of the mutiny begging me to see that he had not betrayed me. Sardar Shamsher Singh was carried off by the soldiers and kept a prisoner in his own tent, but got out under the walls of the tent instead of the door, on the second night, and, in common clothes and barefooted made his way to my camp, a distance of several miles." Vol. II, p. 622, also L.G., p. 109.

the Raja took an oath of fidelity to the Khalsa and promised to stand by Sher Singh through good and evil. The camp then moved straight to the city of Multan but found that the city-gates were shut against them.

Although he was happy over the action of Sher Singh, Mul Raj was not prepared to admit the Raja and his 5000 men within the fortifications of the city till he was convinced of the honesty of their motives. He, therefore, asked the Raja to encamp for the time being, in the grounds of the Hazuri Bagh gardens. Negotiations then began ; one day Mul Raj and the Raja met in a temple where the latter declared by placing his hands on the scriptures that he and his men had come in good faith and that they would make a united effort to dislodge the "farhangis" from the position they have usurped in their state. To implement that decision two sets of proclamations—one signed by Raja Sher Singh and his associate chiefs, and the other a joint one by Mul Raj and Sher Singh were issued proclaiming a religious war against the British. It called upon all Hindus and Muhammadans who ate the salt of the Maharaja to join in the *DHARMA YUDDHA*. Joint invitations were extended to the Cis-Sutlej Chiefs to take part in the crusade against the British. Mul Raj's suspicions, it seems gradually wore off and the two leaders were planning to deliver a combined attack on the entrenched position taken up by the British army. The news of the intended attack made the British very nervous. But Major Edwardes' cunning and his capacity for intrigue saved the situation. He played a successful ruse at the right psychological moment which not only averted the attack, but also made Mul Raj and Sher Singh part company for ever. This was accomplished by means of a letter addressed to Sher Singh. It purported to have been written by Edwardes to his friend, Raja Sher Singh, in which he praised the Raja for his courage and cunning in so successfully laying the trap for the Diwan.[1] Edwardes had so contrived,

---

[1] My dear Rajah,
What you say about the prey falling into net has pleased me much. In fact, it is the best joke, I have met with for some time. I expected no less from your discretion and management. I must mention to you that I have been obliged, for the sake of appearance, to issue a proclamation calling you a *nimak hurram* (traitor) which among friends, I trust, will be excused. Let me know often how you get on ?

PLATE 8

DIWAN MUL RAJ

## The Hazara Episode and the Defection of Sher Singh

as he tells us himself, that the letter should fall into the hands of Mul Raj rather than Sher Singh.

The letter revived doubts in the mind of Mul Raj concerning Sher Singh's integrity and he resolved to see Sher Singh leave Multan at an early date. Under the circumstances, Sher Singh did not consider it wise to tarry long in Multan. He and his comrades came to realise that the real contest between the British and the Sikhs would have to take place not in Multan but somewhere in the Majha, the homeland of the Khalsa. After celebrating the festival of Dushera, Sher Singh left Multan on the 9 October.

## Chapter 11
### THE CURTAIN FALLS

SHER SINGH Attariwala intended marching back to Lahore and liberating the capital. He came within two miles of the city, but the rising of the citizens which he had expected did not take place. The Resident had imposed a curfew and the streets were patrolled at all hours. The leading Sardars had been arrested. Lehna Singh Majithia had thrown in his lot with the enemy and was using all his influence in Majha, the homeland of the toughest of the Sikh peasantry, in favour of the British. The only chief who had the temerity to defy the British was Ram Singh of Nurpur; but his declaring for freedom was more of symbolic than of material assistance to Sher Singh.

Sher Singh got information that Lord Gough was bringing a large army with heavy guns across the Sutlej. He withdrew from Lahore to join forces with his father. The Attariwalas decided to hold the British on the Chenab—'the dark river'.

The situation in the autumn of 1848 was somewhat as follows: The Chaj and the Sindh-Sagar Doabs had declared for freedom; the other Doabs were under the heel of British military power. In the north-west, people were flocking to the Punjab standard unfurled by Chattar Singh Attariwala; in the south, Mul Raj was fighting a lone battle against odds that kept mounting against him day by day.

Early in November 1848, Lord Gough crossed the Sutlej with an army composed of English and Hindustani mercenaries and marched on to Lahore. Young Dalip Singh, who had done everything he had been told to do by the Resident, waited on the British Commander to pay his respects. Gough refused to receive the Maharajah. On 16 November when the Resident himself took Dalip Singh to Mian Mir where the British force was encamped, Gough did not get off his elephant to return Dalip's greetings. It was a deliberate act of discourtesy to signify that the British now looked upon the Maharajah (who was still under their protection) as an enemy.

PLATE 9

**SHER SINGH ATTARIWALA**

MAHARAJA GULAB SINGH OF JAMMU & KASHMIR

## The Curtain Falls

Gough advanced northwards to the Chenab and came in sight of the Attariwala's forces on the other side of the river. Sher Singh, who had captured some forts on the eastern bank, sent detachments to harass the British. Minor skirmishes between the Punjabis and the British took place along the left bank of the Chenab. In the last week of November 1848, British forces under Brigadier-General Campbell marched towards the fort of Ram Nagar. The Punjabis forestalled the move to capture the fort. They crossed the Chenab on 22 November and placed themselves between the British and Ram Nagar.

General Campbell opened the attack and forced the Punjabis back to the river. Punjabi artillery posted on the opposite bank opened fire. With the support of the artillery, more Punjabi cavalry crossed the Chenab and in a determined counter-attack routed Campbell's force, captured one of his guns and the colours of a regiment.

Ram Nagar was not an engagement of any great consequence but it gave a much needed booster to Punjabi morale. *The British Subaltern* wrote: 'The enemy are in great feather, and ride along within half a mile of our camp and close to our pickets.' Three senior British officers: Lt.-Col. Havelock, Brig.-Gen. Cureton and Captain Fitzgerald were killed at Ram Nagar. Sher Singh Attariwala sent a note to the British offering to stop hostilities if they promised to get out of Lahore. No notice was taken of this offer.

A week after the Punjabi victory at Ram Nagar, General Gough arrived on the Chenab but instead of assaulting the fort as the Punjabis expected him to do, went further upstream to Wazirabad, bribed the local boatmen and crossed the river under cover of darkness. While Sher Singh Attariwala went up to hold Gough's advance down the western bank of the Chenab, the rest of the British force was able to cross the river over the fords which were left unguarded.

On the afternoon of 3 December an artillery duel was fought in the sugar-cane fields around the village of Sadullapur. The cannonade from either side was fierce. *The Subaltern* described the gunfire as: 'A roar that shook the very earth and shot ran through the air with a noise like a mighty winged spirit till the atmosphere was stunned.' British superiority in guns gave

## Sunset of the Sikh Empire

them the edge over the Punjabis. Sadullapur was also not an engagement of any military consequence but was exaggerated by the British Commander as a great victory to offset the reverse suffered at Ram Nagar. He even had it noised about that Sher Singh had been killed in the engagement. Attariwala was very much alive. He retreated from the Chenab to the Jhelum. The British pursued him across the Chaj Doab.

The Punjabis took up their position in the village, Rasul, which was surrounded by an expanse of thick brushwood intersected by deep ravines. The Jhelum was behind them. The enemy came up and took his position at the village of Dinghy about three miles south-east of the Punjabi entrenchments. For some time the two armies jockeyed for position. The Punjabis began to run short of provisions and tried to draw out the enemy from Dinghy. On 13 December, Sher Singh made a feint attack on the British positions but the British refused to budge. Next day came news of the liberation of Attock. Chattar Singh sent troops he could spare to his son and promised to join him with the rest of the army.

The British received an even greater fillip with the news of the fall of Multan. On 30 December, a British cannon-ball fell on the magazine in the fort blowing up 400,000 lbs of gunpowder and killing over five hundred of its defenders. The odds turned heavily against Mul Raj, particularly, as the British received more reinforcements and siege-guns from Bombay. On 22 January, Mul Raj was compelled to lay down arms.

### Victory at Chillianwala 13 January 1840

Lord Gough decided to attack at once. His forces had been augmented by detachments of Dogras under Col. Steinbach (one-time employee of Ranjit Singh) and Rohillas who had deserted the Punjabi camp. His plan was to avoid the jungles and ravines by going a few miles downstream and then attacking the Punjabi flank. Sher Singh forestalled this move and took up formation at the village, Lulliani—with the jungles and ravines still separating him and the enemy.

At noon on 13 January 1849, the Punjabis sighted the British advancing towards them from the direction of the village, Chillianwala. General Elahi Bakhsh's artillery brought the

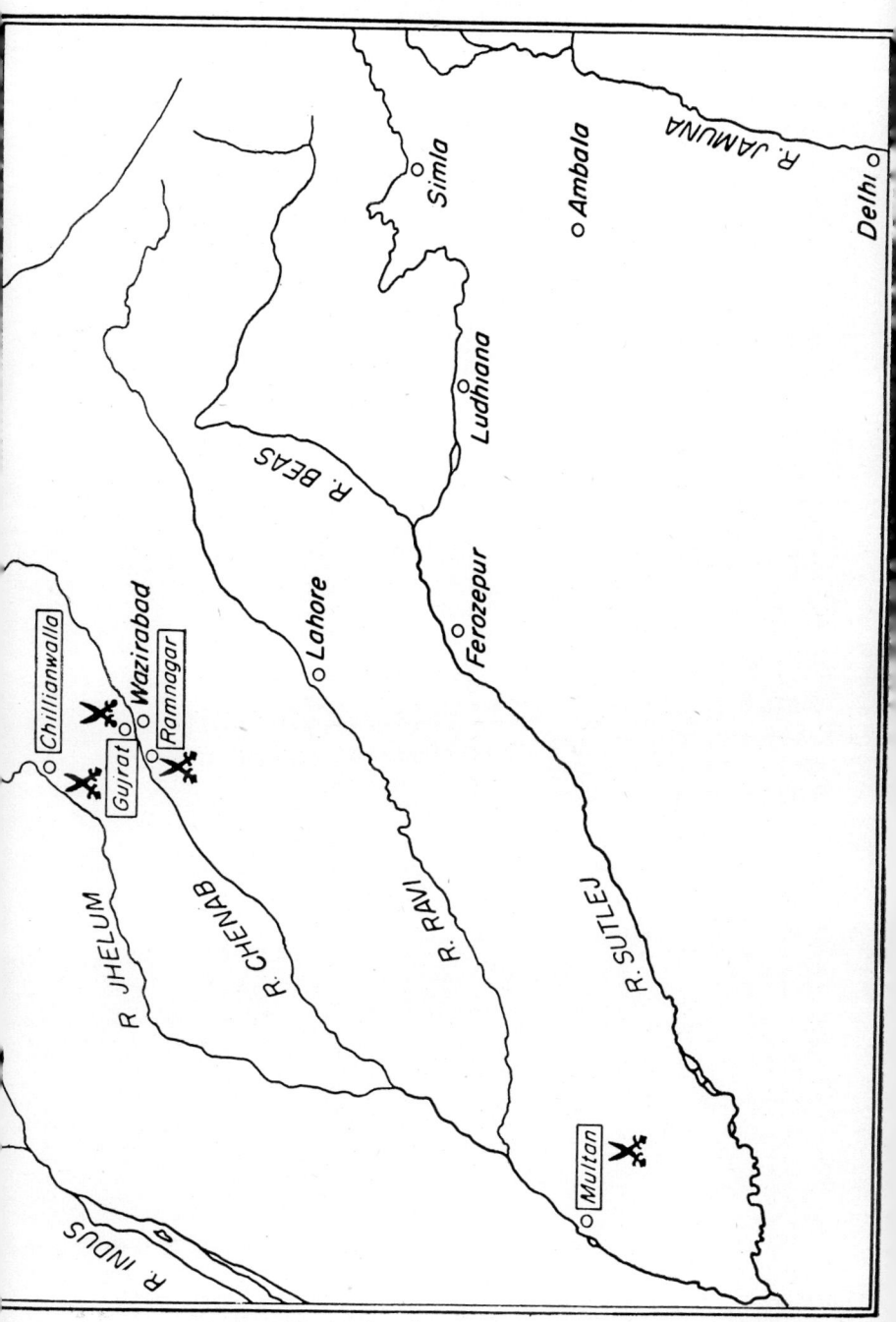

**SECOND ANGLO-SIKH WAR 1848-1849**

(*By courtesy of the Princeton University Press, Drawn by Serbjeet Singh.*)

## The Curtain Falls

enemy advance to a standstill. For one hour Punjabi guns kept the British at a distance. When their fire slackened, the British, who had the advantage in numbers, charged in an attempt to force the Punjabis into the river. The assault was led by Brigadier Pennyuick. The Khalsa found the conditions to their liking. They scattered into the brushwood jungle and began their harrying *dhai-phut* (hit and run) tactics. Their snipers took heavy toll of British infantry and cavalry. Those that got through the brushwood and ravines were easily repulsed in the hand-to-hand fight with the main line of the Punjabi troops. Pennycuick, his son and hundreds of the enemy were killed in most savage fighting between the Punjabis and the British. *The British Subaltern* wrote: 'The Sikhs fought like devils ... Such a mass of men I never set eye on and as plucky as lions: they ran right on the bayonets of the 24th (Regiment) and struck at their assailants when they were transfixed.'

The bloody battle lasted till darkness fell. The Punjabis captured four British guns and the colours of three regiments. The night was one of great terror for the British. General Thackwell wrote: 'Confusion pervaded the whole army. Fears were generally entertained that the enemy (the Punjabis) would attempt a night attack. If they had been enterprising and could have perceived the extent of their advantage they would assuredly have thrown themselves on us ... the jungle which had befriended them in the commencement of the action now formed a protection to us.'

The scene of the next morning is also painted by General Thackwell: 'Prince Albert hats and military shoes might be seen in all directions strewn on the ground in great abundance ... the camp next day was overspread with funeral gloom.' And it might well have been, for nearly 3000 British lay dead or wounded in the ravines and brushwood.

Chillianwala was the worst defeat the British had suffered since their occupation of India. Gough was superseded and Napier was asked to come from England to take over command.

Sher Singh Attariwala's guns boomed a twenty-one gun salute to the Punjabi victory.

The British awaited their doom with stoic resignation. And once again, as at Ferozeshahr, the Punjabis failed to drive home their advantage to a conclusive victory. Their own losses had been considerable and they were not aware of the magnitude of the punishment they had inflicted on the enemy. They were short of powder and their Artillery Commander, General Elahi Bakhsh, in a moment of weakness laid down arms. The supply situation became acute, particularly, as three days after the battle Chattar Singh with his troops joined his son with not enough provisions for themselves. The elements also came to the rescue of the British. As soon as the fighting stopped it began to rain; and for the next three days it poured incessantly, turning the ravines which separated the Punjabis from their quarry into deep moats. By the fourth day when the sun shone again on the sodden plain, the British had pulled out of Chillianwala and retreated across the Chaj to the banks of the Chenab.

The English poet, George Meredith, composed the following lines in commemoration of the battle.

> Chillianwallah, Chillianwallah!
>     'Tis a village dark and low,
> By the bloody Jhelum river
>     Bridged by the foreboding foe;
> And across the wintry water
>     He is ready to retreat,
> When the carnage and the slaughter
>     Shall have paid for his defeat.
>
> Chillianwallah, Chillianwallah!
>     'Tis a wild and dreary plain.
> Strewn with plots of thickest jungle,
>     Matted with the gory stain.
> There the murder—mounted artillery,
>     In the deadly ambuscade,
> Wrought the thunder of its treachery
>     On the skeleton brigade.
>
> Chillianwallah, Chillianwallah!
>     When the night set in with rain,
> Came the savage plundering devils
>     To their work among the slain;

## The Curtain Falls

And the wounded and the dying
   In cold blood did share the doom
Of their comrades round them lying,
   Stiff in the dead skyless gloom.

Chillianwallah, Chillianwallah!
   Thou wilt be a doleful chord,
And a mystic note of mourning
   That will need no chiming word;
And that heart will leap with anguish
   Who may understand the best;
But the hopes of all will languish
   Till thy memory is at rest.

Sher Singh Attariwala again sent a proposal for settlement. Since the Maharajah was in British hands, all he asked for was the reinstatement of Dalip Singh and the evacuation of British forces from Lahore. Sher Singh sent George Lawrence, who was a prisoner in his hands, as an envoy. The terms were rejected. More reinforcements were sent up from Hindustan.

One may be permitted to disgress on the Punjabi treatment of British prisoners. It was always favourably commended by British soldiers—though not always by British historians. *The British Subaltern* wrote: 'Two of the 9,000 lancers who were taken prisoners the other day were sent back this morning with Sher Singh's compliments. They seemed rather sorry to come back as they had been treated like princes, *pilawed* with champagne and brandy to the mast head and sent away with Rs. 10 each in his pocket.'

## The Disaster at Gujerat, 21 February 1849

Sher Singh Attariwala advanced towards the Chenab and entrenched his forces in horse-shoe formation between the town of Gujerat and the river. At the ends of the horse-shoe were the dry beds of two streams. The British forces re-assembled at the village of Lassori and then advanced on Gujerat: their right flank touching the Chenab, their left across the same dry stream-bed a little lower down. General Whish, who had been freed from the Multan campaign, came up and added to the enemy strength.

The Panjabis were weaker both in guns (fifty-nine to the British sixty-six) and in man-power. The Afghan cavalry was led by Dost Mohammad's son, Akram Khan, but it could barely be relied on in a struggle which was essentially between the Punjabis and the British.

The engagement was fought on a bright, sunny morning, with larks singing in the sky. The British advance began at 7.30 a.m. The Punjabis were as usual lacking in confidence. They opened fire too soon and blew away ammunition of which they were short and betrayed the position of their guns. The British halted when they were within range, adjusted their sights and in a cannonade lasting an hour and a half silenced the Punjabi artillery. Then with their guns still belching fire, British cavalry and infantry stormed the Punjabis. The Afghan cavalry tried to deflect the enemy but withdrew without effecting their purpose and thus exposed another Punjabi flank to the enemy. The Punjabis received the British assault as they had done in the earlier engagements. 'In this action as well as at Chillianwala', wrote Thackwell, 'Seikhs caught hold of the bayonets of their assailants with their left hands and closing with their adversary dealt furious sword blows with their right... This circumstance alone will suffice to demonstrate the rare species of courage possessed by these men.' The gunners, both Mussalman and Sikh, literally stuck to their guns to the last. General Thackwell remarked: 'The fidelity displayed by the Sikh gunners is worthy of record: the devotion with which they remained at their posts, when the atmosphere around them was absolutely fired by the British guns, does not admit description.' The Punjabis began to retreat. By noon they had evacuated Gujerat. The British occupied the town and pressed home their advantage by relentless pursuit. The Punjabis were hemmed in from all sides: Gough in front, Steinbach's Dogras on their right, Imamuddin on their left and Abbott's Pathan mercenaries behind them. The Commanders (except Sher Singh Attariwala, who had three horses shot under him) fled, leaving the common soldiers to fight a delaying rearguard action. The men fought late into the night: their bodies were found scattered for many miles beyond the field of battle. The night was made more fearful by explosions of unfired Punjabi ammunition dumps and by the thunder and rain which followed.

## The Curtain Falls

The enemy gave the Punjabi wounded no mercy. *The British Subaltern* wrote: 'Little quarter I am ashamed to say, was given and even those we managed to save from the vengeance of our men, I fear, were killed afterwards. But, after all, it is a war of extermination.'

The Battle of Gujerat was a disaster to Punjabi arms from which they could scarcely hope to recover. The coup de grace was, however, delivered by the arch-traitor, Gulab Singh Dogra. He helped Abbott to cut off Sher Singh Attariwala's retreat towards the frontier. The prospect of continuing the fight with Afghan help was thus obviated. He also arranged for the supply of boats for the British army to cross the Jhelum. Sher Singh tried to negotiate terms but the British insisted on unconditional surrender.

On 14 March 1849, both the Attariwala Sardars, father and son, came to the British camp at Hurmel near Rawalpindi with their faces covered under their shawls and gave up their swords to General Gilbert. They were followed by batches of hundreds. 'The reluctance of some of the old Khalsa veterans to surrender their arms was evident. Some could not restrain their tears; while on the faces of others, rage and hatred were visibly depicted', wrote General Thackwell. The remark of one veteran greybeard, as he put down his gun, summed up the history of the Punjab: 'Aj Ranjit Singh mar gaya (Today Ranjit Singh has died).'[1]

The concluding portion of the fateful story which deprived the boy-Maharaja, Dalip Singh, of his throne and turned the sovereign state of the Punjab into a province of British India, may better be told in the words of Lord Dalhousie and his able Secretary, Sir Henry Elliot, who was commissioned for the actual accomplishment of the task of annexation or more precisely of confiscation. In a letter marked private dated 30 March 1849, addressed to Brigadier Mountain, Lord Dalhousie writes:

"On the night of the 26th, I received General Gilbert's despatch from Peshawar. On the 27th, I sent Elliot to Lahore—on the 28th he arrived and on the 29th he crowned the work for

---

[1] Sita Ram Kohli's manuscript dealing with the battles of the Second Anglo-Sikh War have been lost. The editor has inserted these from his own *'Fall of the kingdom of the Punjab'*.

me. I am truly grateful for his aid and applaud highly his skill.

Last night after I had learnt that by my orders, the Maharaja had been deposed, and the Punjab had been declared a British province, I prayed God with a clear conscience to prosper the work; and I laid head on my pillow without being troubled by even the vision of a doubt as to the justice or necessity of the deed I had done...

My judgement may have erred. Time alone can show. But this I know my motives are untainted and my conscience is at ease. I believe the policy will be successful; I know that it is honest. With this conviction I rest content till the decision of the Government will come. I have assumed a tremendous responsibility; but I neither quail under it nor repent it. I thank God that whatever may be the issue, I shall have the tranquil mind.

In all probability I shall be gone before you reach this place. I hope to meet you at Simla much improved."[1]

Besides the letter from which we have quoted above, there are several others which Dalhousie wrote to Sir Frederick Currie which also confirm the view that long before the battles of Chillianwala and Gujerat were fought, he had made up his mind to put an end to the Sikh rule in the Punjab. Therefore, when the official news of the surrender of the Khalsa army was received by him, he hastened to despatch his Foreign Secretary, Sir Henry Elliot, to Lahore and put his resolve into action. But the irony of the situation is that Dalhousie not only wanted to confiscate the kingdom of Dalip Singh but in that he wanted the minor Prince himself and his Regency government to be a party to this suicidal transaction of renouncing their own independence and of replacing Sikh *raj* by British *raj*, in the Punjab. How Elliot managed this delicate affair and earned the gratitude of his align master, we leave it to him to tell. He writes, in his report dated 29 March 1849:

"Immediately on my arrival, I communicated to Sir H. M. Lawrence and Mr. J. Lawrence the instructions with which I was charged, and regretted to find that both these officers were fully

---

1 Pp. 170-171, Currie's Correspondence.

## The Curtain Falls

persuaded that the Council of Regency would, on no account, be induced to accede to the terms which were offered for their acceptance, in as much as they had already incurred great odium amongst their countrymen for what were considered to be their former concessions."[1]

Elliot was disheartened at first, but his resourcefulness did not fail him. He then hit upon the more artful device of working separately on the personal interests of each member of the Council and studying their reaction. He requested Henry Lawrence immediately to send for the two most influential members of the Council as he wanted to talk to them. Raja Tej Singh and Diwan Dina Nath were accordingly summoned. The Raja at first excused himself on the ground of sickness. But the messenger was sent again and was told to inform him that the mission on which Sir Henry Elliot had come was urgent and could not be accomplished without him, so he should come to the Residency unless he was really very seriously ill. Upon this Tej Singh came. His looks, Elliot's report states, gave no warrant for his excuses. Diwan Dina Nath came with him.

How the talks went on and ended is explicitly stated in Mr. Elliot's report of 29 March. He writes: "I explained to them the purpose for which I had come, that the Punjab would be annexed to the British dominions at all events but that it was for them to decide whether this should be done in an unqualified manner, or whether they would subscribe to the conditions which I was about to lay before them."

"The Rajah......opened out in a strain of invective against Sher Singh and all the rebellious Sardars;......acknowledged that the British Government had acquired a perfect right to dispose of the country as it saw fit, and recommended that it should declare its will without calling upon the Council to sign any conditions. I replied that if they refused to accept the terms which the Governor-General offered, the Maharajah and themselves would be entirely at his mercy, and I had no authority to say that they would be entitled to receive any allowance whatever."

"The Diwan ... commented on the severity of the conditions and particularly on the expatriation of the Maharajah... I

---

1 This has reference to the Bhyrowal Treaty, December 1846 which is aptly called, 'The Prologue to Annexation'.

promised that the Maharajah should not be sent anywhere to the east of the Ganges, pointing out Hardwar, Garhmukteswar, Bithoor, and Allahabad (Prayag) as being all of them places of high sanctity in their religion. They seemed to be thankful for this as a concession...They seemed fully satisfied with the personal allowance assigned to the Maharajah, which I told them would be about 10,000 rupees per mensem."

"Other subjects were then discussed, and they enquired anxiously about their own future position. I told them it was not intended to deprive them of their *jagirs* or salaries, and that, for this indulgence they would be expected to yield the British Government the benefit of their advice and assistance whenever called upon to do so; that if they did not subscribe to the conditions, I could not promise that any consideration would be shown to them."

"After much more parley, during which ... I convinced them of my resolute determination to yield to no point, they expressed their willingness to sign the paper and signed it accordingly, not without evident sorrow and repugnance on the part of the Diwan."

Having succeeded with Tej Singh and Dina Nath, Elliot next summoned Bhai Nidhan Singh and Fakir Nur-ud-Din, the only other members of the Regency Council who were residing in Lahore at the moment. Nidhan was the doyen of the celebrated priestly family of Bhai Basti Ram, and Fakir Nur-ud-Din that of the most influential Muhammadan family of Lahore. "When they came and were told what had passed," writes Sir Henry Elliot, "they said they would abide by whatever their colleagues were prepared to do. They then affixed their seal and signatures to the paper in duplicate and Sir H. M. Lawrence and myself then added our counter-signatures. The members then took their leave after the conference had lasted about two hours". The remaining two members of the Regency Council, namely, Sardar Shamsher Singh Sindhanwalia and Sardar Attar Singh Kalianwala not being present in Lahore, their accredited agents (*vakils*) signed the documents on their behalf.[1] The

---

[1] The two members of the Council namely Raja Sher Singh Attariwala and Sardar Ranjor Singh Majithia were left out—the former for reason of his open rebellion and the latter was suspected of his leanings towards the rebels and was placed under restraint throughout the period of the war.

## The Curtain Falls

question of the dissolution of the kingdom of the Sikhs and of the confiscation of its property including the world-famous gem *Kohi-Noor* was thus finally decided, and agreed upon.

That the destiny of a ruling Prince and of his twenty million subjects should have been decided by four of his timid and selfish councillors and this, too, within the brief space of two hours, is one of the very grim facts of history. Even the deal over the sale of a flock of sheep, between a shepherd and a butcher, perhaps, takes longer time than was taken by Mr. Elliot and Raja Tej Singh and Co., in making over to the British, the fortunes of the two crores of people of the Punjab.[1]

All that now remained to be done was the formal ratification of this business by the minor Prince and Mr. Elliot; which the latter desired should be done in a public Darbar. A Darbar was accordingly arranged for the next morning viz. 29 March at 7.00 a.m. At the appointed hour Sir Henry Elliot arrived at the Darbar Hall accompanied by the Lawrences (John and Henry) and other officials of the Residency. The party was escorted by a squadron of the Governor-General's bodyguard which Lord Dalhousie had specially sent for the occasion from his Ferozepore Camp. The Darbar Hall in the Lahore fort was suitably decorated—English and Indian spectators lining the walls on either side. The Maharaja and his Ministers who were waiting at the gate of the citadel to receive the Governor-Generals's representative then joined the small cavalcade which together moved to the audience hall. The boy-king was conducted to the throne at the end of the Hall (being the last time he occupied this seat) and the British envoys with the members of the Regency Council sat on either side. A deep silence prevailed in the Hall. The proceedings began with the reading aloud of the 'fatal edict' in English which declared that henceforth the sovereignty of the

---

[1] In order to give the transaction an appearance that it had the approval of the masses, the towns of Lahore & Amritsar were ordered to be lit up with coloured lamps on the night of the 29th. About Amritsar, in particular, the remark of Captain Trotter who had taken part in the Anglo-Sikh wars & had continued to be in service for 6 years after annexation is significant. He writes, "On the very day after the reading of the Proclamation, Amritsar their (Sikh) holy city, lighted up its thousands of coloured lamps, and listened contentedly to the hymns which a train of long-bearded priests chanted in honour of the victorious *Farhangi*". Vol. I, p. 229.

Punjab was assumed by the British.[1] Then followed the reading of the Persian and Hindustani translations of the decree for the 'comprehension of everyone present.'

Upon the conclusion of the Manifesto, the paper was passed on by the Chief Minister, Raja Tej Singh, to the Maharajah who affixed his signature 'by tracing the initials of his name in English letters'. This completed the ratification of that farcical transaction which formally and finally transformed the sovereign state of the Punjab, into a British province, and its ruler, Dalip Singh, into a throneless pensioner of the British Government. Elliot concludes his report with a feeling of pride and exultation over his achievement. "As I left the place" says he, "I had the proud satisfaction of seeing the British colours hoisted on the citadel under a royal salute from our own artillery, at once proclaiming the ascendancy of British rule, and sounding the knell of the Khalsa Raj".

Contemporary writers as well as later historians have expressed diverse opinions about the annexation of the Punjab. Lord Dalhousie's own view of this affair is stated in his letter addressed to Brigadier Mountain from which we have quoted above. He says he had not even the vision of a doubt as to the justice and necessity of the deed he had done. It seems, he was thoroughly obsessed with the thought—though wrongly and unjustly—that the Sikhs will never desist from war till all power of making war was permanently denied to them. He may have believed so honestly and genuinely. However, when the circumstances under which the annexation was made are examined in their context, firstly of the obligations undertaken by the British Government in March 1846 for reorganising the Government of the Lahore state; and secondly, of the events immediately preceding the annexation, we are unable to accept the view taken by Dalhousie that his measure was at all consistent with justice and equity.

By the Treaty of Bhyrowal, 16 December 1846, the Governor-General of India had undertaken to protect the Maharaja and

---

1 The silence which prevailed in the audience hall, remarks a British writer, was broken by Raja Dina Nath who, heaving a sigh, remarked that the decree of the Governor-General, however hard upon Dalip Singh, must be obeyed.

## The Curtain Falls

his kingdom during the period of the latter's minority, and for this purpose a British garrison was maintained in Lahore at an annual cost of rupees twenty-two lakhs which sum was charged to the Lahore treasury. The administration of the state was to be carried on by a Council of Regency under the direction of a British Resident assisted by a number of European Officers. The Resident was vested with full power 'to direct and control all matters in every department of the State'. 'The Indian members of the Council', as Lord Hardinge states in his letter 'are entirely under his (British Resident) control and guidance, he can change them and appoint others, and in military affairs his powers are as unlimited as in the civil administration, he can withdraw Sikh garrisons replacing them by British troops in any and every part of the Punjab'. A subsequent letter dated 23 October 1847, from him (Lord Hardinge) to the Resident further clarified the relative positions of the government of Maharajah Dalip Singh and that of the British Government. "In all our measures", states the letter under reference, "taken during the minority, we must bear in mind that by the Treaty of Lahore the Punjab was never intended to be an independent state. By the clause I added, the Chief of the State can neither make war nor peace, nor exchange nor sell an acre of territory, nor admit an European Officer, nor refuse us a thoroughfare through his territories nor, in fact, perform any act (except its own internal administration) without our permission. In fact, the native prince is in fetters and under our protection, and must do our bidding..."[1].

Apart from the position of a "ward" and of a subordinate ally assigned to the Sikh Prince, Lord Hardinge, had also urged upon the Resident, (Sir Henry Lawrence) the advisability of keeping a tight hand on all native officers, and making his own personality felt in every department of the government; and the Resident did exercise an effective overall check on day-to-day administration. In fact, the British Resident was the government of the Lahore State; and Sir Henry Lawrence wielded that unlimited authority which was, at one time, exercised by the late Maharaja Ranjit Singh. In his report on the practical working of the

[1] See Articles 11-14 of the Treaty of Bhyrowal, and also page 113, Login and Dalip Singh. Login quotes from Hardinge's letter dated 23-10-1847.

## Sunset of the Sikh Empire

Regency Council, Lawrence writes, "On the whole the Darbar gives me as much support as I can reasonably expect. I allow nothing that appears to me wrong to pass unnoticed, the members of the Council are gradually falling into the proper train and refer most questions to me, and in words, at least, allow more fully even than I wish, that they are only executive officers—to do as they are bid".[1]

What has been stated above leaves little room for doubt that the relative position of Maharaja Dalip Singh and the Governor-General was that of a 'protector' and 'the protected' or of 'guardian' and 'ward'. Since 18 August 1847, viz. the day on which Dalip Singh's mother, Rani Jind Kaur, was removed from Lahore to Sheikhupura and later from the Punjab to British India, the minor Prince came to be an entire responsibility of the British Resident. This responsibility implied above all, the protection of the Prince's person and the preservation of peace in his kingdom. The act of annexation denied the very basis of this position.

As for the events immediately preceding the annexation, these are too well known to merit repetition here. The trouble started in Multan as the result of an accident. It was not a preconceived plan on the part of Mul Raj or of the discharged garrison of the Multan citadel, as Dalhousie and Currie would have us believe.[2] For months together (April-August) the rising in Multan remained localised and if the British troops stationed in Lahore (vide Treaty of Bhyrowal) had been despatched in time, the subsequent trouble could have been averted altogether. The rising in the Punjab might never have taken place. But, as we have stated early in these pages, the triumvirate, namely, the Resident, the Governor-

---

[1] Parliamentary papers 1848-49 p. 32. Sohan Lal's remark on p. 14 dV of his book *'mayan tabia marzi-i-sahiban em'* conveys exactly the same sense.

[2] Some of Dalhousie's own letters would show that when he had asked Sir Frederick Currie to furnish him proof of the existence of an organised conspiracy to convince the Home Government that Multan and Mul Raj were merely the opportunity for the outbreak and not the causes of insurrection, 'the Resident could not produce evidence. The Governor-General had not only to send reminders twice on this point, but had also pointedly to mention that it would be of advantage to the Govt. of India to be able to establish the fact of an insurrection having been in the course of preparation and it will be of essential moment to the reputation of your own administration'. Dalhousie to Currie 14 December, 1848, p. 135 also p. 122, Currie's Correspondence.

## The Curtain Falls

General and the Commander-in-Chief were impelled by different motives. They did not, therefore, take effective and speedy action. These motives they kept concealed, and the Lahore Darbar and the subjects of the Maharaja were put on a wrong scent. Even as late as the month of November, when Lord Gough at the head of his main invading army marched into the Punjab, it was given out that the British army had come to punish the rebels and restore peace and order in the kingdom of the Maharaja. Leaflets to this effect were published and distributed. Promises of pardon and general amnesty for their past conduct were held out to such of the insurgents as would return to the allegiance of the Maharaja. In other words, what the British Government would have the people believe was that in fighting against Mul Raj or against Sher Singh, they were putting down an armed insurrection by the Maharaja's subjects, and as such were discharging their obligation towards their 'ward'—the minor, Dalip Singh. But, after obtaining victory at Multan and Gujerat, "Lord Dalhousie", to quote Major Evans Bell, "turns round, and declares the Treaty (March 1846) to have been violated, and therefore (rendered) null and void, and explains that the successful campaign... so ostensibly carried on for the suppression of a rebellion against the government of Maharajah Dalip Singh—really constituted a war against the Maharajah and the State of Lahore, by which the British Government has conquered the Punjab".[1] This was strange logic indeed, but the logic of the strong against the weak.

We cannot ignore the fact that treaties made by the British were made with the Sikh Government and the people of the state and not with any individual Sardar or chieftain. These treaties could not, therefore, be dropped or declared 'null and void' because a discharged governor of the Lahore Darbar had rebelled or because a certain regiment had been treacherous or because the mother of the Prince (Rani Jind Kaur) who had no legal status in the government of her son was suspected of intriguing against the Resident. The action of Lord Dalhousie in deposing the boy-sovereign from his throne and confiscating his state and property, therefore, was wrong, unjust and uncalled for. That

---

1 Retrospects and Prospects of Indian Policy, p. 157-58.

## Sunset of the Sikh Empire

Dalhousie himself entertained partly, if not wholly, similar feeling becomes manifest when we examine his manifesto with some care. We notice a studied attempt on his part to give specious arguments to seek support from his predecessor's actions in justifying his own harsh treatment of the Sikh Prince.

"The Governor-General of India", runs this document, "unfeignedly regrets that he should feel himself compelled to depose from his throne a descendant of Maharajah Ranjit Singh while he is yet in his early youth.........But the sovereign of every state is responsible for, and must be effected by, the acts of his people over whom he reigns........As in the former war, the Maharajah, because of the lawless violence of his subjects, whom his Government was unable to control, was made to pay the penalty of their offence in the loss of his richest provinces, so must he now be involved in all the consequences of their further violence, and of the deep national injury they have again committed."

"When a renewal of formidable war by the army and the great body of the Sikhs has forced upon the Government of India the conviction that a continuance of Sikh domination in the Punjab is incompatible with the security of the British territories, the Governor-General cannot permit that mere compassion for the Prince should deter him from the adoption of such measures against the nation as alone can be effectual for the future maintenance of peace, and for protecting the interests of the British people"[1].

The reason which really prompted Dalhousie in adopting this ruthless policy of annihilating the kingdom of the Punjab was his belief that the integrity of the British Indian Empire required that course of action. In the very year that he assumed the office of the Governor-General of British India, (1848), this young imperialist[2] stated in the course of writing an official minute".......

---

1 Manifesto to the Lahore Darbar by Lord Dalhousie. Quoted from pp. 136-37, Sir John Login and Dalip Singh. This is only evading the issue. Dalip Singh was no doubt, the reigning sovereign, but he was a minor and those who ruled during the minority were the British Resident and the members of the Regency Council—all nominated by the Governor-General. They were responsible for not suppressing the insurrection in time. The boy-sovereign was made a scapegoat.

2 Dalhousie was in his thirty-sixth year when he landed in India (Calcutta) on 12 January 1848, as Governor-General.

## The Curtain Falls

that in the exercise of a wise and sound policy, the British Government is bound not to put aside or neglect such rightful opportunities of acquiring territories or revenue, as may from time to time, present themselves."[1] This short sentence unfolds Dalhousie's mind and in a nutshell, explains the policy he pursued during his term of office. We would, however, like to add that when the action taken by him in regard to the Punjab is judged in the context of the measures adopted by his predecessors, the entire blame must not be thrown on Dalhousie. A persual of these measures makes it abundantly clear that the absorption of the kingdom of the Punjab into the expanding British Indian Empire formed part of a long-range programme set before them by the British rulers of India; and that, if Dalhousie had not done it, someone else among his successors would have completed this programme. The military and political interests of the British empire and its Indian appanage could not be served fully and satisfactorily so long as the Punjab continued to exist as an independent sovereign state. Its subversion, therefore, had become a matter of necessity with them; and we find that the British Indian statesmen endeavoured to conform their Punjab policy to meet that end during the course of half a century preceding the annexation.

In the opening years of the 19th century, when there was apprehension of Napoleon's invasion of the East, the British Indian Government resolved to make the river Jumna their boundary line, and treat the province of Sirhind as a neutral zone between their own and Ranjit Singh's dominion. Thirty years later, when the danger from Russia began to loom large in their eyes, the older view was abandoned and the creation of a much wider neutral zone came to be considered a strategical necessity. This was to include Sirhind, Punjab, Sindh and Afghanistan. The Sirhind Sikh chiefs, during these three decades, had been reduced to the position of subordinate allies; and the new Durrani kingdom of Kabul to be formed under Shah Shuja-Ul-Mulk was intended to be established as a British protectorate. The sovereign state of the Sikhs thus came to be sandwiched between the two. The shaping of the course of its dissolution, therefore, now engaged the earnest attention of

3 Lee-Warner, Vol. II, p. 116.

British Indian Officers. We find, accordingly, Sir William Osborne recommending the immediate occupation of the Punjab on Ranjit Singh's death; and Sir William MacNagten proposing to lop off the Sikh province of Peshawar and adding master to the newly constituted Durrani Kingdom of Kabul. Governor-General Lord Ellenborough during his regime of office worked on a regular scheme of action and had scheduled November 1845 as the approximate date by which he could muster a force large enough to occupy the Punjab. But he was not destined to see his scheme through. He was recalled from his office in July 1844. His successor, Sir Henry Hardinge, considered it inexpedient to swallow the whole of the Sikh kingdom in one mouthful. He preferred to take it in instalments. Therefore, he separated the hills from the plains and gave away the former to Raja Gulab Singh. He kept the plains between the rivers Sutlej and Beas for his own government and left the rest with Dalip Singh to be taken on a more appropriate occasion by his successors. However, before he left India, Hardinge had taken necessary steps to reduce even the truncated Punjab to the position of a subordinate state, completely governed and controlled by the British Resident. Except for the fact that after the treaty of Bhyrowal the saffron-coloured flag of the Khalsa was still permitted to flutter over the citadel of Lahore, the kingdom of the Punjab had lost its sovereign character. Hardinge's successor, the Marquess of Dalhousie, however did not approve his plan. He neither considered it expedient to govern the country through the agency of the "Native Councillors" working under a British minister; nor thought it safe to keep on a trained Sikh army 'to enact over and over again such scenes as were witnessed on previous occasions. Since it was necessary to maintain an adequate force on the British Indian frontiers to watch a hostile power (particularly Russia), Dalhousie held that it should better be maintained in the Punjab. The two million sterling which the country including the Jullundur Doab (annexed two years earlier) was expected to yield by way of annual revenue was, he considered, more than sufficient to pay the cost of the additional army to be maintained there for purposes of defence of the Indian Empire. It would be 'cheaper, better and securer to take the Punjab and rule it ourselves directly rather than indirectly through a native agency.'

PLATE 12

LORD DALHOUSIE

## The Curtain Falls

The Punjab kingdom of Ranjit Singh included the whole strip of territory beyond the Indus and adjoining the hills about 450 miles long from north to south and 250 miles broad at its widest part; its annexation would, therefore, at once carry the frontier of British India to the boundary provided it by nature. "With our outposts at the mouths of the passes (in these hills) it is absolutely and definitely impossible that any power can obtain entrance—whereas, on the Sutlej, we have no defence and the slightest alarm must be signal for a preliminary contest—a Punjab war or a Kabul expedition."[1] This was indeed the objective which the British Indian statesmen had kept before them for long and which it was left for the Earl of Dalhousie finally to accomplish. Thus in less than ten years after his death, the foreboding of Ranjit Singh turned out to be true and the Punjab like the rest of India, came to be painted red[2] on the political map of the country.

How inscrutable is the way of the working of destiny! Could any English statesman at that time imagine that within ten decades his people would also have to wind up their empire and erase the red from the political maps of Asia and Africa. So turns the cycle of Time. Verily has a Persian poet observed:

*Dar en wurta kashti fro sudd hazar*
*Ki paeda na shudd takhta ra ba kinar*

(In the whirlpool of Time, thousands of boats were drawn in and sank. But not a plank (splinter) of any one of them came up to the surface (to tell its sad tale).

---

1 Letters by "Economist", letter No. 111, 1849.
2 The tradition has it that on one occasion C.M. Wade, Pol. Agent, Ludhiana during his interview with Maharaja Ranjit Singh exhibited the map of India to show it to His Highness. The Maharaja either casually or deliberately enquired of him what the red patches on the map denoted. 'The British possessions' was the Agent's reply. Ranjit Singh is said to have turned aside and with a heavy heart told his courtiers *'ek din Panjab bhi lal ho jana hai'*.

# INDEX

## A

Abbott, Major James, political adviser at Hazara, 158; attitude towards Chattar Singh, 158-9; instigated Pathan chiefs, 159
Abdali, Ahmad Shah, 1; northern India invaded by, 2; eighth invasion of India by, 4
Afghan War, between the Afghans and the British, 51 et seq.
Afghanistan, British garrisons withdrawn from, 50
Afghans, the, 1, 2, 3; arms and training superiority of, 4
Agnew, Mr. Vans : political adviser in Multan, 142; attacked by Amir Chand with a spear, 143; was murdered, 144
Ahluwalia, Jassa Singh, 3
Ailadar, Sunder Singh, 122
Ali Masjid, 53, 55
Aliwal, a battle was fought at, 112
Allard, Jean Francois, 59
Almora, British outpost at, 47
Ambala, British troops in readiness at, 105
Anderson, Lt., Assistant political adviser in Multan, 142; was murdered, 144
Attariwala, Chattar Singh, 95, 96, 174; was asked to bring Khan Zaman to book and restore order in the region of Gandgarh, 19; governor of Hazara, 158; family tradition and family of, 158; precautionary measures, 159; was removed from his office and his jagir was confiscated, 159; decided to go to war, 161; requested help in liberating the Punjab from the 'oppression of the Farhangi', 163; communication with his son Sher Singh, 168; joined his son Sher Singh, 176
Attariwala, Gulab Singh see Singh, Gulab
Attariwala, Raja Sher Singh see Attariwala, Sher Singh
Attariwala, Sardar Chattar Singh see Attariwala, Chattar Singh
Attariwala, Sardar Sham Singh see Attariwala, Sham Singh
Attariwala, Sher Singh, eldest son of Chattar Singh, 125, 126, 144, 149, 173; was fighting for the British at Multan, 162; defection of 163 et seq.; decision to join Chattar Singh, 164-5; communication with Chattar Singh, 168; jointly with Mul Raj proclaimed a religious war against the British, 170-1, 174; intended to liberate Lahore, 172; peace proposal to the British by, 177
Attariwala, Sham Singh, 6, 31, 92, 113; Hira Singh and his party were chased and killed by the troops of, 88; dressed in white and on a white horse, fought at the front and fell dead, 116
Attock, the Fort of, 7, 95; liberation of, 174
Auckland, Lord, 12, 23, 50n, 59, 108n.
Avitable, General, 52, 53, 55; constrained to abandon Peshawar, 40; the British received information and help from, 59
Aziz-ud-din, Fakir, 22, 26, 28, 31, 57, 60, 62, 63

## B

Badozye, Nassar Khan, 150
Bahadur, Banda, 2
Bajwa, Chet Singh see Singh, Chet

Bakhsh, General Elahi, his artillery brought the enemy advance to a standstill, 174-5; in a moment of weakness laid down arms, 176
Bedi, Baba Bikram Singh, 18, 39, 61
Bedi, Baba Mian Singh, 92
British Government, Lahore Darbar's relation with, 20-5; passage of troops via Dehra Ismail Khan, 23; revision of commercial treaty with Lahore Darbar, 25; clauses of treaty with Lahore Darbar, 49-50; British garrisons were withdrawn from Afghanistan, 50; war with the Afghans, 51 *et seq.;* conquest of the Punjab contemplated by, 56 *et seq.;* the Italian, General Avitable, governor of Peshawar, gave help and information to, 59; Suchet Singh's 'treasure' in the hands of, 80-1; movement of British troops at Ferozepore and other places, 82; alliance proposal of Rani Jind Kaur to, 98; during Ranjit Singh's period the activities of, 101; against the Punjab war preparations of, 101 *et seq.;* strength of British garrisons on the Punjab frontier, 120; severed diplomatic relations with the Lahore Darbar, 105; proclaimed war on the Lahore Darbar, 105; a battle with the Sikhs, 114-6; treaty with the Lahore Darbar, 118-20; Governor-General's alternative form of administration of Lahore Darbar, 126 *et seq.;* Governor-General's scheme supported by the Sardars, 129; authority of the British Resident under Governor-General's scheme, 131-2; Sher Singh's peace proposal rejected by, 177 Broadfoot, Major, 97*n.*, 98*n.*, 100, 102, 109*n.;* a letter to Eilenborough on the administration of Hira Singh & Pandit Jalal written by, 89; in search of an *agent provocateur* in Lahore, 104
Burns, Sir Alexander, 18*n.*, 51

## C

Calcutteea, Gulab Singh, 78; was shot dead by Attar Singh, 79
Campbell, Brigadier-General: marched towards the fort of Ram Nagar, 173; opened attack on the Punjabis, 173
Campbell, George, on unjustifiable action against Lal Singh, 104
Canora, Col., an American in Sikh service, 159
Chand, Amir, attacked Mr. Agnew with a spear, 143
Chand, Mian Prithi, 18
Chand, Mian Rattan, 18
Chand, Misr Diwan, battle with Azim Khan, 8
Chand, Mohkam, 151, 152
Chand, Tek, 120
Chenab, the : Attariwalas decided to hold the British on, 172; minor skirmishes on the bank of, 173; the Punjabis crossed the river and placed themselves between the British and Ram Nagar, 173; battle in the region of, 173-4
Chillianwala : victory at, 174 *et seq.* the British had suffered the worst defeat at, 175; George Meredith composed a poem to commemorate the battle of, 176-7
Chinese, launched counter attack against Zorawar Singh and recovered lost lands, 48
Clerk, Mr. George Russell, 10*n.*, 22, 23, 24, 27*n*,, 36, 47, 57; in the fight against the Afghans assistance of Sher Singh obtained by, 52-3
Connolly, Lt., conferred *khilaats* on Yuzafzai subjects of the Sikhs, 21
Cortland, 148, 150 *and n.*, 153, 154, 155
Court, General, fled to Ferozepore, 40 *and n.*
Craigie, Captain, 52
Cunningham, Captain J.D., 20*n*, 47; on the battle of Sabraon, 113-4

Cureton, General, killed at Ram Nagar 173
Currie, Sir Frederick, 110, 125, 130, 132, 134, 142, 145; regarding the action on Multan, Governor-General's letter to, 146-7; Lord Dalhousie's letter to, 148-9; despatch of four armies to Multan was arranged by, 149-50; strong letter to Abbott on the intention of the Pakhli brigade and murder of Commandant Canora, 160

# D

*Dal Khalsa*, National Army of the *Panth*, 3 rise of the, 2-5
Dalhousie, Lord, 146 *and n.*, 147*n.*; a letter to Currie regarding action on Multan, 148-9; regarding the troubles in Multan and Hazara, 161, private letter to Brigadier Mountain, 179-80; on the end of the Sikh rule in the Punjab, 179-80
Dass, Har Bhagwan, 153
Devi, Rani Mehtab, 10
Dick, Sir Robert, 115
Dogra, Dhian Singh, 10, 12, 14, 16, 17*n.*, 20, 26 *and n.*, 31, 42*n.*, 45, 50, 56, 62, 63; in the saddle, 13; for a change of Government, 16; Chet Singh was hacked to pieces by, 17; serious difference with Nau Nihal Singh, 27; suffered injuries, 28; a personal letter to Sher Singh by, 28-9; aspersion on his integrity, 29; compromise between Rani and Sher Singh suggested by, 31, 32; supremacy at Lahore planned by, 33; indispensability of, 33; terms for peace to Rani Chand Kaur by, 37; plot to kill Rani Chand Kaur, 43-4; Ferozepore celebration joined by, 60-1; a plot of murder of, 64; murder of, 65; to negotiate terms of peace a team from Lahore Darbar led by, 117
Dogra, Gulab Singh, 31, 34, 35, 37, 43*n.*, 49, 55*n.*, 59, 71, 80*n.*, 83, 84, 93*n.*, 100, 112, 117*n.*, 124*n.*, 125*n.*, 179; elder brother of Dhian Singh 20; help to the British by, 54; expansion of the estates of, 72-3; conflict with Hira Singh, 76-7; tax arrears of, 87, 91; negotiation with Rani Jind Kaur's term, 92; came to Lahore and made a settlement with Rani, 92-4; British help asked for by, 98; negotiation with the British by, 113; treaty with the British, 118; came forward with an offer, 119; by the treaty of Amritsar, Kashmir, Jammu and Kohistan were transferred to, 123; Shaikh Imamud-din defeated the troops of, 124
Dogra, Raja Gulab Singh *see* Dogra, Gulab Singh
Duggal, Diwan Rattan Chand, 92

# E

Eden, Miss Emily, 12
Edwards, Capt Herbert, 122, 149; Imam-ud-din tendered his submission to, 125; arrogant and rude behaviour towards Diwan Daulat Rai the Governor, 137; was replaced by Commandant Cortlandt, 137; on the annexation of the Punjab, a letter to Major Hodson by, 147; a letter to Currie by, 147; to win over the Pathans, endeavours by, 150 *et seq.*; a letter to Mustapha Khan in Multan, 153; forces of, 153-4; battle of Multan, 153-7; on Sher Singh, 164
Ellenborough, Lord, 24, 37, 49, 50, 56, 59, 60, 65, 78*n.*, 80, 100, 102, 103*n.*; on the future of Afghanistan, 55; letters to Field Marshal the Duke of Wellington, 58
Elliot, Sir Henry, 145, 179; his way of replacing Sikh *raj* by British *raj*, 180 *et seq.*
Elphinstone, General, surrender to Muhammad Akbar Khan, 52

## F

Fane, Sir Henry, 12
Ferozepore, celebration at, 61; British war preparations, at, 102; British troops from different places were on the move towards, 105; first battle fought at, 105; one brigade and a few *ghorcharas* with 20 guns were left by Lal Singh to watch over, 106
Fitzgerald, Captain, killed at Ram Nagar, 173
Ford, Major, murder of, 40
Foulkes, Commandant, murder of, 40
*Friend of India* newspaper, on the king-killing in the Punjab, 66

## G

Gadwai, Rattan Singh, 11
Gandgarh, 19
Ghazni, refugees, 22; a British garrison at, 52
Gilbert, Sir Walter, 109, 115
Gough, Sir Hugh, 108*n*., 115*n*., 116*n*.; Lal Singh's troops attacked the force of, 107; attack on the Sikh entrenchments, 109; assessment of British and Sikh losses made by, 116 with an army the Sutlej was crossed; by, 172; discourtesy shown to Dalip Singh, 172; arrived on the bank of Chenab, 173; the British force towards Chillianwala, 174; was superseded by Napier, 175
Granthi, Bhai Gurmukh Singh, 11, 31, 63; well-known Sikh priest, 14; became a victim of the purge by Hari Singh, 69
Griffin, Sir Lepel, 63*n*., 82*n*.; on Sher Singh's army, 46; on heroic acts performed by the Sikhs, 116; *The History of Lal Singh*, 126
Gujerat, the disaster at, 177 *et seq*.

## H

Hardinge, Sir Henry, 81, 108, 109, 115 and *n*., 117, 120, 124, 131, 185; regarding the alliance proposal of Rani Jind Kaur a letter written to Lord Ellenborough by, 98; men and war equipment increased by, 102; was determined to make the state weak, 118; an alternative form of administration for Lahore Darbar, 12 *et seq*.; stratagem of, 129 *et seq*.
Hathu, Nidhan Singh, 7
Havelock, General, 107; killed at Ram Nagar, 173
Hazara, trouble in, 84, 158 *et seq*.
Hugel, Baron, 70

## I

Idgah, a well-fortified building in Multan, 143; residence of Mr. Van Agnew & party, 143; gun duel at, 144; Agnew and Anderson murdered in, 144
Imam-ud-din, Shaikh, 120; succeeded his father, the Governor of Kashmir, 124; Lal Singh encouraged Shaikh to resist the occupation of Kashmir by Gulab Singh, 124; defeated the troops of Raja Gulab Singh, 124; tendered his submission to Capt. Herbert Edwards, 125
Iskardu, expedition to, 19-20

## J

Jalalabad, a British garrison at, 52; failure of the first attempt to relieve 53
Jalla, Pandit, 74*n*., 75, 87, 88 and *n*.; was appointed *Mashir-i-Khas*, 70; was killed, 88
Jind, Rani *see* Kaur, Rani Jind

## K

Kabul, 21, 23; passage of British troops returning from, 22; British prisoners in, 52; force replanted the British flag on the Bala Hisar, 56

# INDEX

Kalianwala, Attar Singh, 96, 125, 131, 149; Prime Ministership aspired to by, 90; joined Edwards, 156
Kandahar, 21; a British garrison at, 52
Kangra fort, 13n,; defence of, 122-3
Kanhya, Nidhan Singh, 7
Karshman, J., editor of the *Friend of India*, 65
Kashmir, transfered to Gulab Singh, 123; revolt in, 124
Kaur, Chand *see* Kaur, Rani Chand
Kaur, Ishar, of Kharak Singh's favourite Ranis, 15
Kaur, Kanwarani Sahib *see* Kaur, Sahib
Kaur, Rani Chand, Kharak Singh's senior Maharani, 16, 27; a claim to rule, 30; supporters of, 31-3; indispensability of Dhian Singh admitted by, 33; battle with Sher Singh, 34-7; negotiation with the British for help, 36; Dhian Singh's terms for peace to, 37; a victim of Sher Singh, 43; death of, 44
Kaur, Rani Jind, 69n., 88, 90, 91, 100; mother of Dalip Singh, 70; for negotiation with Gulab Singh a team was sent by, 92; Gulab Singh was offered the position of Wazir by, 93; installed her brother Jawahar Singh in the position of Wazir, 94; alliance with British proposed by, 98; as regent, 121; outwitted by British statesmanship, 132; from Lahore, removal of, 132-4; reduction of allowance of, 134
Kaur, Rani Mehtab, 12, 70n.
Kaur, Sahib, the widow of Nau Nihal Singh, became the first victim of Sher Singh, 42; miscarriage of, 42-3
Kaur, Tej, daughter of Sardar Chattar Singh, was betrothed to the boy Maharaja Dalip Singh, 158
Keen, Sir John, 25
Kelat-i-Ghilzal, a British garrison at, 52

Khalsa army, expenditure table of, 86; behaviour of, 91-2
Khalsa Panth, the, 3; proclamation of sovereignty of, 4
Khalsa power, rise of the, 1, 2
Khalsa soldiers, corruption of, 34
Khalsa, the, *Raj Kareyga Khalsa*, 3 *see also* Dal Khalsa
Khan, Bahawal, 152; army of, 153
Khan, Dost Muhammad, 22, 24, 21n., 50n., 51, 61, 95; treaty of amity and friendship with Lahore Darbar, 50-1; guest of Sher Singh, 50
Khan, Fateh, 83, 84, 95, 96
Khan, Kaura, 151n.; a Bilochi chief, 151, 152; was honoured and rewarded by Edwardes, 151
Khan, Mitha, the Muslim Bilochi chief, 151
Khan, Muhammad Akbar, son of Dost Muhammad, General Elphinstone surrendered to, 52
Khan, Mustapha, 153
Khan, Nassar *see* Popalzai, Nassar Khan
Khan, Painda, seized the frontiers of Kishengarh, 18
Khan, Peer Ibrahim (or Bahawalpur), 153
Khan, Sardar Habib-ullah, 84
Khan, Sardar Mohammed Azim, against the Sikhs, 8
Khan, Sultan Mahmud, 50
Khyber Pass, 9, 21
Kishan, Ram, 16; became a victim of the purge by Hari Singh, 69
*Koh-i-Noor* the world-famous gem, 37, 183
Kulu and Mandi; expedition to, 20 *and n.*

# L

Ladakh, 48; conquered by Ranjit Singh, 19; important wool producing centre, 46
Lahore, 4, 7, 12, 36
Lahore Durbar, 7, 9, 48; Sikh priests

of, 14; restored Paind Khan's jagir, 18; relations with the British, 20-5; double-dealing by British strongly resented by, 22; revision of British Government's commercial treaty with, 25; clauses of Treaty with British Government, 49-50; a treaty of amity and friendship with Dost Muhammad, 50-1; dismissal of Europeans from the service of, 79; financial position of, 85 *et seq.*; British Government severed diplomatic relations with, 105; British Government proclaimed war, on, 105; to negotiate terms of peace, a team led by Gulab Singh was sent by, 117; Treaty with the British, 118-20; the powers of government were invested in a council of four, 126; alternative form of administration as shaped by the Governor-General, 126 *et seq.*; Henry Lawrence established appellate courts in, 136; administrative reforms of, 137-40

Lahore Government, *see* Lahore Darbar

Lake, Lt., 154, 155; appointed as Political Agent to Bahawalpur, 152

Lal, Misar Rup, 122, 123

Lal Munshi Sohan, 10, 11 *and n.*, 16 17*n.*, 29*n.*, 42, 50, 65, 68; on Khalsa soldiers, 91-2

Latif, Sayyed Mohammad, on Nau Nihal Singh's death, 29

Lawrence, Mr John, 125, 128, 131, 136*n.*, 179; a letter to Sir Frederick Currie, 127*n.*; brother of Sir Henry Lawrence, 138; becomes acting Resident and his administration, 138-40; exempted certain articles from duty in Multan, 141-2; on Multan revolt letters to Currie, Millot and Brigadier Wheeler, 145; a letter to Sir Henry Elliot by, 145

Lawrence, Sir Henry, 53, 54, 59 *and n.*, 113, 121, 125, 126, 128, 129, 135*n.*, 179, 185, 186; meeting of Sardars held in the tent of, 129-30; 'Prema Plot' of, 132 *et seq.*, appellate courts established by, 136; went to England on furlough, 138; discussed with Mul Raj about payments of arrears, 141; on the conquest of the Punjab, 148

Lhasa, important wool-producing centre, 46; Lhasa army recovered Tuklakote, Gartok, Rohtak and Iskardu, 48

Littler, Sir John, 107, 108, 109, 125, 129

Ludhiana, the only British military station on the Sikh frontier till 1839, 102; war shifted to, 111

Lumley, Sir James, 57

# M

Mackeson, Lieutenant, 53, 54, 55

Macnaghten, 24, 57; established contact with the Yusafzai chiefs, 21; charge against the Lahore Darbar concocted by, 22; murder of, 56

Majithia, Ranjodh Singh, 111 and *n*, 131

Majithia, Sardar Lehna Singh, 12, 26, 30, 31, 40, 60 and *n.*, 62, 87, 172; brought to Lahore in chains, 61; released from jail, 62; Prince Pratap Singh son of Sher Singh murdered by, 65; put up a stout resistance to Hira Singh's attack on Lahore fort, 68; was killed, 68-9

Majithia, Sardar Ranjodh Singh, *see* Singh, Ranjodh

Mal, Chetan, governor of Mangrota fort, 150-1; was killed, 151

Mal, Diwan Lakhi, Governor of Dera Ismail Khan, 83

Mal, Diwan Sawan, of Multan, 40, 120; ordered to clear arrears, 19; sudden death of, 84, 141; tax arrears of, 87

Mal, Logan, Governor of Dera Ghazi Khan, 151; was made captive, 151

Malleson, Colonel, on the battle of Pherushahr, 110

Malwai, Dhana Singh, 11, 31; portion of the village Mauran transferred to, 81

Man, Kahan Singh, was appointed as in charge of Multan in place of Mul Raj, 142; 143
Man, Sardar Fateh Singh, 30, 92
Mandi and Kulu, expedition to, 20 *and n*.
Mauran, a village, 81-2; British interference, 82
Mazhabi, Godar Singh, with the rabble entered into Idgah and murdered Agnew and Anderson, 144
McGaskill, Sir Joseph, killed in the battle of Mudki, 107
McGregor, on the government of the Punjab, 121
Meerut, British troops in readiness at, 105
Mehtab Devi, Rani, 10
Meredith, George, the English poet, composed a poem on Chillianwallah, 176-7
*Misldari* a semi-military organisation 2, 7
Mohammed, Pir, 8
Mohammed, Sultan, 8
Mohi-ud-din, Sheikh Ghulam, governor of Kashmir, 30, 84, 91; tax arrears, 87; death of, 124
Mudki, Lal Singh with his army moved towards, 106-7; battle of, 107-8
Muhammad, Amir Dost, *see* Khan, Dost Muhammed
Muhammad, Dost, *see* Khan, Dost Muhammad
Multan, the province of, 141; rising at, 141 *et seq.;* Mul Raj was persuaded by the soldiers to lead their revolt, 144; outbreak at Multan was a premeditated movement of the Khalsa, 146; Currie arranged to despatch four armies to, 149-50; siege of, 149 *et seq.;* battle of, 153-7; fall of, 174
Muzaffarabad, captured by rebels, 84; reconquered by Hira Singh, 85

## N

Nalwa, Hari Singh, 61; tutor of Prince Nau Nihal, 17*n*.

Napier, Sir Charles, 102; to take over command from Lord Gough, 175
Nath, Diwan Dina, 32*n*., 91, 96, 97, 99, 120, 122, 125, 126, 130*n*., 144, 181
Nicholson, Captain, report on Sardar Chattar Singh, 160
Nott, General, 52; knighted for recapture of Kabul, 56
Nur-ud-din, Fakir, 91 96, 97, 182
Nur-ud-din, Khalifa, 119, 126

## O

Osborne, Sir William, 12, 18*n.;* invasion of the Sikh kingdom proposed by, 57

## P

Palmer, Colonel, 52
Panipat, battlefield of, 1
Peshawar, 8, 21, 57; status of the Muhammedan troops at, 22
Pollock, General, 53, 55; knighted for recapture of Kabul, 56
Popalzal, Sardar Nassar Khan, 152
Povindia, Sardar, Gulab Singh, 30
Pherushahr, 107; Sikh army in the field at, 108; 'a battle gained after it had been lost', 110
'Prema Plot', 132-3, 133*n*
Punjab, the, kingdom of, 5-9; British scheme for the conquest of, 75 *et seq.*, trouble in the frontier districts of, 83-4; financial position of, 85 *et seq.;* the last year of freedom of, 90-100; British war preparations against, 101 *et seq.;* strength of British garrisons on the frontier of, 120; evacuated Gujerat, 178; annexed to the British Empire, 179-80; ceremonial transfer of, 183-4; *see also* Lahore Darbar
Punjabis, the, minor skirmishes on the bank of the Chenab, 173

## Q

Qassuria, Shams-ud-din, confidential

messenger, 106; Lal Singh conveyed secret information to the enemy through, 109; detailed information regarding the dispositions of the Sikh army sent to Major Lawrence by, 114

## R

Raj, Mul, 168n., 172; son of Diwan Sawan Mal, 141; heavy *nazrana* demanded by Hira Singh from, 141; Lal Singh's troops repulsed by, 141; at the exemption of certain articles from duty the reaction of, 142; decided to resign, 142; was confined in his house, 143; to stand in the territory between the Indus and the Chenab threatened by Edwards, 153; failure of the army of, 154; troops led personally by, 155; battle of Multan, 155-7; jointly with Sher Singh proclaimed a religious war against the British, 170-1, 174
Rakhi, 3, 4
Ram, Bakhsi Bhagat, 91, 97
Ram, Bhai Gobind, 27, 28, 30, 87
Ram, Diwan Kirpa, 63
Ram, Ganga, was hanged for subversive activity, 134
Ram, Misr Beli, 25, 27, 37; head of the treasury, 16; release of, 26; a victim of the purge by Hira Singh, 69
Ram, Misr Rallia, 120
Ram Nagar, British officers killed at, 173
Ram, Tulsi, sentenced to life, 134
Rang, Ram, 143, 153; fight with Edwards' army, 154
Ratnu, Wazir, 48
Richmond, Colonel, 78n., 80, 81, 82
Rupa, Bhai, 14

## S

Sabraon, a decisive battle fought at, 112; battle between the Sikhs and the British, 114-6
Sadullapur, the village of, fighting at, 173-4
Sahai, Diwan Devi, 122
Sale, Sir Robert, 52; killed in the battle of Mudki, 107
*Sarbat Khalsa*, 3, 42, 74, 96-7, 112
Shah, Nadir, 1; Delhi occupied by, 1
Shah, Zaman, grandson of Ahmad Shah Abdali, 6, 103
Shams-ud-din, *see* Qassuria, Shams-ud-din
Shuja-ul-Mulk, assassination of, 49
Shujah, Shah 21, 23, 24, 50n., 51, 103
Sikhs, the, 1; repressive measures and its effect on, 2; *dhai-phut* tactics of, 4; the British or the subordinate alliance cordons the kingdom of, 101; near Sabraon a battle with the British was fought by, 114-6
Sindhanwalia, Ajit Singh, 27, 30, 35 *and n.*, 39, 42, 61, 62n., 64; was received by Sher Singh, 62; Sher Singh murdered by, 64-5; was shot dead, 69
Sindhanwalia, Attar Singh, 39, 40, 42, 61; *see also* Singh, Attar
Sindhanwalia Sardars, ambition of seizing sovereignty by, 63
Sindhanwalia, Sardar Shamsher Singh, 144, 149
Sindhanwalia, Sham Singh, 131
Singh, Ajit *see* Sindhanwalia, Ajit Singh
Singh, Amir, 7
Singh, Attar, 27, 30, 39, 63-4, 82; killed by Hira Singh's army, 79; *see also* Sindhanwalia, Attar Singh
Singh, Avtar, youngest son of Chattar Singh, 162
Singh, Bhai Bir, 77, 78, 79; was killed by Hira Singh's army, 79
Singh, Bhai Gurmukh *see* Granthi, Bhai Gurmukh Singh
Singh, Bhai Mohan, 28
Singh, Bhai Nidhan, 131, 182
Singh, Bhai Ram, well-known Sikh priest, 13n., 14, 16, 27, 30, 36, 87,

# INDEX

91, 93, 94, 98, 113n., 119
Singh, Chattar, see Attariwala, Chattar Singh
Singh, Chet, 14, 15 and n., 16, 17n.; assassination of, 15-17; hacked to pieces by Dhian Singh, 17
Singh, Commandant Kahan, was hanged for subversive activity, 134
Singh, Dalip, see Singh, Maharaja Dalip Singh, Davinder; recovery of Mauran by, 82
Singh, Dhaunkal, 34
Singh, Dhian; see Dogra, Dhian Singh
Singh. Diwan Hari, 4; was ordered to wind up the Lhasa expedition, 48
Singh, General Mian, of Kashmir, 85n; order to clear arrears, 19
Singh, Gulab see Dogra, Gulab Singh
Singh, Gulab, second son of Chattar Singh, placed under arrest in the Lahore fort, 162
Singh, Gurdit, brother of Chet Singh was murdered, 17n.
Singh, Gurmukh, 16
Singh, Guru Gobind, 5, 41
Singh, Hari, see Singh, Diwan Hari
Singh, Hira, 60, 80n.; received news of the assassination of his father Dhian Singh, 67; obtained promises of help from troops, 67-8; a substantial increase in pay for the army promised by, 68; Lahore fort attacked by, 68; Dhian Singh's body was cremated by, 69; purged some Sindhanwalias for the murder of his father, 69; assumed the position of Prime Minister, 69; as Prime Minister of the Punjab, 67 et seq.; salary of soldiers increased by, 70; Jawahar Singh conceived the idea of ousting Hira Singh, 71; conspiracy against, 73; certain demands of army *panchayats* conceded by, 74; troopers had been won over, 75; conflict with Gulab Singh, 76-7; Attar Singh's journey through British territory, protested by, 82; for the movement of British troops at Ferozepore and other places, the attitude of, 82-3; Muzaffarabad was lost and reconquered by, 85; left residence with cash and jewellery, 88; was killed in fight, 88
Singh, Jamadar Khushal, 27, 28, 30, 40, 60
Singh, Jassa, 3
Singh, Jathedars Gujjar, 4
Singh, Jawahar, brother of Rani Jind Kaur, 70, 91, 92; idea of ousting Hira Singh conceived by, 71; was imprisoned, 71; release of, 74; Prime Ministership aspired to by, 90; in the position of *Wazirat*, 94; death of Peshaura Singh rejoiced by, 96; death of, 96
Singh, Jawala, 34; hostile attitude towards Sher Singh, 45; was led to Lahore in chains, 46; death of, 46
Singh, Jiwan, 7
Singh, Kahan Man see Man, Kahan Singh
Singh, Kanwar Nau Nihar see Singh, Nau Nihal
Singh, Kanwar Pratap, son of Sher Singh, 39, 56, 61; was murdered by Lehna Singh, 65
Singh, Kanwar Sher, 13, 14, 42n., 58n., 61, 108n; step-brother of Kharak Singh, 11; bid for the throne, 11-12, 26,; 30; British Agent's courtesy call on, 23; a personal call from Dhian Singh on, 29; supporters of, 31; proceeded to Lahore, 33; battle with Rani Chand Kaur, 34-7; army of, 34; was invested as Maharaja, 39; army out of control of, 39-40; pay scale of army was raised by, 41; pregnant Kanwarani Sahib Kaur became first victim of, 42; Rani Chand Kaur was the next victim of, 43; Dost Muhammad a guest of, 50; to fight the Afghans, the British received assistance of, 52-3; royal duties neglected by, 62-3; plot for murdering Dhian Singh agreed by, 64; murder of,

64-5; synopsis of the reign of, 66
Singh, Kashmira, 30, 71, 72; Kapur Singh was flogged to death by, 73
Singh, Kehr, was brought to Lahore in chains, 61; was released from jail, 62
Singh, Kharak, 11, 14n., 18n., 34n.; eldest son of Ranjit Singh, 10; acceptance by the British as Maharaja of the Punjab, 13; investiture of, 14-15; fall of, 15-17; forced retirement of, 17; strained relation with his son Nau Nihal Singh, 25; death of, 27
Singh, Lal, 93, 119, 125n., 129; was appointed wazir, 99; Major Broadfoot picks up quarrel with, 104; friendly assurance conveyed to the British by, 106; moved towards Mudki, 106; troops lost their way and reached Pherushahr instead of Mudki, 107; regarding movements of troops, betrayal of, 107; reached Mudki, 107; army's secret information conveyed to the British by, 108-9, discredited himself with the army, 112; was re-imposed on the army, 114; detailed dispositions of the Sikh army sent to Major Lawrence by, 114; was confirmed in the position of wazir, 121; trial for his role in the Kashmir debacle, 125-6; was ordered to leave the Punjab, 126; Mul Raj repulsed the troops of, 141
Singh, Lehna see Majithia, Sardar Lehna Singh
Singh, Maharaja Dalip, 30, 81, 100, 131, 132; proclaimed Maharaja by Hira Singh, 69; illness of, 103; meeting with the Governor-General 117; was recognised by the British as Maharaja, 121; Lord Gough showed discourtesy to, 172; deprived of his throne, 179; personal allowances of, 182
Singh, Mahtab, 72, 73, 95
Singh, Man, governor of Srinagar, hacked to pieces, 40
Singh, Man Udham, 28
Singh, Multana, 30
Singh, Nau Nihal, 13 and n., 15 and n., 16, 28n.; only son of Kharak Singh, 14; became ruler of the Lahore kingdom, 17; administrative ability of, 17-19; problems regarding his father, Maharaja Kharak Singh, 25; internal administration, 25 et seq.; serious difference with Dhian Singh, 27; illness and death of, 28; news of his death was kept secret, 28.; his death was officially announced, 29
Singh, Peshaura, 30, 69, 72, 91, 94; death of, 95
Singh, Pratap, see Singh, Kanwar Pratap
Singh, Prince Dalip, see Singh, Maharaja Dalip
Singh, Prince Kharak, see Singh, Kharak
Singh, Raja Gulab, see Dogra, Gulab Singh
Singh, Raja Hira, see Singh, Hira
Singh, Raja Lal, see Singh, Lal
Singh, Raja Sher, see Attariwala, Sher Singh
Singh, Raja Suchet, see Singh, Suchet
Singh, Ram, see Singh, Bhai Ram
Singh, Ranjit, 6, 41n.; settlements with *misldars*, 7; annihilation of Pathan colony of Kasur, 7; clash with Gurkhas, 7; Sutlage as the eastern limit of his dominion, 7; fort of Attock fell into the hands of, 7; Khyber Pass dominated by; 9; troops, revenues & area of the kingdom of, 9; composition of the court of, 9; death of, 9; funeral of, 10-11; meeting with Lord Auckland, 13; Ladakh conquered by, 19; passage of British troops refused by, 23
Singh, Ranjodh, 111, 122
Singh, Sardar Chattar, see Attariwala Chattar Singh
Singh, Sardar Sham, see Attariwala, Sham Singh

# INDEX

Singh, Sham, *see* Attariwala, Sham Singh
Singh, Sher, *see* Singh, Kanwar Sher
Singh, Sobha, murder of, 40
Singh, Suchet, younger brother of Dhian Singh, 60, 64, 67, 71 and *n*, 72, 120*n.;* fought against the army of Hira Singh and was killed, 75; 'treasure' of, 80-1
Singh, Tara, 30
Singh, Tej, 97, 112, 124*n.*, 125, 126, 132, 182; was appointed commander of the armies, 99; four brigades of Sikh troops were on move under, 105; camp was pitched at Ludhiana by, 106; discredited himself with the army, 112; as head of the State Army, 121
Singh, Zorawar, 20; Ladakh conquered by, 19; hostilities against the Tibetans resumed by, 46-51; Gartok & Tuklakote occupied by, 47; Chinese government launched counter attack against, 48; Lhasa army recovered all lost lands from, 48
Smith, Sir Harry, 109, 111, 115
Soltykoff, a Russian traveller, on Nau Nihal Singh's death, 29
Suri, Sohan Lal, *see* Lal, Munshi Sohan

## T

Thackwell, Sir Robert, 115
Tibet, 19, 20; Zorawar Singh resumed hostilities against, 46-51
Tiwana, Fateh Khan, *see* Khan, Fateh
Tiwana, Malik Fateh Khan, *see* Khan Fateh
Treaty, between the British and the Lahore Darbar, 118; between the British and Gulab Singh, 80; clauses and conditions of, 118-211 Kashmir, Jammu and Kohistan transferred to Gulab Singh by treaty of Amritsar, 123; Governor-General's scheme, 129 *et seq.;* Treaty of Bhyrowal, 184 *et seq.*

## V

Ventura, Jean Baptiste, 34*n.*, 59

## W

Wade, Captain, 13, 15*n.*, 26*n.;* invited the chiefs of Jalalabad, 21
War, between Rani Chand Kaur and Sher Singh, 34-7; Afghan War, 51 *et seq.;* against the Punjab, the British preparation of, 101 *et seq.;* war compensation demanded by the British, 119-20; battle of Multan, 153-7; situation in the autumn of of 1848, 172; battle at the Chenab area, Ram Nagar, Sadullapur, 173-4; battle of Chillianwala, 174 *et seq.;* battle at Gujerat, 177 *et seq.*
Whish, Major-General W.S., 177; troops from Lahore and Ferozepore led to Multan by, 156-7; troops of, 166-7
Wilde, Brigadier, 52, 53

## Y

Yusafzai, the, 21, 22

## Z

Zaman, Khan, 19